STRENGTHENING FAMILY BONDS

"Authors of previous self-help books, the Birds present the third in their trilogy that includes the popular *Marriage Is for Grownups* and *Power to the Parents*. The extensive text is clearly written and based upon the Birds' experiences as parents of nine children. Granting that upheavals in social patterns over the last decades have threatened the family unit, the authors insist it is still possible to form bonds in the home that will help each member support the others, with benefits for all. The advice here is basic but sound, covering situations that arise from the time of taking the marriage vows through the years when the children are grown and on their own. The chief message encompasses the essentials of sharing love, responsibility, respect and faith."—*Publishers Weekly*

The authors on. . . .
SEXUALITY: "Discussions of sexual love within the family have to be 'ongoing.' Children are constantly changing, growing month by month. There can therefore be no single point in time or age at which the child is 'ready' for a discussion of sex."

FAMILY LOYALTY: ". . . strong family loyalty, rather than inhibiting the development of friendships outside the family, aids the emotional development and self-assurance of children thereby making it easier for them to relate to others."

To Live As Family

To Live As Family

An Experience of Love and
Bonding

Joseph and Lois Bird

COMPLETE AND UNABRIDGED

IMAGE BOOKS
A DIVISION OF DOUBLEDAY & COMPANY, INC.
GARDEN CITY, NEW YORK
1983

Image Book edition published March 1983 by special arrangement with Doubleday & Company, Inc.

Excerpt from POWER TO THE PARENTS! A Common Sense Psychology of Child Raising for the 70's. Copyright © 1972 by Joseph & Lois Bird. Publishing by Doubleday & Company, Inc.

Library of Congress Cataloging in Publication Data
Bird, Joseph W.
To live as family.
1. Family. 2. Parenting. I. Bird, Lois F. II. Title
HQ734.B629   306.8   AACR2
Library of Congress Catalog Card Number: 81-43392

ISBN-10: 0-385-19020-4

ISBN-13: 978-0-385-19020-6

BVG 01

To:
Paul, Ann, Susan, Kathleen, Joan,
Stephen, Michael, Mary, and Diane

*You lived this book; we merely put it on
paper. You taught us the meaning of bonding.
You permitted us to share in the lives of
nine truly remarkable human beings. For this
you have our gratitude and love. Always.*

Contents

To Live As Family

1

In the Beginning

The family begins in a commitment of love. It is germinated and nurtured in the mutual love of a man and woman joined together as husband and wife. Ideally, this is a love which strives toward perfection and is seldom satisfied with less. The word *family* has in recent years been subjected to any number of definitional vagaries and distortions. We speak of the "family of man." The sociologists talk of the "extended" family. There is the "family" of free nations. We now read a lot about the one-parent family. And extending the word to the bizarre, the media reported on the murderous perversions of the Charles Manson "family." Recently, a leading feminist defined *family* as no more than "a group of caring people." It is perhaps important, therefore, that we begin with an explanation of *family* as we will be using the word in the chapters to follow. Our view might be called "traditional." Some will accuse us of limiting our concept of the family unfairly in an age in which we are told the traditional nuclear family is in the minority and some prophesy is fast fading from the scene. We respect such opinions, but we feel comfortable writing only of what we have experienced and believe to be valid. Throughout the pages to follow, therefore, *family* will be used to mean father, mother, and their children. We will focus our attention on others outside of the family—friends, relatives, teachers, etc.—only as they interact with and influence the *family*. Central to all of this will be the thesis that it is upon the love of a man, the father, and a woman, the mother, that the family is built.

We enter marriage as adults. We have, in our progress toward adulthood, experienced years of loving and rejecting, of being loved and suffering rejection, and during those years we have learned, often painfully, that loving and being loved is the most crucial, life-giving, transcending experience of all.

Therein lies the great enigma. No word has more definitions than the word *love*. No emotion, if in fact love is an emotion, has more conflicts. No virtue has more interpretations. And no skill, if love is in fact a skill, is more steeped in controversy. Or confusion. Yet we marry for love, don't we? Isn't love at the very least, our dream?

Erich Fromm, psychoanalyst and philosopher, raised the question: "Is love an art? Then it requires knowledge and effort. Or is love a pleasant sensation, something 'one falls into' if one is lucky?" Arguing for the former, while admitting the majority of people today subscribe to the latter definition, Fromm presented the components of loving as *giving, caring, responsibility, respect,* and *knowledge.* These components, we agree, are present in all loving—to greater or lesser degree. On a human level (apart from the divine love of which the mystics speak), this love is most often discovered in a relationship between one woman and one man. It is romantic, committed, and at least in the eyes of the lovers, unique.

It is a love which has presented a high challenge to psychologists, philosophers, and poets as well as to all lovers throughout the ages. And today it is as much a mystery as it must have been when prehistoric man traveled in bands across the plains of Africa and the Outback of Australia, experiencing feelings and desires beyond a mere biological drive. Romeo and Juliet rejected hatred and prejudice, defied their families, and died in a profession of their love. Why do we find beauty and inspiration, rather than sadness and tragedy in their story? Is it because it touches something in each of us that defies logic but raises us above the realities of our lives? And is it because we feel a deep need for such transcendence?

Perhaps the love of a man for a woman must always remain shrouded in poetic metaphors. Shakespeare portrayed such love; he made no attempt to analyze it. Certainly if love is more profound than the lyrics of a popular song and more demanding than even the closest friendship, it must encompass at least all of the components of which Fromm spoke. But whenever we attempt to translate these components into a living reality, we find ourselves enmeshed in a thicket of self-interest, misunderstanding, and troublesome emotional reactions. Communication, that keystone of all relationships is of course the essential ingredient of loving. It is the challenge (and frequently the stumbling block) as well as the source of the *knowledge* of which Fromm spoke. If love is a "giving of self," what does the giving involve? What does my loved one want me to give? What do I feel free to give? And where do romance and emotion come in? If "God is love," as the Evangelist John proclaimed, what do we say of that love of self that so many claim to be essential to mental health? Does love witness God or merely evidence the vanity of a narcissistic society? On the other hand, if love is a transpsychic reality in which the lovers try to enter one another's emotional "worlds," a reality centered on empathy and understanding, what can we say of the powerful attraction we call "chemistry"? To go further, if as Fromm says, "One loves that for which one labors, and labors for that which one loves," what is this "labor"? Am I laboring if my labors give me as much or more satisfaction than they do my lover? Must love be self-sacrificing in order to qualify as loving? And if the labor is satisfying, is it no longer labor? Or is it no longer loving? Even further, we might ask if love demands "labor" to legitimize the loving. Can we claim too, in carrying it one step further, that parents who have acted out their roles of parenting with little or no satisfaction and with considerable inward but never expressed resentment are the most loving parents? Parenthetically, we can never subscribe to such parental approaches as even the most remote indication of loving.

Unquestionably, *responsibility* must be at the heart of loving within the family, but even this component is not free of ambiguity; it raises a number of questions. Is "responsibility" a duty imposed from without, a collection of social imperatives, or is it a free choice to respond to the needs of another human being? If it is a free choice, are we free to decline? Husband and wife pledge their love, yet they may hold very different realities of loving—and these realities may shift from encounter to encounter, time to time. One spouse may "love" by meeting specific obligations; the other may "love" by empathy and understanding. As a result, they may reject the claim of their partner to being "loving." Only when they each can accept the other's gift of love, and only when they are capable of incorporating and developing modalities of love beyond their own, can they aspire to a mature, far broader love which is the cornerstone of any successful family.

The committed loving relationship between husband and wife provides a nurturant environment within which children can grow in self-esteem and their own ability to love. Children are an extension of the love between the parents. Therefore, parents can never make their love for one another subordinate to their obligations as parents. Not only can a child accept the loving relationship between the parents, their loyalty to one another and their romantic bond as having precedence over the obligations of parental concern for him, he can find security in it. Rather than resenting the fact that he is an extension of the parental love and will always remain secondary to it within the family, he grows to take pride in it. Initially, of course, he will probably quite naturally attempt to intrude on the parental relationship. A boy will attempt to rival his father for the mother's affections; a girl will attempt to compete with her mother. But once the child learns that he or she cannot "win," that there is no hope of splitting the bond of love between the parents, a transformation will take place. The child will take a major step toward adulthood. Out of the initial frustration will come the motivation to venture forth in search of a relationship as loving and as fulfilling as that enjoyed by the parents. The loving marriage the child witnesses in viewing the parents will become the ideal for which the child searches in later years when he or she seeks a mate.

When a boy and girl, man and woman, fall in love, it generally takes on the characteristic of a romantic fantasy relationship. At that point, they are free to revel in the luxury of such a relationship, free of the price inherent in serious caring. As yet, they have few responsibilities toward one another and their relationship. They have little more than the intensity of their emotional responses. But at that stage, that's enough. These intense emotions will not, however, convey them beyond the dating phase and into the commitments and unity which will be demanded of marriage and parenthood. Only later, as they seriously begin to contemplate marriage, will they recognize that their love must be expanded to include the components of exclusivity, permanence, and dedication. How rapidly

and successfully this realization occurs and growth takes
place will depend upon the maturity both bring to the
relationship. And this maturity will be a reflection of the
marital relationships they have each observed in their parents. By any measure, the family—good, bad, or mediocre
—will seldom be better or worse than the relationship between husband and wife. Through this relationship, not
only do children learn the meaning of love, they learn the
virtues of loyalty, forbearance, perseverance, and integrity.
These form their abilities to understand others.

Romantic love involves a lot of petty, but powerful
emotions. It is a wild roller coaster. Crazy. Wonderful.
And anguishing. But beyond all that, if the man and
woman are to glean any sense out of it and build it into
what is both rewarding and sustaining, it demands *knowledge*. It isn't enough to say "I love you," nor to defend
such a claim of loving, as did Browning, by counting the
ways. To love, we must each learn how our loved one
wants to be loved—in times of joy, in illness, in disap-
pointment. No small task.

The learning will be painfully slow, sometimes tedious,
frequently frustrating. Attempting to *know* is a major
undertaking. Partners may spend hours exchanging personal information and opinions, but the messages are
often confusing and contradictory. If we don't know ourselves (and do we ever?), how can we help someone else
to try to know us? There will always be parts of us, real or
imagined, which we want no one to know. Little wonder
so many attempts at loving during those first months,
even years, fail. When we have scanty knowledge of each
other, loving gestures may easily be misinterpreted and
rejected. And with a loving gesture rejected, the lover
feels personally, as a person, rejected.

Every couple is advised to "get to know one another,"
often by married friends and parents who tell them, "You

can never hope to know someone until you marry them."
Unfortunately, the couple is seldom told how to go about
it. Communication is obviously easier to counsel than to
teach. Nevertheless, all hope does not have to be abandoned. Communication skills can be learned. Knowledge
of another person can be acquired. We can learn a lot
about one another before as well as after we marry, if we
work to develop the skills, if we ask the right questions,
and if we listen carefully to the answers.

Most couples begin to share views on marriage and
family life before they make any commitment to each
other. It is all part of the general information-gathering
process by which they hope to decide, "Is this the person
I want to spend my life with?" The underlying motives in
such information gathering are obviously more serious
than those involved with, "Do you like anchovy pizza?"
We go about searching for answers to the difficult questions of "Who are you? What do you believe in? Where
do you plan to go with your life?" and especially, "Tell
me your dreams of the future."

Interpretations of human behavior, especially those
most influenced by the writing of Freud, have focused on
the past rather than the future. They have emphasized
the importance of parental and social influences from earliest childhood on, rather than paying attention to the
hopes and aspirations we all have. Psychology has begun
questioning whether or not, however, it might be wise to
look to what we *hope* to do with our lives to give us a picture of who and what we are. While no one can deny the
importance of prior experiences, our so-called "track record," and its importance on our present choices and actions and in predicting what we may do in the future, perhaps our expectations of that future, regardless of what
influences may have touched those expectations, may be
more important in determining the direction of our lives.

We might say that what we are is what we dream and aspire to. As the young couple exchange their views, interests, past experiences, and especially their goals, they take the first tentative steps toward not only getting to know one another, but if they are to eventually join their lives together, to determine where they may go together. In a not unfriendly way, they test each other. No testing can be more important.

They meet, are attracted to each other, and almost at once this evaluation process begins. They search for mutual values, common interests, and compatible goals. They measure one another against the image they each hold of the ideal spouse and parent. She measures him against all other men she has known, against those who have played significant roles in her life, against the ideal lover, husband, and father. He makes a like evaluation of her. If they are realistic, they will not demand perfection. They will recognize that we fall in love with humans, not gods. Nevertheless, if they are realistic, their standards will not be minimal. They will not settle for a second or third best. The commitments and responsibilities that will be demanded in marriage and parenthood will call for most serious "comparison shopping." The choices involved are difficult. The consequences potentially severe. Their mutual evaluations will be approached with utmost sobriety.

The ideals they each seek in a mate have been forming long before they seriously ask the question, "Do I want to marry this person?" Throughout childhood we are all exposed to a number of potential role models—some good, some bad. Some role models we accept, and others we reject. The young man may search for a wife "just like the girl that married dear old dad." On the other hand, he may look for qualities in a future wife that he feels his mother lacked. If he was fond of his sister, he may measure all women against her. If the girl toward whom he is attracted does not measure up to his sister, he may drop her. More commonly, he will have an ideal that is somewhat of a composite, made up of aunts, teachers, female friends and relatives, and even women from history or fiction. For most of us, the initial attraction and the basis for comparison is strictly physical. We find someone physically attractive, and we are drawn to them. At that point, attractiveness is all we have to go on. Beauty being in the eye of the beholder, we are attracted to physical qualities that may not appeal to our friends and/or potential rivals. This is a decided break for most of us, who may be less than the movie ideal of attractiveness. In any case, the physical attributes may play a decreasing importance following the initial dating selection. They become even less important when we reach the stage of contemplating marriage. The beauty queen may have scores of men ringing her telephone, but her less attractive sister may get more proposals if she comes closer to matching what most men are looking for in a wife.

A pleasing personality, a giving nature, emotional stability, common interests, moral and ethical values, education, occupation, earning potential, age, health, family background, and perhaps a dozen or more other factors will be weighed and evaluated. Some will be more important than others. In a hundred hours of conversation, the average couple will have gone through no more than a preliminary "screening." There is simply too much to learn along the way toward knowing each other to expect more than a preliminary "screening." Even the second or third hundred hours will leave more questions than answers. When they meet, let's say in their early twenties, they each bring in to the relationship two decades of experiences. They have the cumulative life experience of over 350,000 hours. If they spend 8 hours a day together (hardly likely) for a period of a year, they can expect only to share the highlights of what they have lived through. But more important, how can they exchange reactions and values based upon their total life experiences, such that they can be sure they have clarified them? Perhaps one of the most dangerous assumptions we can ever make is to assume that we *know* another human being. Dangerous and presumptuous.

Every husband and every wife brings to the marriage a *visual image* of a family, one shaped by individual experiences and hopes. To each one of us, the word "family" triggers a montage of emotional reactions, a jumble of memories, both positive and negative, from our childhood. On these memories, we superimpose a fantasy image of the *ideal* family. If we recall our childhood years as pleasant, we may incorporate into our image of the ideal many of the activities, traditions, and values from those years. The effect of such incorporation on the building of the family we will establish may be very positive or very negative. Much will depend on our spouse, his or her experiences and values, and innumerable circumstances which may be similar to or dissimilar to those in our past. When a couple sit down and begin to share memories, before they talk seriously of marriage, the relating of backgrounds is part of the testing. They want to know how similar or dissimilar they are. Almost surely they will quickly discover just how dissimilar family patterns can be. Chances are, if they are in love they will unconsciously emphasize the similarities and tend to ignore the dissimilarities. Hopefully, they will be able to recognize that there is no single "correct" image of a family. And should they ultimately marry, they will, again hopefully, work to establish their joint image of *their* family. To do so will call for what is essential to the success of marriage and the family in every area of their existence: an autonomy which permits both husband and wife to be comfortably free of any dependence upon their parents. If we feel that departure from the values and traditions with which we were raised is somehow an affront to our parents and therefore "wrong," it may act as a severely inhibiting factor toward the establishment of a new family, one in which the members can take pride in a bonding they have created. We will return to the importance of autonomy and how it can be achieved in subsequent chapters. For now, we will state this as a given: the makeup of a family should never be formed from the ill-fitting and often disputed, hand-me-down practices of a prior generation.

In attempts to share concepts, dreams, and images of a family and aspirations for it, misunderstanding can easily arise if the wrong questions are asked. "What role do you believe a father should play?" is not only an impossibly broad and vague question, it can be one which is very threatening. Certainly he wants to be a good father, but does he have any idea what answer is expected of him. He can hardly answer, "I want to be a good father." That isn't sufficient. But is he prepared to describe all the various roles fatherhood may entail? Does he have any idea, even in his wildest imagination, what fatherhood may entail or can entail? Since all such roles are played out within a social context (the family) can he hope to cover how he sees his future role as a husband and father without knowing what roles his wife and children may play? Asked such a question, he may even respond to the question defensively. And she may answer with a counterattack. These are areas for discussion which should always be approached as if "walking on eggshells." We usually suggest that the couple employ a less confrontational approach. They can begin by sharing their *visual images* of their "ideal" family in various settings and situations

—e.g., "Let me tell you how I see us on Christmas Eve . . ." "How do you see our family on Sunday mornings?" "When I come home from work, I picture myself . . ." "My favorite image of a family outing is to . . ." Such visual images are similar to daydreams. They allow the listener to form a similar image and then to evaluate it as positive or negative—not "bad" or "good" (because that would be making a value judgment in an area in which value judgments are not appropriate). Out of visual images, goals can be formulated. Over the course of days and weeks and months, the couple spend evaluating and testing each other, they may explore literally hundreds of visual images together, recognizing that these visual images are neither "right" nor "wrong" but merely the expression of a human being and who he/she is on an increasingly intimate level. They might explore the following:

• What picture do you have of a family in prayer or in spiritual practices? Do you see us going to church together? Praying together as a family?

• Where do you see yourself living five years from now? In an apartment? Condominium? House? In this locale? In another state, or another country?

• What sort of social life do you picture for a husband and wife? How about for just the two of them? What would it be with others? With their families? How would it fit in with vacations, weekends away, evenings out?

• How do you see the handling of a financial crisis in the family, say the car just gave out or the hot-water heater just split? Do you see the husband handling it? Or the wife? Or the two of them sitting down and working it out together? And do you have some image of how you might react emotionally to such an unexpected event?

• What would you picture doing on a vacation? First of all, what would be your image of the perfect vacation? What would be your image of a vacation in Hawaii? Or in New York City? Or in a national park? And would the image be any different if it were a vacation just for two or a vacation which included children?

• Suppose we had a twelve-year-old son/daughter, what can you see yourself doing with him/her? What can you picture yourself doing differently with a son than with a daughter? What can you see yourself talking about differently with a son than with a daughter, or teaching a son rather than a daughter?

• What is your picture of a husband-wife relationship—an ideal relationship—after five, ten years of marriage? Do you see it as growing and getting better, and if so, in what ways is it better?

• How do you see a husband and wife taking responsibility for the income in the family and the management of the finances? In your image, do you see them making their financial decisions jointly, do you see the wife handling the payment of the monthly bills or the husband handling all of that? And how do you see them agreeing upon financial long-range goals?

This exchange of visual images—the "picture postcards"—we believe is very effective in terms of learning who the person is to whom you are married. It calls, of course, for a great degree of openness. And, in a word, it demands sitting back quietly listening to the other one. Through listening to each other and entering one another's visual images, partners are offered an opportunity to shift individual perceptions and values from those which are singular—mine alone—to mutual—yours alone —to the most rewarding perceptions—ours. In engaging in these exchanges and visual images before marriage, and even before a commitment to marry has been made, the couple are in a far better position to evaluate the future of their relationship. As a result, they may either reject the relationship or embrace it. If they listen to each other's images and the various elements which make such images attractive, they will most likely find that they seldom reject the other one's images. Nor will they feel that their images—their dreams—are rejected. Seldom do any of us give up a cherished visual image. Even those images which engender guilt take on a life of their own and a value to us which causes us to embrace them for a lifetime. What can, and hopefully will, happen is that he will accept and enhance her images. He will find ways to integrate them into his own. She will, in turn, accept his images and expand them in a way which will tell him that she values him. This does not mean, however, that either of them will go against their own moral and ethical values. She will not "play along" with his fantasies simply in order to "catch" him, anticipating that she can reform him once they are married. He will not verbally assent to her images expecting that she will be argued out of such expectancies once they have started their family.

She may, for example, share a visual image of a family vacation on a houseboat cruising along the Mississippi Delta. He may, in evaluating it, decide that her vacation image is not unacceptable to him and he may therefore pick it up from there and elaborate on his image of, perhaps, a family anchored on an isolated beach, broiling fish over a charcoal fire, the father of the family reveling in his new, and somewhat humorous role of "captain of the ship." As they continue to share their images, their daydreams, they will find that they add brush strokes to the "picture postcards" they paint. Thus, in a non-demanding, non-threatening manner, they learn each other's values and goals. To anticipate their future together,

knowing that their visualizations of the future are not incompatible. They are not miles apart. Any union of husband and wife must be, at least to some extent, a mixture
of oil and water. Understanding, communication, and
love provide the catalyst which makes it possible to unite
this man and this woman. Shared imagery we believe is
one of the most effective communication techniques in
furthering these goals.

2

Family Bonds

We are drawn to others when some *value* we hold is felt to be enhanced by the relationship and by our interactions with them. We may join a Bible study group because we feel our religious values will be fostered by participation with the other members of the group. We marry because we believe that our personal goals will be frosted within the relationship with that "special" person —whatever our goals may be. Similarly, the bonds which develop between the parents and their children, and the values the parents hold as they develop a family, hopefully reflect the rewards the parents, and later the children, seek in their relationships.

The strengths and satisfactions to be found within a family result from *bonding*. When the question is asked, "What attracted you to him/her?" the usual answer given is, "I loved him/her." It is sad indeed to find a husband and wife who married for reasons having nothing to do with love. We all find deepest satisfaction in loving, and we hope to be loved in return. But explaining attraction in terms of "love" tells us very little, if anything. It doesn't explain the "chemistry." And it does nothing to help us understand why some couples (and some families) grow closer over time, while others seem to drift

apart. What most of us think of when we use the word
"love" is a strong, sometimes overpowering, emotion. And
through this emotion, we believe a bonding results. But
this interpretation may lead us off the track. Love itself,
by whatever definition we use, is not bonding. Nor does
the presence of love, regardless how strong and dedicated
it may be, explain what goes on in the bonding experience.

We may have some picture, however clear or unclear,
of the values and experiences which bond us to those with
whom we feel close. On the other hand, we may have little or no conception. When the experiences or values are
clear, the bonding has usually occurred in a situation in
which mutual goals were well-defined. For example: a
swollen river threatens to overflow its banks, flooding all
homes in the neighborhood. We join with our neighbors
in sandbagging the river banks. During those hours we
spent fighting time and the rising waters, a bond will undoubtedly develop between the neighbors involved where
none may have previously existed. With a joint goal and
cooperative effort, we find we are drawn closely together.
The ties may, of course, weaken when the danger passes,
but they could conceivably strengthen if we subsequently
work together to lobby the legislature for effective flood
control. This type of bonding is very evident. Other bonding factors are not as apparent. In the relationship of husband and wife, as well as in the interactions between all
family members, the bonds are seldom so clear. We may
wonder what keeps some tragically unhappy, even destructive marriages together. Some writers on marriage
have suggested the marriage vows be changed from "as
long as we both shall *live*" to "as long as we both shall
love." These social innovators, however, may be ignorant
of how bonding occurs and how bonding strengthens over
time. Where the husband-wife relationship is mutually

advantageous—socially, emotionally, or economically—
bonding may keep a marriage intact even when little or
no love exists. Permanence is not always happiness, sad to
say. Counselors and psychotherapists are all too familiar
with "neurotic interaction" marriages in which the bonds
are incredibly strong. Activities which bond such couples
are only minimally *cooperative* (both working toward the
same, mutually desired goal). Most frequently, these relationships are *symbiotic*. Symbiosis, a concept borrowed
from biology, describes a relationship of mutual benefit in
which the goals of the participants are not shared, but in
which they need each other for the satisfaction of their
separate goals. There are small birds that eat insects from
the mouths of alligators. The birds find the source of food
while ridding the alligators of pesky insects. This is a clas-
sic case of symbiosis.

Today, a non-neurotic symbiotic relationship may be
somewhat rare. In the rural society of a century ago, such
relationships were common. Plowing the land from sunup
to sundown, the farmer needed a wife to care for his children, house and clothes, and prepare meals. She bore him
sons who would, in time, join him in the fields. For her
part, she needed a husband to provide her with a home,
the social status of a wife, and the economic security
rarely attained by a single woman. The relationship was
fully symbiotic, but that is not to suggest that love could
not grow in such a relationship. It could and often did.
Love and bonding, however, are not synonymous. When
bonding experiences are positive, strong feelings will often
develop which are then identified as love. Loving emotions do not form bonds. The bonding which grew out of
mutual labors of our pioneer ancestors, what the sociologists call task bonding, is still, to this day, a component of
the total bonding experience in most marriages and families, but seldom perhaps to the degree it was in those

bygone days. As the economy changed, task bonding lessened in importance. Husband and wife no longer needed one another in their labors to the degree they once had. We can only conjecture how much this lessening in need may have contributed to our ever-rising divorce rate and to the disintegration of family unity. In the chapter to follow, we will return to the subject of task bonding, its applications, and the contributions it makes to the building of a close, loving family.

Mutual effort, however, whether cooperative or symbiotic, is only one of many contributing factors to the closeness the couple may develop, and to the closeness they seek in the early days of their relationship. Do likes attract, or do opposites? This is one of the oldest arguments. Do likes have a better chance of building a successful family, or do opposites? Stated a slightly different way, do husband and wife, bringing divergent backgrounds and views to their relationship, have more to contribute to the richness of their marriage? There are, of course, numerous studies going back over several decades which find correlations between religious affiliation, family background, education, moral values, ethnic derivation, etc., with success in marriage. The strength of the correlation varies from study to study. But even where high correlations are found, rather than proving that likes attract and/or build more successful marriages, they may prove only that we tend to marry persons from our background, neighborhood, school, church, and community. They are the people we are most likely to come in contact with. And these persons obviously will be more like ourselves.

Similarities in interests, tastes, and backgrounds may themselves create bonding of a sort. A young man with whom we spoke had traveled from a small town in Nebraska to New York City. He was hoping to establish himself in a career in theater-set design. At first, he was quite miserable. He found himself in a strange, somewhat hostile environment, one in which strangers seldom smiled or spoke. For several weeks he survived in this unaccustomed cold environment. Then, by chance, he met an aspiring young actress from his home town. She wasn't really from his home town, but from a town of about the same size, forty or fifty miles distant. It was as if the sun had broken through after days of cloudy skies. And this was true for both of them. There was an immediate bonding. From their first meeting on, they lived in a scenario recycled through countless motion pictures. As they talked long into the night, day after day, and explored their backgrounds, they discovered they were both Catholics, both supported environmentalist causes, were both enthusiastic joggers, and both liked Chinese food. The initial force of attraction—and bonding, stemmed from their common Nebraska backgrounds. The backgrounds were enough to motivate them to explore further. A few months later, they married. In years to come, they may be convinced that a benevolent God ordained that they should travel hundreds of miles to find each other— "We just knew we were meant to find each other."

Still, we are left with a question: "Should one seek a partner with compatible interests and values?" Logic says yes—but so much for logic. Sexual "chemistry," social pressures, loneliness, and a half a dozen other psychological and social variables enter the picture. Important as they may be, and as strong an influence as they may be, how can we be sure they will not cloud our reasoning? Mating, as many of us have discovered, seldom follows the rules of logic. While it is true that a couple who share virtually no interests and values will be unlikely to cast their lot together in matrimony, and will rarely even date a second time, the breadth of common interests and values may vary from slight to very great. We have spoken to many, many couples who have complained of a lack of common interests. But just what interests are important? If he likes Italian food and she prefers Chinese, is this a dissimilarity in tastes which cannot be resolved? The answer might seem to be "no" unless they choose to make such differences incompatible. An attraction may be built upon shared interests which prove to have little or no relevance to the challenges the couple may face in their marriage and parenthood. One of the authors participated in a survey of college students' choices in marriage partners. Students were asked to list the interests and values they would look for in a potential mate. Now, if we consider marriage a commitment for life, and if we recognize that men and women of twenty to twenty-five will in many respects be very different when they find themselves the parents of teenagers, the replies we got failed to show much maturity or foresight. For example: "I want her to share my interest in drag racing." "I want him to be a member of Sigma Chi or Phi Kappa Psi." "I want a girl who is into anthropology." "He has to support the Equal Rights Amendment." "He can't be a Dallas Cowboys fan; I'm a Pittsburgh Steelers nut." "I love backpacking; so of course I want a guy who feels the same way." Unfortunately, our survey did not ask the question, "Where do you see yourself ten years from now?" Had they been asked the latter question, and had they put some effort into answering it, we feel sure the answers would have been very different.

The values and interests expressed in imagery may cut through many deceptions which have a way of creeping into the usual dating period. They may, in a word, help us to be honest with ourselves. If the images called for are selected with thought, they will aid in examining what will be relevant to the roles of lovers and parents.

Honestly examining our goals and motives is never an easy task. But it is a very rewarding one.

This sort of rational, "cold-blooded," evaluation of a prospective spouse may seem to have little to do with loving. And if we think of love as nothing more than a physical/emotional attraction, it does have to do with love. And we suppose it is "cold-blooded." But when visual images are employed rationally, they do not lack compassion, understanding, and deep caring. In fact, exchanging our visual images can be a form of loving. Often, it is a deep, trustful sharing of dreams and hopes. It is an exposure of self. If we share our dreams, we do so in the faith that you will not ridicule and reject them. We do so in trust that you will accept the dream as an acceptance of the dreamer. You may not join in the dream. That is understood. You are asked only not to smash them. You will have your own dreams and goals. Hopefully, you will express the same trust. And out of it, there is always the chance that we may discover common reactions, values, visions, and dreams. And a bond will be formed. Perhaps even a committed love.

According to surveys, a depressingly high percentage of men and women say that, given the opportunity, they would not marry the person they married. Many express frustration at what they describe as a change in the other person since the wedding. They complain, "I've grown, but my husband/wife hasn't." Or, "He/she was not the same person before we married." The fact of the matter, however, is that adults rarely go through radical changes in either values or personality. We pretty well stay the same once we reach adulthood (although circumstances, relationships, and significant events—either positive or negative, may bring out facets of our personality and reveal reactions not previously in evidence). Certainly it is true that the man and the woman may not fully know each other during the courting period. Perhaps they might have known each other better had they spent more time in serious discussion, and over a longer period of time, but all too frequently these steps were slighted. Then, after several years of marriage they may begin to discover things about the person they married which seemingly come as a great surprise. It may be too late to avoid tragedy.

It is natural to assume that all others want the same things in life as we do. It is therefore only to be expected that the one we hope to marry shares our view of life. Little wonder, then, most couples give little attention to these discussions. Most of us spend more time planning the wedding than planning for the marriage and family to follow. The fact remains, however, we are going to have to live with the outcome of our planning or lack of planning. Wherever we find ourselves in life, we have *reached our goals*. Many of us may reject such a notion, but it is an undeniable fact. If life has not turned out as we consciously claim to have hoped, we will understandably say our goals have not been reached. But perhaps they have. We may have unconsciously accepted the belief that failure is our destiny, and acting on this belief, however unconsciously, we may have pursued it. We all know people who seem to structure their entire lives so that they will repeatedly fail. Others seem to succeed at whatever they pursue. The view that we act upon our own expectancies and therefore "achieve" our goals may, of course, be argued, but one fact is indisputable: what we do not embrace and pursue as a goal can never become our achievement. To a couple considering marriage, nothing should be more important than goal-setting—clear goal-setting. This will go beyond the exchange of images. Our images express our individual hopes and dreams. It is when we find that our hopes and dreams merge that we can then begin to explore how they can be transformed into goals. In setting goals, we couple those images with rational plans to turn them into reality. This distinction between images (daydreams, hopes) and reality is significant, yet too often the distinction is ignored. The husband-to-be may, for example, share the following image with his fiancée: "I see us living in a condominium on the island of Maui in Hawaii, a place overlooking the beach. I can see us with a couple of kids, a sailboat, and plenty of time to have a lot of fun together as a family. It would be an idyllic life, the sun and surf and a lot of laughter."

It sounds like a wonderful life. But his dream (and let's assume she shares it) will remain only a dream, an idle fantasy, until they make rational plans to attain it. Only then can these dreams be called a "goal." And a lot of questions would have to be asked, a lot of conditions discussed, before the two of them could say, "Yes, this is what we want." How does he picture earning a living on Maui? If he is presently working to earn an advanced degree in petroleum geology, with hopes of a lucrative position with an oil company, his only chance of combining career dreams and his dreams of Maui may rest with the discovery of oil in Hawaii, at present an unlikely event. To make the dream a goal, therefore, would demand some radical changes. Most of us have some unfulfilled dreams. We keep them on the "back burner" because to turn them into goals would put them in conflict with existing higher-priority goals.

When a young man and woman begin to plan a life together, they first very tentatively present their individual goals to one another. Initially, these are goals apart from those which involve their future family. They are career goals, social aspirations, recreational aims, and financial desires. Only when they first present these "individual" goals to each other, can they measure them against goals

they each may have for a family, and only then can they
begin to *attempt* to resolve and compromise these aspirations. Some they may find to be incompatible. If so, the
discovery may raise a red flag. And if they are wise, they
will seriously re-evaluate their pending lifetime commitment. In any case, presentation of individual goals will
clear the way for serious discussions of their goals for a
family.

And what are these goals? At the fore, they will be
goals which contribute to their individual *actualization as
persons,* individually, including actualization of children
they may have. Discarding any sociological jargon, what
we interpret this to mean is *parenthood and family building which contributes to the self-esteem and feelings of
achievement of all family members.* When these goals of
self-actualization are met by the parents, we have found
that a similar resulting self-image will show itself in their
children, and will be reflected in family unity and pride.
The family will become a "whole" rather than merely individuals "doing their own thing." And the self-esteem
enjoyed by all members of the family will be more than
the mere vicarious satisfaction to be found in the achievements of one or another member. The self-actualization
and self-esteem will spring from the satisfaction of
achievement derived from the contributions the individual makes to the cumulative status of the family. In a
word, each family member will feel better about himself
or herself because of the pride that can be found in the
family.

Personal rewards, and these can be measured in self-esteem, from the achievements of family members are substantial, whether the rewards are one's own or those of another family member. This isn't to say that we "borrow"
rewards from the achievements of others, but rather we
share our achievements with the other family members as

they share their achievements with us. Such sharing of achievements, however, has become virtually a thing of the past as it has been disparaged during the "do-your-own-thing" generation of the sixties and seventies. During two decades in which both parents and children have been encouraged to ignore the needs, desires, and values of others, it is understandable that pride in family would be viewed with suspicion. There is no way we can take pride in the values and achievements of others if we do not espouse the same values and applaud the same achievements. "Doing your own thing" can only be interpreted as isolating each of us to our *own* thing. We can take no satisfaction in joining hands with others—physically, emotionally, or philosophically—if we have made a "statement" that says, in effect, "I will not reach out to join you; I will pursue solely my own goals." This has proven to be a tragedy. Since self-esteem can be derived only from achievement, where do we then, today, look to find achievement if we continue to promote the egocentricity of the sixties and seventies? Most men and women toiling in the marketplace today find difficulty justifying how they are earning their living. Their efforts are probably not unethical. They hold honest jobs, and they work hard. But the product of their labors seldom provides any substantial pride and achievement. In previous days, the expert blacksmith could take great pride in shoeing a horse well or in repairing a plow. The cook could gain considerable self-esteem in turning out a succulent stew. Today, however, in an age in which services outnumber products on the market, many of us find ourselves questioning the value of what we do, the contributions we make. Certainly our occupations may be worthwhile. They may even be needed. But we may find ourselves hard-pressed to say, "This is what I have produced, and it is good. I can take pride in it." Perhaps the frustration that many feel in this is reflected in the increasing number who have turned to raising beets and carrots in backyard plots, weaving cloth to make their clothes, constructing furniture on their weekends, and baking their own bread. It may not be the necessity to save money. It may be that they are seeking the satisfaction that can be found in saying, "I did it myself." There seems to be ample evidence that we have a deep need, buried somewhere in our psyche, to produce tangible evidence of our achievements, our contributions.

But what of the family, and the role of the parents? We firmly believe that there can be no achievement so rewarding, so fulfilling, as the achievements to be found in parenthood well done. If we can point to the children we have brought into the world and have nurtured into healthy, mature, loving, responsible human beings, and if we can say with pride, "We have done well; we have the responsibilities of parenting and have not turned our backs on what has been expected of us," we will find the need for achievement more than sufficiently met. Other achievements will, in fact, pale in comparison. There are no other achievements which will long outlive most of us. The works of Shakespeare have long outlived Shakespeare's life. Edison's inventions have contributed to the lives of all of us far beyond the inventor's life. But the procreative "achievement" of parenthood offers an "immortality" seldom to be found by any of us in any other area of our existence. When a couple plan a family, they are truly planning the future.

"Do we want to have children, and if so, when?" are two of the key questions a soon-to-be-married couple should face. Since most couples, despite talk of the "growing trend" toward childless marriages, do look forward to having children, these questions should be addressed long before they begin planning their wedding.

In subsequent chapters, we will return to this all-important question, but for now, let's look at some of the initial issues they should face. "Family planning" and "planned parenthood" have come to mean little more than spaced births and programs of contraception—even abortion "on demand." The argument of the planned parenthood advocates is that every child should be wanted. The argument seems rather self-evident, but *wanted* for what? and by whom? We have spoken to unhappy, rejected, fifteen-year-old girls who have cried, "I want to have a baby in order to have something that belongs to me." We have also listened to women married five or more years and still childless who have said, "I want a baby in order to catch up with my kid sister, who already has two." And we have listened to more than a few couples who have said they want to start a family "because our parents can't wait to become grandparents." On the other side, there are those who present arguments for every imaginable means of avoiding parenthood. In California, there is even an organization promoting state funding of abortions employing the incredible euphemism of "procreative rights." They apparently claim the "right" to become pregnant, the "right" to decide to bear the child or to have an abortion, and the "right" to have others, the taxpayers, pay for the consequences of their choice. It seems an irony that those who argue for "rational" planned parenthood and "responsible choice" are the same ones in the forefront of the proponents of abortion "on demand" for those who have done no planning and have assumed no responsibility. Perhaps those who loudly cry that a woman should have the right to control her own body, should be made aware of a simple maxim: every right carries with it a correlative duty, and duty, by its very nature, implies responsibility. The responsibility which comes with adulthood and the ability to procreate is a heavy one, and it cannot be passed off to others under the name of "a right."

In our contemporary society, children are an economic liability; they are not an asset. Most of us find the rewards of parenthood far exceed the "price" we have to pay, but the fact remains that there are no "practical" reasons for having a family. Children are the ultimate luxury, the gift husband and wife give to each other. Children do not ordinarily contribute to the economy of the family. They do not add to the emotional well-being of the parents. And they do not increase, in our present day and age, with family limitation being a paramount value, the status of the family. When children therefore, are brought into the world, it is very permissible to question why. Most certainly, they should be desired out of *love*. A love which is first the fruition of the love of husband and wife and second, a love both parents give to the child. In loving her husband, the wife has a desire to bear his child and to give her love to it. In loving his wife the husband wants to share with her the miracle of procreation. Both will then recognize the responsibilities such a commitment entails, and both will be motivated by love to assume it. Since love demands maturity, such maturity will make clear their motivations. They will not bring a child into the world in an attempt to satisfy their neurotic needs or social pressures.

Once they have established their goals for a family, there will still remain other feelings and motives—secondary goals—to be formulated. Most of these secondary goals will serve to implement their primary goals. And their primary goals will be centered on a single goal: a family which is rooted in love. The secondary goals will include such things as the financial, educational, spiritual, and social support of the family. They will involve the respective roles to be played by parents and children. Again, there will be a lot to be gained in the exchange of visual images, the "picture postcards." On the threshold of their wedding, a couple may understandably find exchanging visual images and goals a year or more down the road very difficult. The honeymoon and a furnished apartment may be the furthest they project into the future. But the long-range goals of a family can be ignored only at the peril of the marriage and the ultimate welfare of the family which may be established. Many couples will say, "So long as we both love each other, the future will take care of itself," but this is both a naïve view of love and a denial of any personal responsibility. No one would deny that our loved one's goals may be adopted by us out of love, nor that we may abandon certain of our goals out of love, but it would be folly to suggest that love carries with it the mutuality of goals with the loved one. Even when the goals are the same, lovers may reasonably differ in how best to achieve them. Often there is no "best" way. If the man and woman are mature and caring, they may disagree, even strongly, on both goals and means of achieving them without diminishing their mutual love and respect. Nevertheless—and this is important—if the goals, whatever they may be, are directed toward the building of a family and demand a cooperative effort of the highest order, it is important that such goals be held mutually, and that their direction be charted before the couple embark on their path through life.

If there is a common thread running through the fabric of family planning, it is *communication*. What communication is, what it can be, and what it is not, however, is not something on which we all agree. It is often as broadly or loosely defined as the word *love*. We all can agree that it is more than just talking, and that it goes beyond mere gathering of information. It is not simply an "exchange" or a "touching," no matter how easily these

words are tossed about by the "sensitivity" group thera-
pists. Communication, verbal or non-verbal, is an interaction through which we attempt to understand and ultimately know one another. And even this definition is
admittedly vague. Wanting to know each other, to enter
each other's "worlds," we reach out through our words
and actions. We do not always succeed, even after hundreds or thousands of hours of striving. There are always
barriers of semantics, emotion, and intellect which get in
the way. The effort, however, is more certainly worth the
prize. We would all like to be able to confidently say, "I
understand you; I know what you're saying and feeling,"
and to have our loved one reply, "Yes, I know you do."
Unfortunately, it is an all-too-rare occurrence. Communication demands an effort which few couples are willing to expend. If a couple tell us, "We're going to get
married, and we have spent two hundred hours talking
over our plans for a family and the life we will have," we
will rejoice and congratulate them. Their two hundred
hours are a fine beginning—but only a beginning. They
will have thousands of hours to go before they can begin
to claim good communication, perhaps not even then.
Listening to another human being and attempting to understand him or her, can be the challenge of a lifetime. In
the chapters to follow, we will return again and again to
the concept of bonding, and the various means by which
it is implemented and strengthened, but it is well to emphasize that at the core of nearly all bonding will be the
development of ever-sophisticated systems of communication.

For a husband and wife, motivation to communicate
will, in its more mature form, be much the same as the
motivation to love: to meet the needs and desires of the
other. So we see that we come to a circle: which is cause
and which is effect? The successful family begins in love,

the love of one man and one woman. It is built on love. It is nurtured by love. It is sustained by love. And where love exists, lovers strive to know each other, to share each other's worlds. They strive, always, to communicate. Through countless hours, and a closeness that is both physical and emotional, they share their values, their convictions, and their goals. These goals are moral, ethical, spiritual, material, and social. They are a composite of the world as they dream it can be, as they want to shape it, and as they want to share it. The communication begins the moment they meet. The effort toward the attainment of the goals begins the moment they begin to formulate visual images of their life together.

Dr. Aaron Stern, a psychiatrist, in pondering the nature of love has said, "*It is communication, a communication far broader than the written and spoken word. It is the entire range of human sensory behavior, both verbal and non-verbal, through which two people experience each other. We love each other to the extent that we are able to communicate with each other, a communication that extends into all areas of life: social, intellectual, emotional, and physical.*"

And it is out of the cornerstone of this communication that a family, bonded together in common goals and in love, is formed and sustained.

3

"We're Expecting!"

Within a few weeks after the doctor confirmed that, sure enough, our first child was on the way, we plunged into preparations. We were knee-deep in brochures for baby furniture, home magazine illustrations of nurseries, and books, books, books: everything from the latest theories on obstetrics to Spock. We approached nest-building with a fanatical zeal. Birthing and parenthood became our obsession. No project was more thoroughly researched. We were ready. We weren't exactly sure what we were ready for, but *we were ready*.

If there was one thing we didn't lack during those months, it was advice. We needed it, of course, but we were not prepared to be buried in it, and we came close to being just that. The advice was often contradictory, often offered with no rationale, but we had no experience with which to evaluate it.

The opinions and advice split into three areas of concern (reflecting, we later learned, the concerns of the advice-givers):

1. The problems and difficulties (?) of pregnancy
2. The serious effects the arrival of a child can have on the husband-wife relationship

3. The horrendous expenses the couple can expect

Then there were the countless lists: receiving blankets, diapers, bassinet, booties, Bathinette, bottles, nipples, swabs, thermometer, scales, etc., etc., etc. The opinions were at times valuable. At other times, what friends and relatives had to offer was not only of little value; it was downright destructive. Little by little, however, we began to picture parenthood as more than a set of concerns and lists. It would mean an almost total change in the lives— individually and together—we had known. Would we be able to keep the "you and I" while assuming the responsibilities toward "the three of us"? Would the newborn be the awesome, almost overwhelming, intrusion some warned of, or would it be the "bundle from heaven" of which grandmothers spoke? Would the birthing itself be a glorious fulfilling experience, or an unspeakable agony? And would the gestation period be a situation comedy of pickles and strawberry ice cream at midnight, an enigmatic "transformation into womanhood," or an aching back and swollen feet? Or would it be all of these?

During those first weeks following the doctor's announcement, "Yes, you are," we reacted like sponges: we listened, we questioned, we absorbed, we digested the congratulations, counsels, and caveats of the authorities: housewives and house painters, dentists and den mothers, appliance salesmen, aunts, home economists, pamphlet writers, plumbers, pharmacists, and real estate appraisers: in a word, anyone who claimed even a remote association with the procreative process. They couldn't all be right. Their pronouncements were not consistent. It is truly amazing how many and varying are the opinions on the birthing process. Slowly, a question emerged: are pregnancy, birth, and the new role of parenthood such individual, idiosyncratic experiences that they cannot be reduced to platitudes and dictums? Of course! We could learn from others, and we did, but perhaps the most important learning occurred in discovering each other in new and often bewildering roles.

We both wanted a baby very much, so we rejoiced in the news. Our own experiences as parents, as well as the experiences of hundreds of parents we have counseled, have since validated how important it is that the pregnancy is anticipated with desire by *both* parents. Unfortunately, it too frequently is not. Financial considerations, housing, career and educational choices, feminism, peer influences, desire for travel and recreation, and age (too young or too old) are but a few of the reasons expressed for not wanting children (or, more commonly today, "postponing the start of our family"). A couple may agree before they marry to have no children for five years. Yet two or three years later something—who knows what— may loose a strong parental drive in one or the other. Let's say it's the wife (although it may as probably be the husband). If she now expresses a strong desire to start the family and he has not changed his views on postponing parenthood, he may understandably accuse her of "breaking the contract."

At that point, she probably has not broken any contract—yet. She has simply reopened negotiations. But she may also have been demanding new conditions for their relationship. Communication, mutual concern, and rationality will never be more crucial. To bring a child into the world only to later say, "I really wasn't ready to have a baby, but I guess we never talked about it much; I'm not sure she knew how I felt," is grossly unfair to all three of those concerned—especially the child.

Where husband and wife do not mutually and equally desire the child, however, communication will seldom resolve the issue satisfactorily. The decision to start a family

or to add to it should never be a matter of compromise or
"giving in." The risks are far too great. The entire future
relationship of husband and wife and, most important,
the environment of love and acceptance to which every
child is entitled are jeopardized if the child is not wanted
and the responsibilities of parenthood not freely accepted
by *both* parents. The strains of parenthood (and there
will be strains even in the best of circumstances) easily
turn to resentment and hostility when the baby was not
fully desired. If there is any single maxim to be followed
in initiating a family it is this: *Do not plan to bring a
child into the world until both of you have discussed the
matter thoroughly, have both arrived at independent, informed decisions, and both of you want the baby and are
ready, with love and generosity, to assume the responsibilities that will follow toward each other and toward
the new member of your family.*

A generation ago, the child conceived out of marriage
was often called a "love child." What an indirect
calumny on marriage! The euphemism may have been
more charitable than the legal designation *bastard*, but its
implications did serious violence to reality. A child conceived in adolescent passion cannot, by reason of the circumstances, be said to have been conceived in the mutual
love of the parents. Mutual love does not bring forth irresponsibility. Nor are all children conceived in marriage
given life by loving parents. Yet it is mutual love which
should be the primary motive in the decision to start a
family. Every child enters the world as the greatest mirac-
ulous statement of life, entitled to be cherished and loved
unselfishly. The child stands the best chance of being
loved in such manner if he or she is born into an environment of love and commitment between husband and
wife. When husband and wife love each other deeply, it
seems the most natural thing in the world that they desire

to give that love a physical expression in conceiving and bringing into the world *their* child. Even in the months before birth, they speak of it as "our baby." Thus we would say there are two very important tests involved in the mature decision to have a child: Do we share a mutual commitment in love to each other? and, Do we both want to bring this child into the world? Almost always, the most *loved* child is the child born out of the serious, loving, commitment of a husband and wife and their mutual desire to conceive.

In marriage, pregnancy makes a statement to the world. It reaffirms the wedding vows in that it is a serious assumption of responsibility in reliance upon the deepest trust and mutual commitment. It also symbolizes a rite of passage: the couple are no longer a boy and girl in love playing house; they are now adults, recognized as such. To see them together the first time she ventures out wearing her new maternity clothes is like meeting strangers. They have at once become a family. They have taken a leap in maturity—regardless of their ages at the time. If marriage acted to separate them somewhat from their single friends, parenthood will act to separate them still more. At the same time, it will draw them ever closer as a couple. Everything they have shared in the past will pale in comparison. They now share a miracle. Their shared parenthood will set them apart from the world in a unique bond. They may rush to tell their parents and friends of the baby they are expecting, but there will be something of a secret and a mystery which only they can share. They cannot express it in words.

This very special bonding which hopefully will always occur during the months of pregnancy has a "two of us against the world" quality to it. It has an echo, however faint, of what the frontier families of the last century must have shared. Homesteading land in isolated, often hostile, regions of the great plains and western territories, the bonding of husband and wife in pregnancy must have been very real indeed. They had no one else. In the movies, when the frontier wife entered labor, the husband would ride over to the nearby farm to fetch a neighbor wife to assist at the birth. The father-in-waiting would then help out by boiling huge quantities of water (no one ever explained what was done with the hot water). But in fact, the nearest farm might have been a full day's ride away. The baby's father was the only one present to assist at the birth. It was into his hands the baby was delivered.

With the coming of the automobile, and the increased number of doctors and hospitals, the father found he no longer had much role in the pregnancy and delivery. He was not only pushed out of the delivery room, he was often denied virtually any participation in the nine-month experience of pregnancy. In the first half of the twentieth century, childbearing was viewed as strictly "women's business." As soon as it was known that the young bride was expecting, an informal matriarchal support group would spring up. The expectant mother had been told, "Every girl needs her mother when a baby is on the way." In most hospitals, only two people were permitted to visit the expectant mother in the labor room: her husband and her mother (not her father, brother, or best friend). Home birth was considered risky and to be avoided. Babies were born in hospitals, and the birthing was treated as virtually a medical crisis, thereby excluding the husband still more. Often the expectant mother would develop a closer relationship with her obstetrician than that which she shared with her husband. It became popular to portray the expectant father as a helpless, hand-wringing buffoon pacing the floor of the fathers' waiting room while his wife underwent an unknown ordeal. Fortunately, about fifteen years ago, expectant parents began to demand that the father be permitted to participate in the birth process. This was not readily accepted by the medical profession and hospital staff, but the parents finally won out. Popularity of the Lamaze method of natural childbirth, coupled with an increasingly holistic and humanistic approach to obstetrics, opened the doors of the delivery room to fathers. Recently, an increasing number of couples have chosen to have their babies born at home, assisted by a doctor who was willing to do so outside of a hospital setting or by a nurse-midwife. Although this option is still controversial within the medical profession, it is interesting that the current generation of parents are discovering the benefits their great-grandparents must have found in the family setting as a birthing environment: husband-wife-newborn bonding. In any case, whether the baby is born at home or in the hospital, the father's presence at the birth is of such importance in solidifying the bond of parenthood that no compromises should even be considered.

The months preceding birth move swiftly. First, there are the physical changes. Often, the physical changes during the first trimester (three months) are what signal the pregnancy. The woman in early pregnancy feels tired, physically exhausted. She may undergo the rigors of so-called "morning sickness," the bouts of nausea (which are as apt to occur at midday or early evening as in the morning hours). The symptoms of pregnancy, however, vary widely from woman to woman. There is an old saying, "No two women alike, and no two pregnancies alike for the same woman." Some women experience very little fatigue and no nausea. Individual expectancies may play a major role in determining symptoms. If the mother-to-be has become convinced such symptoms are inevitable, and that pregnancy is a nine-month ordeal of aches, pains, and vomiting, her pregnancy may confirm it. It becomes a self-fulfilling prophecy. One young wife told us her aunt had advised her that pregnancy was the perfect excuse, and could be used to avoid anything the woman wanted to avoid—sex, housework, enthusiasm for life, and the relationship her husband might enjoy. Fortunately, she was smart enough to ignore her aunt's advice. She decided to view pregnancy as a normal condition and to play down any discomforts that might occur along the way. Needless to say, her aunt was furious. "You could have had that husband of yours under your thumb for nine months if you had played your cards right," was her embittered aunt's critique. "I kept my husband on a guilt trip both times I was pregnant." The guilt trip apparently didn't work. The aunt's husband left her a year later.

Not long ago, perhaps less than three decades, conception, pregnancy, and parenthood were viewed as the singular "end" of marriage. Bringing a child into the world was strictly a causative chain: marriage/sexual intercourse/pregnancy/parenthood. It was all very biological. Some, but not all, theologians espoused the medieval notion that sex was to be morally tolerated, no more, as essential to perpetuation of the species. Husband and wife engaged in this physical act consciously desiring to bring offspring into the world. There was no other purpose. In fact, if pleasure was found in such actions, it was at least somewhat shameful if not sinful. We would like to believe such a narrow attitude is no longer with us. We would like to believe the sexual union of husband and wife is accepted as an expression of love and physical desire apart from, although not necessarily excluding, the goal of procreation. But we are realists. We have spoken to a number of couples who somehow view expectant parenthood as incompatible with sexual loving. More than a few wives have told us they expect their husbands to lose sexual interest during pregnancy. They expect that some-

how the pregnancy will serve to turn off the normal desire
he had before she began carrying his child. We have tried
to understand this, not entirely with success. We suspect,
from talking to a number of men, that it is a myth per-
petuated by those who have become embittered by the
failure in their marital relationship. It may be that they
are the same sad minority who claim that women lose sexual responsivity during pregnancy. But the pregnancy itself is a sexual experience. It was born out of a sexual relationship, one which expressed sexual desire and love and
the wanting to bring forth a viable representation of that
desire. We can only assume, then, that many of those
husbands or wives who find their sexual desires diminished during pregnancy are the victims of self-
fulfilling prophecies they have been given earlier in their
marital lives. They have been handed the myths of the
diminished sexual drive during pregnancy and they have
accepted these myths and turned them into inhibitions.
Without such pernicious influences, sexual lovers find
their physical relationship is enhanced, not diminished,
during the months of pregnancy. The husband sees his
wife as the object of his sexual desires, desires which are
stimulated even more by the knowledge that she is carrying within her the child he has joined her in conceiving.
And as for her, she finds her sexual response to him is in-
fused with a new and exciting element: the shared fruit of
their sexual loving. Many women have expressed it by saying, "it is as if for nine months, I am carrying him within
me." Far from diminishing in pregnancy, the sexual drive
of both of them may be stimulated. Certainly, from time
to time she may be uncomfortable when engaging in sex.
During the early months she may be tired. But sexual
desire, like love itself in all ways, will find a way. There is
no reason when love exists for romance or sexual desire to
wane in any degree. In a word, if the wife responds to her

husband before pregnancy, and if he finds her sexually desirable before her body swells with the child she carries, their sexual chemistry will not be altered, they will love and want each other as they await becoming *three*.

Those first months of pregnancy often serve as an introduction, sometimes a harsh introduction, to reality. Often it is the reality of other people, not that of the expectant parents. Following all those gloomy predictions of financial strain, physical debility, and sexual atrophy, we might say it is the strong (and deeply in love) couple who can face nine months with anything short of panic. And certainly with anticipation of the first child, there is bound to be a degree of anxiety. After all, you have been loaded with "just wait until . . ." The last month of pregnancy can bring on a mixed flood of emotions. At that point, perhaps more than ever before, husband and wife feel a need for each other. She may have discovered that the physical symptoms so vividly described by the scare stories of the old wives do not reflect her experiences, but she will have discovered her body as she has never known before, and she will have struggled to adjust to it. She will be using it every day and attempting to find what she can do with it. It is a new body, and one which will demand continual adjustments. The child she carries will strain at her back, wake her at night with its kicking, and send pain down her legs. She will feel clumsy, vulnerable, and apprehensive. And all with good reason. While she may have previously prided herself on her self-sufficiency, she will now feel an increasing need for support and reassurance. Her husband will be looked to with increasing urgency. She will cry out for his strength and nurturance. She will be rewarded and an increased bonding will result, or she will be bitterly disappointed and an irreparable rendering of the relationship may occur.

For him this may be a time of frustration, bewilderment, and anxiety. In all probability, he will want to be able to do something to help her, something to ease her discomfort and apprehension. But he will feel helpless. The birthing process will not rest in his hands even partially. If he is the average male, he will feel guilt without knowing why. And much of the time he may feel he is living with a stranger. In reality, he probably is. As she approaches the time of her labor and delivery, she will most likely slip into a world of her own, a world shared only with the infant she carries. One husband described it as, "a frustrating experience. It's as if she was keeping some deep, dark, secret from everyone, even me." Another said, "They say the smile of the Mona Lisa is enigmatic. I never knew what that meant until I watched my wife during pregnancy. *She* was enigmatic. She was totally in her own world much of the time. I would try to reach her, and I can't say we were not close, but there was always some mysterious barrier I couldn't penetrate."

Most wives, we feel sure, do not want to exclude their husbands. They want closeness and sharing. They want what they have enjoyed in the past, with an even stronger intensity if possible. But they do carry a "secret" that cannot be articulated. The woman herself can only faintly understand it. Here, within her body, is a human being she has never seen, never spoken to, but one she knows, feels, responds to, and loves enough to live for and to die for. The inexpressible secret she carries is one she feels she shares with the life within her. Yet it is a secret she herself will never comprehend.

Considerable bonding can develop as husband and wife share in preparing for the arrival of the baby. One of the first considerations they face will, of course, be that of housing. Even such a very small person can demand a considerable amount of space. In a two-bedroom house or apartment, a newborn infant can take over nearly half the available square footage. That may seem an exaggerated figure until expectant parents start acquiring baby furnishings. First of all, the second bedroom will of course become the nursery. And nurseries never (or almost never) serve a double function. Fitting the image of the "loving, expectant parents," husband and wife will probably be busying themselves repainting the room in pastels or papering it in a nursery-rhyme motif. They will then furnish it with a six-year crib, a chest of drawers, a bassinet (if the parents have not decided to save this initial investment and sleep the baby in the crib), a Bathinette (although the bathtub or the kitchen sink may be a more practical place in which to bathe the baby), a stroller or baby buggy, and whatever other accouterments a persuasive salesperson in a baby department can convince them is a "must." To this they will probably add prints of Hummel children, a mobile for suspending over the crib, a music box that plays a lullaby, and a rocking chair. But it won't stop there. The furnishings of the newborn may have a way of spilling over from the nursery into what may have previously been a fashionable, well-structured, two-adult residence. The furnishings and properties of the baby grow at an amazing rate and invade almost all available space. Even before the baby comes home from the hospital, a major transformation begins in the redefining of privacy and space. Preparing for this, as much bother as it may be, provides a great opportunity for the parents! Planning and shopping for the third member of the family can create incomparable memories. Neither parent may be an authority on the furnishings required for infants, or the quality of high chairs, playpens, and six-year cribs, but the mistakes that may result from their naïveté may be more than compensated for by the bonding they experience in doing it together. We won't argue with those who say it would be more sensible to take a neighbor or one of the grandmothers along on those shopping trips. Of course they may have an expertise the parents lack. Yet we feel the memories of selecting the first items of baby clothing and furniture should be exclusive to the expectant mother and father.

In all such preparations, the couple will face one of those paradoxes with which we all are vexed. At a time when husband and wife, individually or together, are declaring their autonomy, severing their dependency on parents and others, establishing their own family and another generation, they are told they need support of parents and other adults upon whom they have been dependent in the past. After all, the challenges of parenthood, they are told, are many and complex. They will need "expert advice." And who better to give such advice than an experienced mother? But wait a minute, even if they believe Mother or the next-door neighbor knows more about baby furniture and crib blankets than they do, and even if they overlook the fact that much has changed in the intervening years since Mother or the neighbor had an infant, we would still argue that parents-to-be cling to each other, establish their own parenthood, and build their own nest. Stumble they may, and all of us have stumbled, but the memories are worth it. It is not a matter of defiantly excluding all others; it *is* a matter of consistently and increasingly clinging to one another. Nest-building is done by two. It is not a community project.

Restructuring time and space to accommodate that first child will call for adjustments and compromises never anticipated. Deciding on where you're going to locate the nursery may result in a hobby room or den being moved to the rafters of the garage. A playpen in the living room will never blend with the other furnishings. And unless you have a large kitchen, the high chair will always be in the way. Couples usually discover, and very quickly, that the living space which was more than ample and comfortable for two is now terribly overcrowded for three—even when the third one can fit easily inside a bureau drawer. So what to do about it? One solution might be to move to a larger home or apartment. Unfortunately, suitable and spacious housing is beyond the means of many young couples. It will come as no news to any reader that an inflated housing market has put home ownership in the realm of the nearly impossible dream. But perhaps not totally. It simply may take more time and work to attain that dream than it did in previous generations. In the meantime, apartment dwelling may be the only answer. And it is an answer which is far from intolerable. Although some cities have in recent years passed laws prohibiting landlords from banning families with children, finding a suitable apartment for your family where children, and particularly infants, are acceptable may still present a major challenge, one a couple should rationally confront long before they bring their baby home from the hospital. Newborn babies make a lot of noise, and it is a noise which greatly annoys most adults. The parents may be able to tolerate it (although at a 2 A.M. feeding, even that might be questionable), but neighbors may not operate on such a parental level of tranquillity. The apartment owner, kind soul that he is, may not evict the parents; they may even find themselves surrounded by understanding, patient neighbors, but who would want to test the patience of such indulgent souls? So parents try to keep the crying noise to a minimum. Soundproofing the nursery might help. It is seldom, however, a practical undertaking. Covering walls with heavy blankets or carpeting might also help, but you may find carpeted walls less than desirable. You may even consider moving the baby to the far side of your apartment, away from your next-door neighbor, but this may mean turning the kitchen into a temporary sleeping room. Finally, you will probably do what most parents do: you will pick up the baby when it starts to cry; you will take care of its needs; and you will hope and pray the baby will stop crying before it riles your neighbors.

Coping with necessary accommodations and space can strain the always-fragile relationship between husband and wife unless the problems are approached jointly and with maturity. The child is the child of both parents, and in justice both parents will be called upon to compromise and adjust to its intrusions. Maturity and parenthood go hand in hand. Beginning a family, both parents will reassess their priorities. The frustration and stress that are so much a part of parenthood, especially new parenthood, are lessened if the parents can recognize and accept the choices they will be called upon to make. These are not sacrifices; they are choices. It is a fact of life that adulthood presents us with a series of choices. We can't, as the "now" generation proclaimed, "have it all—now." If only five hundred dollars is available, and the vacation we've dreamed of costs five hundred dollars and a new television set also has a five-hundred-dollar price tag, a choice will have to be made. If we choose the vacation, it makes no sense to say that we have *sacrificed* in not purchasing the television set. When a couple marry they recognize marriage as a choice which involves giving up the advantages of single life for what is expected will be the greater advantages of married life. Again, it is not a sacrifice, it is a choice. Having a baby is also a choice. All arguments about "social conditioning," peer-group or parental pressure, do not erase the fact that the decision to begin a family is almost always one which is mutual and freely entered into by both parents. Even if conception was an "accident," once the baby is *there*, a fact of life; the choice is made.

The respective lies of both parents will be significantly altered. What this may demand can never be fully known in advance. Responsible parenthood can call for a job change, a housing move, temporary or even permanent abandonment of career or avocational goals, certainly a revision of the family budget, more extensive planning for evenings out, weekends away, and vacations. It will entail a rescheduling of everything from mealtimes to lovemaking, and each decision along the way will challenge the maturity of both parents. In all such decisions, it will be essential that they keep firmly in mind, "this is the child of both of us." Only such an *adult* view can prevent rivalry between parents and strain on the marital bond. Once the baby arrives, nothing will be the same until the last child leaves home. And perhaps not even then. New parents find themselves looking about the living room trying to anticipate what can be broken, pulled off, or put in a small mouth. Sunday outings will be planned to include a diaper supply, a baby-bottle heater which plugs into the car cigarette lighter, a stroller stored in the trunk, and an arrival time back home in time for a bath and early bedtime. Any and every parental activity will be subject to interruption by the loud, and always persistent, demands of the baby. Is it true that baby rules the home? Few experienced parents would argue the question. In time, and with careful planning, parents may be able to build, and maintain, a life for two worked in around the baby's schedule, but in the meantime, time and work demands of the baby will be a responsibility both will face. With maturity and love, however, they will face it with equanimity, patience, and perseverance. Parenthood brings with it joy, a joy which can only be experienced by two loving adults.

Every newborn is smaller than we imagine it will be and appears more fragile than it really is. Certainly it takes more time than parents expect. And it fails to live up to those norms that Spock and others tell us a baby should fit. The fact that we parents may be able to look back a few years in the future with amusement on the first months or even years of frenetic concern and needless activity centered around that baby is scant consolation when we are waiting for a bottle to warm at two in the morning, changing clothes after the baby has up-chucked on us just before on our way to an important engagement, or trying to get that last burp from a fussy baby, knowing that if we don't, we won't have any sleep for an hour. The tasks call for a partnership of parents, each contributing to the parenting. As with loving in the husband-wife relationship, it is without reservation or qualification. It isn't something which is measured. Both parents give whatever the opportunity for giving requires. They both stand willing to be first to volunteer to meet the demands of the baby.

Certainly babies demand a lot. It may not be as much work as some claim, but it will be more work than most new parents anticipate. One or both of them may have had baby-sitting experience. They may have helped care for younger brothers and sisters. But there is no surrogate-parent experience which can prepare one for the twenty-four-hour-a-day responsibility of parenthood. This responsibility really is not overwhelming, although at times it may seem so. It can be handled by one parent alone, but sharing the responsibilities of parenthood whenever possible is not only fair, it can add greatly to the creation and the strengthening of the bond between the parents. If working together painting a living room is a bonding experience, how much more can be derived from sharing in the tasks of caring for one's own child. During the late

1960s and 1970s, most women's magazines carried articles on the "new role" of the father of the family. In most of these articles, the authors described the family structure of previous generations as one in which all child-rearing (except discipline which usually was corporal punishment) was left to the mother. The father was cast in the role of patriarch. *He* never changed a diaper or warmed a bottle. *He* never risked his masculine image by tying the bow on his daughter's dress. *He* never made the sandwiches for a child's lunch or gave an infant a bath; *he* never read his child a story or tucked his children in bed with a goodnight kiss. The authors then go on to proclaim the new age of liberation and equality. The father, in the new age, is to be as nurturant as the mother. He may be more ill-equipped (as they portray him), but he is willing to try. The articles, however, may reflect less reality than the authors would like us to accept. They present a stereotypic view of the patriarchal father, a straw man of three or four decades ago which can be easily knocked down. We have talked with many grandparents and great-grandparents of that era. How did the men of those days act toward their children? Most often they diapered, burped, bathed, and cuddled their children as a matter of course. If there is one responsibility which is not tied to sex role, it is parenthood. These earlier fathers did not see parenthood as sex-role-determined, and they did not feel that their masculinity exempted them from the responsibilities of nurturance. In fact, they felt the nurturant role was a privilege, one that they recalled with great satisfaction.

And while we are refuting sex-role myths, we would like to take on another one. It is the one which suggests that either parent, usually designated as the mother, is by reason of gender more knowledgeable or skillful at one or another of the tasks of child-rearing, or that one parent is by reason of gender better able to understand the needs of the child. Parenthood is not an inborn, natural, or instinctual attribute of either sex. Parents most probably bring equal understanding and skill to parenting the firstborn child of both. *Sharing* what they observe and learn will become a component of their bonding.

Task bonding and parenting is a major component of the total bonding between husband and wife. It is, however, only one component of the cohesivensss that comes with parenthood. It may not even be the dominant component. There is gratification derived from membership in the family, just as there is gratification which comes from membership in any selective group. Even close pals gain prestige from the fact that they share interests and confidences which exclude outsiders. Members of any clique gain prestige from membership as well as an incentive for further involvement in their membership. Marriage itself creates an in-group for the husband and wife, but nothing so strong as the in-group membership that they find in parenthood. From the moment of conception they form a new, far more exclusive "clique," a stronger bonding. The marriage contract itself creates a bonding. Its substance is derived primarily from the social sanction, but it is a social sanction and a bonding which is shared by countless other couples. While any adult male may marry any adult female, only *this man* and *this woman* can give birth to *this child.* It is a unique bonding that they share. Their baby, the child that carries the genetic endowment of the two of them, gives them something that sets them apart from all others. It is a truly incomparable bonding. Even couples who have fallen into open hostility and bitterness cannot cast off the bond of parenthood which links them. To share parenthood with another human being is to establish a bond with that person which will prevail throughout the life of the child to whom life has been given—and beyond. The father of that child will always be the father and the mother will always be the mother. *They* will always be the parents. Even in the face of the grossest irresponsibility on the part of one or the other, even in the face of one or the other deserting or repudiating the parental responsibility before the baby is born, the bond of parenthood will never be destroyed.

There is status in parenthood, and we enjoy it. We take pride in the children we conceive and bring into the world. It is a pride shared with the one we love, the one with whom we share this "achievement." *Our* son or daughter, will be the prettiest, smartest, the most talented, child ever. So when our friends and relatives rave over our little angel, we are sure they are simply perceptive, not flattering. Now of course we may not be entirely objective when it comes to our child (although we are sure we are). But we do expect great things from him or her. Why shouldn't we be proud? Why shouldn't we occasionally brag? Pride in those we love is no vice, is it? To boast of the talents, attributes, and attractiveness of one's spouse or children is only to acknowledge the esteem in which we hold them. "Hey! Look at me! This is *my* wife, *my* children!" If a man can justifiably take pride in his membership in a fraternal organization, how much more is he entitled to take pride in his children and in their mother? His wife is someone wonderful and special. He can say the same of each of his children, and he hopes they will feel similarly about themselves and about their membership in the family. Membership gratification bonds are among the most powerful of all bonding elements, and they contribute the most to self-esteem. Memberships in which we take no pride, we either drop or deny. The girl who is embarrassed to admit she comes from a small farm town may claim to hail from San Francisco or New York City. The graduate of a small technical college may go out of this way to avoid mentioning his school when he is in the company of those who hold degrees from big-name universities. Our affiliations are important to all of us. We want to belong to the best, the greatest, the most prestigious. And above all, our primary membership, the one with which we most closely identify, is our membership in the family. What could be more natural than to want to brag about it?

From membership bonding, it is then only a short step to *identity* bonds. In a psychological interpretation, "identification" occurs when we experience ("feel") what happens to another person as if it happens to us. It is at the core of the family relationship. In its purest, most literal, form it is the emotional reaction of empathy, the pain we feel when someone we love is injured. On another level of complexity, it is the temptation most of us have from time to time to "name-drop." The success of someone with whom we can identify becomes our success, even if in small measure. In the Salinas Valley of California the residents today boast that their home is "Steinbeck Country." John Steinbeck painted a not altogether favorable portrait of their area and its inhabitants in his novels, but with his universal literary acclaim and his Nobel Prize, the criticism he previously received from the residents shifted to identification. He was now someone in whom they could take pride. Within the family there is constant identification. It may be positive or negative. The wife of a successful businessman may develop a higher opinion of herself than the wife of a man less successful. If his success is outstanding, her status is assured. If he is a failure, she may blame him for her loss of status, the status she acquired only through identification. With the birth of a child, the husband acquires additional status, not only through his paternity but through identifica-

tion with that child and with the child's mother. This
beautiful child is *his* baby, the genetic extension of him.
This woman is one who chose *him* to father her child.
His pride and his "name-dropping"—"*my* wife," "*my*
daughter," are understandable. The same holds true, of
course, for the mother of that child.

This identity bonding is not, however, effective in en-
hancing the relationship within the family unless it is
carried beyond merely taking pride in the talents and
achievements of others. It must be more than a one-way
street. We may admire someone. We even identify with
them. But a substantial bond will not flourish unless our
responses to them are *rewarding to them*. Identity bonding is reinforced (supported) only through the response
of the person with whom we identify. And what form
does this "response" bonding generally take? We each
differ in the kinds of response we find rewarding. Some of
us may respond to flattery. Therefore a bond is established with anyone who flatters us. We may respond
to a challenging confrontation, and a bond is then established when our adversary responds to our logical argument. A wife may respond to babying. A husband may respond to mothering. Responses are often tied to cultural
roles (the macho male; the passive female) or to the emotional needs of the individual. Between members of a
family, especially husband and wife, the most common
and rewarding responses are verbal and physical expressions of affection. Unfortunately, they are the most often
neglected. Praise, compliments, and words of love, coupled with touching and holding are the essential heart-
beat of family bonding. We previously said that bonding
is not a result of love, love is a result of bonding. But expressions of love and admiration act to reinforce the
bonding behavior. Needless to say, infants have a need for
physical affection. Enclosing the baby in one's arms is a

warm and gratifying experience for most of us. Hopefully, the pleasure will not decrease as the baby matures into the child and the child matures into the adult. Whatever our fears and inhibitions, we all have a strong need to hold and be held by those we care for. Several decades ago pediatricians and psychologists discovered that severe problems may arise when infants are deprived of such nurturant touching. Without it, babies may sicken and even die. The need to be touched and to be held may be as strong as the need for physical nurturance, food and water. Many psychiatrists and psychologists contend that human beings never outgrow this need. We count ourselves among them. Yet there are countless individuals, even entire families, in which affectionate touching is almost nonexistent. Americans in general do not have a reputation for touching and embracing.

The bonding effects of affectionate touching, however, are too important to the growth of both the marriage and the relationship of parent and child to be dismissed with, "I'm just not a touching person." The newborn infant is not a "walking" person, nor is he a "conversing" person. But he learns how to walk and how to converse. The infant does not have to learn how to enjoy being touched. There is an innate desire to be touched, to be held, to enjoy the satisfaction of close physical intimacy. The child needs touching and holding as much as it needs mother's milk. But, then, so do parents. Without touching, we are left to feel cold and alone in the world. We touch with tenderness and affection that which we value. It is almost a compulsion. The exquisite softness of a jade brooch, the smooth marble of a Michelangelo statue, the warmth and softness of the tiny, grasping fingers of a newborn. We value them. Hence, we have the urge to touch them. Husband and wife, valuing each other above all else, express their feelings through kisses, embraces, and passing touches throughout the day. His arm circles her shoulders as she nurses their baby. She leans over to kiss him as he rocks their sleeping child. The touches and strokes which are so much a part of new love do not diminish with time. They do not fade as time demands increase with the arrival of their child. If they were to diminish, it would not be the result of the "intrusion" of the new member into the family. It would signal that their relationship was itself atrophying.

We once asked a group of men, all of whom admitted to having troubled marriages, when they felt their relationship began to sour. To a man, they all gave the same answer: following the birth of our first child. It might be tempting to explain the answer by saying the wife was now absorbed with new demands on her time or the husband became jealous of the attentions she paid to the infant, but we feel it goes beyond such superficial explanations. When the baby enters the home, and they become a family of three rather than a man and woman living in a relationship, the roles change. The newborn is a stranger. The parents cannot expect to know him/her immediately. After all, if any other stranger appeared at their front door, they wouldn't expect immediately to know and understand him. Learning about anyone, learning to know them, is a slow process. It is almost sure that husband and wife will have only scratched the surface in knowing one another in their roles as husband and wife. Now, they will be called upon to try to know a third party, the infant, while at the same time attempting to know one another all over again. He may have been able to predict her reactions to friends, business associates, and family, but now he has to learn how she will react to a stranger who has entered their home, a stranger who demands more attention and concern than all friends and relatives put together. She will have an equally difficult challenge in trying to know him. More difficult still, they will not be able with much accuracy to predict their own individual reactions. They will have ideals and goals pertaining to what they would *like* to be as parents and what they would like their husband and wife relationship to be while they are growing in their parenthood, but prediction is not synonymous with desire. What is important to them for their future happiness and the happiness of the family, is that they learn to love the new person (spouse) as fully as they have loved the former person (spouse). And to be able to nurture that love such that it will grow beyond what it was when they were dating and beyond what it was during the first weeks of their honeymoon.

The sexual relationship far too often goes into a slump during the pregnancy and following the birth of the first child. For some couples, it diminishes with additional children as the wife and husband find work demands within the home increasing. It may be tied to feelings of resentment, exhaustion, or simply distraction. Frequently, they accept this loss of romantic and sexual feeling as somehow inevitable. "I don't believe you can expect the spark to last in the same way after children come along," said one wife. "Children have a way of turning everything upside down. Once you become parents, the romance just seems to dry up. We still love one another, but it isn't the same. How can it be?" Well, it can be, but only if husband and wife do not accept the loss of romance, excitement, and the joys of sexual love as a self-fulfilling prophecy that comes with the start of a family. No matter what demands are made by children, the old saying, "Where there is a will, there is a way," applies. It may take more ingenuity to keep those special moments, those late evenings before the fireplace together, and those occasional weekends away, but it can be done. To deny it, or neglect it, is to invite resentment, depression, or divorce.

Soon after the baby joins the family, events, some planned and some unplanned, begin to form family customs and traditions. These ultimately provide a framework upon which the character of the unique family is built. As the events are repeated, and are found to be rewarding by first the parents and then the children, they establish bonds which set the family members and their relationships apart, distinct from friends, relatives, and neighbors. It may seem a bit farfetched to speak of building family traditions when an infant is less than a year old, but in fact, traditions will probably have been in the planning stage from the onset of pregnancy. Parents-to-be share their dreams of a family, visual images of *their* family and its identity. These dreams, goals, and plans will have been expanded throughout pregnancy and the first months in the life of their child. Later they will both further develop those, and relive in the warmth of nostalgia the early, somewhat tentative "traditions" they initiate.

While many of these traditions and memories will come from accidental, spontaneous events, some will result from planning: what we call "planned memories." Think of the "perfect" evening out together. Sometimes it may "just happen," but more often, it will be the result of planning. Clothes will be selected, reservations made, and flowers purchased. In effect, a scenario will have been "written" for the entire evening. Family memories—and the traditions which result from them and which are cherished most fondly—are usually planned with equal care. It may be a first-month birthday party in which Father-Mother-baby join in a celebration, cake and all. Maybe the one-month-old cannot understand and appreciate the festivities, but the parents can. Who knows, it might be the beginning of anchovy pizza as a birthday meal. In any case, it will form one more memory to be stored in that mental "computer bank" so essential to the development of bonding—first between the parents, and in time between all members of the family. It may be a photographic pose to be repeated year after year. We can recall that for our first child's first birthday, we had a small plastic windup carousel on the dinner table beside the cake. We don't remember where or when we purchased it. It was about a foot high, yellow and orange, and rather garish. It had little birds' heads poking out of it, which rapidly bobbed up and down as the carousel revolved. It became a birthday "tradition," and none of the children ever failed to burst into laughter when we wound it up and set it in motion. And there were other traditions. The "Happy Birthday" on the birthday cake was traditionally the artwork of Daddy, inscribed on a birthday cake traditionally baked by Mommy. Over the years, we found that family traditions can be established through almost anything and everything. Often circumstances or last-minute necessities dictated an action which became a tradition. When our eldest child was six, we decided to do something which has become a Christmas tradition and which has provided countless hours of pleasure to all of us. It has also provided immeasurable bonding. It happened quite by accident. We wanted to take the children downtown to see the decorated store windows, the lighted lampposts, the tinseled tree, and all the glitter which plays a part in putting us in a holiday mood. But we knew that children are children, and that many of the toys and other goodies they would see might touch off pleas of, "Oh, can I have that?" At the time, living in married-student housing as graduate students, we had little money to provide for Christmas. We came up with what we hoped might be an effective way to counter the pleas and to avoid having to say no. We told the children we would go downtown and look at all the lights and the pretty windows, and then before the stores closed for the evening, we would let them select one ornament for the Christmas tree. It would be theirs alone. They would hang it on the tree. And then when the tree was taken down after Christmas, they would put their ornament away in a "special" box, to be hung on the tree in following years. With each passing Christmas, the "tradition" was repeated. And with increasing family members, what began as a practical strategy became a very rewarding and bonding tradition. Like many traditions, it grew. "That one was Stephen's from the year before last." "That green bird up on top. Wasn't that the one Kathy picked out when she was about eight?" The minor scheme, now many years past, generated what have turned out to be a whole set of traditions. We have set aside a special day each year to shop for ornaments. It usually includes lunch at the restaurant, and a day in which to enjoy being together and laughing together. And our Christmas tree becomes, then, not simply one more decorated tree, indistinguishable from any other in the neighborhood; rather it is a tree decorated with memories, wrapped in a tradition.

The nice thing about family traditions is that they can be built out of so little; they are limited only by the imagination and desires of the members. We like parties, and like most families we celebrate the usual holidays, birthdays, and special events with a party. But long ago we decided there was no reason to limit parties to just the usual and commonplace. Having so decided, we discovered an inexhaustible number of reasons for partying. We have admittedly, an edge on this with a large family. We can have eleven birthday parties, two, sometimes three, graduations a year, plus various celebrations of school awards, etc., all of which get us off to a head start in coming up with excuses for a party. But beyond that, there can be something with no more excuse than a TGIF (Thank God It's Friday) party, a getting-out-of-school party, or a party to celebrate Groundhog Day, or the first day of spring. Any party can draw us together and provide an atmosphere of laughter.

But parties, of course, are only a part of family traditions. A picnic breakfast following Sunday church can easily become a summer tradition. Or a traditional snowball fight on the first snow. Or a family diary we share over and over again, which includes highlights of vacations and achievements of family members—a memory journal. "Traditions," as we see it within a family, are met by only three criteria:

1. That the activity is fun for all members of the family

2. That it is repeated, and therefore builds positive memories

3. That it is exclusive, limited to members of the immediate family only—an in-group activity

They may be very, very simple. To outsiders, they might even seem silly. And most probably, in later years they will provoke a warm laughter from parents as well as children over "the crazy things we used to do." But they are an important, very important, ingredient in the mortar which binds together three or more persons united in love.

This chapter has focused on "nest-building," a term which may seem too cute and superficial to describe the actions and attitudes which go into the formation of a family once husband and wife decide to take on the responsibility of parenthood. But if we can be forgiven the metaphor, we would like to expand it into something more than those initial preparatory actions. The "nest" is not built during the nine months of pregnancy, or even during the first few months of having a stranger in the home. Nest-building continues during all the years of family integration. With the first infant occupying the home, father and mother begin the structure of nest-building, the roles they will play, the accommodations in time and space they will make, the ways in which they will maintain their husband and wife love affair, the responsibilities they will assume, and the goals they will set for the future growth of their family. They may feel they are ready for the stranger when he first crosses the front door, but they will quickly find there are many adjustments they have not anticipated. The nest has not been completed. Many further adjustments and additions will be made. The initial lovers, husband and wife, will be strained to the utmost in their flexibility to make these adjustments. They will be challenged. And they will be tested in their love to meet these challenges. She will be asked to be lover and companion and sexual partner as well as mother (often apprehensively) to her newborn. He will be asked to be understanding and supportive and caring as a father, as well as remaining a romantic, attentive husband. Surprisingly enough, none of these roles are incompatible, although the couple may have been put on notice that they were in conflict. They *can* continue to love one another as they did when they first tentatively chose to join their lives and commit their futures to one another. The child they bring into the world is an awesome responsibility, but that child also serves as a visual, living, outgrowth of the emotional contract they have given to each other. If marriage begins as a pledge of love, then the beginning of a family serves as the proof of that pledge when it is acted out in love and responsibility. The nest is not built of twigs and strings, cribs, diapers, and two o'clock feedings. It is built of commitment. It is constructed out of a joint, and equal, assumption of responsibility for human life, attained through the bonding, commitment, and love, of one man and one woman.

4

And Then Another

The second child descends upon the family just about the time the parents feel they've adjusted to the first. It may be a year later or five years later, but one thing is sure: the parents are not ready for the results.

When the first child is brought into the home, everything changes. The parents are no longer two; they are three. And those changes are more than either of them anticipated. But it is still a two-to-one situation, and they can usually cope. When the second child comes along, they not only face all the demands and frustrations (as well as—let's not be entirely negative—the joys) of the first child; they now have compounded the challenges and responsibilities. Just as it has never been true that two can live as cheaply as one, it is equally untrue that two children can be coped with as easily as one.

Sociologists are fond of describing human interactions in terms of what they call a *sociogram*. In a simplifying form, this is a diagram of the lines of influence, conflict, and emotional closeness between various members in a group. The group may be members of a committee, a team of research scientists, or a family. A may feel closer to (or have more influence over) C than B. B may feel closer to (or have more influence over) D than A or C.

And C may be able to relate only to A, negatively or positively. These lines of what might be called intimacy or influence or even antagonism can change from time to time and from event to event. It may help to view the family in terms of an ever-shifting sociogram with lines between husband–wife, husband–child A, husband–child B, wife–child A, wife–child B, and child A–child B. When the first child arrives on the scene, the first thing we notice in most families is a weakening of the lines of emotional closeness between husband and wife. This is not inevitable. It is, we claim, the product of social conditioning. Later, when we discuss the role of sexuality in the family, we will expand on the importance of the maintenance of unity between husband and wife and the importance they should place on retaining the romance and bonding they established before the arrival of children. Initially, the third member of the family will become the primary focus of attention probably of both parents. How they cope with this new demand which can so easily pull them apart will prove crucial to both their marital relationship and the success they attain in their roles as parents.

When jealousy develops outside the family, we seem to find it easier to understand than when those same emotions of jealousy are evident between family members, yet there is no reason why we should. The husband has been "Number One" with his wife. Then the baby arrives. He then may show jealousy when she seems to turn most of her attention to that new crying, demanding, infant. And when you have been Number One in the world of your spouse—it is understandable that having your position usurped by an infant is indeed a frustration, even if the cause is a very rational one. Later on, the wife may react with similar jealousy when the husband makes his son or daughter top priority in his life, a not uncommon occurrence. Now, when we add to these potential problems those that may arise when the second child is added to the family, we can imagine the tensions that may result. The firstborn infant may be mother's boy/girl. The second may be father's. In a short time, the first child may envy the attention the second child receives. The second child may envy the first child. Conflicts can result. Whenever a new member is added to the family—and this holds true whether the new member is a child or a mother-in-law—potential problems will be present. Fortunately, the problems only have to remain potential; they don't have to become realities.

When the parents have the requisite maturity, families have a way of solidifying when faced with change. When a new one enters the family, the existing members shift in their patterns of behavior, they quickly accustom themselves to accommodate the new member and the new routine demanded. They recognize that with the introduction of a new member into the family everything changes, whether that new member is the fourth, seventh, or tenth member of the family. That isn't to say that the accommodations are necessarily lessened by the increase in number. With each addition to the family, the accommodations in space and time will probably be as great as when the first child came home from the hospital. The household has to be shifted around. The parents will face the same questions—perhaps not the same, but questions which will have a *déjà vu* quality: If the new baby is moved into the nursery occupied by the "older" baby, how do we (the parents) cope with the different feeding, bathing, and changing times of the two of them? How do we cope with our very ambulatory three-year-old who wants to play with his slumbering month-old brother or sister? And what do we do when we are rocking or feeding the newborn and our older child wants attention—or perhaps even a lap to climb up on? The answers to these questions will all come down to two basics: *rationality* and *accommodation*. Out of those two will result a third: *flexibility*. The parents will have to be "quick on their feet" to adapt to the demands of a two- (or more) child family while avoiding favoritism. And they will suffer doubts, and perhaps even recriminations, in the process. Happily, *love* has a way of healing the mistakes.

Assuming the parents have met the challenge of high-cost maternity care, the first question is where he or she is to be housed? Remembering those complex preparations and space transformations involved with the first baby, this may seem to be a depressing question. But it need not be. To begin with, when the second child arrives the parents probably still have most of the necessary equipment. If the first child is still sleeping in a crib, a second crib may be needed. The model nursery may feed the fantasy needs of the parents expecting the first child, but perhaps by the second or third they have come to realize that nurseries are short-lived habitats. Therefore, a used-furniture store may offer the best bargain for a second crib. Most other baby furniture will still be around. One high chair is generally enough for any family, unless there are twins. Most of the major space adjustments in the household will have already taken place. Parents quickly grow accustomed to having a playpen in the kitchen or living room, a high chair beside the kitchen table, and a stroller beside the front door. The accommodations, therefore, to a second child can almost be viewed as less than that demanded by the first child. It's simply that the parents will have already gone through the trauma of having a baby invade and take over an entire house.

Each additional family member will call for reapportionment of the space within the home. New questions must be answered. Will an additional bedroom be needed? Will resentments and tensions develop as the territorial per capita space is reduced? During the sixties, those who were most concerned with a predicted population "explosion" cited studies of animals in captivity who engaged in aggressive behavior under conditions of overcrowding. They extrapolated this to humans. Isn't it possible, they said, that the alarming rate of violence in urban ghettos can be attributed to high population density. They apparently overlooked the fact that some of the highest population densities (e.g., Tokyo) have very little violence. Even large numbers of people can crowd into a home environment or neighborhood and live together in harmony. But it will call for accommodation and mutual concern. And some sensible planning ahead so that the existing family members are prepared for the new arrival.

By age two, a child can be talked to about the baby to come. If the news is presented as, "Mommy is going to have a baby," the elder child or children are relegated to the role of observer or even outsider. They may be entertained by the new family member, but they will feel they have no participation. The baby will belong to Mommy and Daddy; it will be *their* "thing." It may seem to be stretching it to put such an interpretation on a brief conversation, but a two-year-old often understands more than we suppose. If the new baby, like new furniture for the master bedroom, benefits only the parents, it may be judged by its elder sibling as simply a stranger invading a territory previously claimed exclusively by the elder children. In a lot of writing by pop-psychology "experts," sibling rivalry is described as almost inevitable. This view is, we feel, patently absurd. We do not believe that children are born with some sort of genetic endowment of rivalry, envy, and jealousy. Envy, like prejudice, has to be learned; it is not inborn. If the parents vie with each other over which television show to watch, or where to spend the vacation that year, or whose turn it is to clean the kitchen, we would expect their children to grow up copying the childishness of the parents. We have counseled many families in which sibling rivalry has been a serious problem. In some of these families the rivalry has developed into intense and long-standing hostility. In every case we observed consistent rivalry and hostility between the parents.

There is no reason to expect the new baby to take attention or love from the older children. Love does not have finite limits; it is not something we must carefully portion out among the members of our families. All of us have the capacity to love without reserve. We may hold it back. We may refuse it, but it is not exhaustible. The parent who can love one child can love twenty; the parent who cannot love twenty, cannot love one. Each family member brings to the family unique gifts of personality, intellect, and creativity. And each brings something of even greater value, the opportunity to love and to share. When baby is moved into the bedroom occupied by an elder sibling, is there any reason why we should expect feelings of resentment to arise, or any reason we might anticipate that the elder child will feel "displaced"? If a puppy joins the family, the parents may have to exercise firmness to convince the child that no, the puppy may not sleep in the child's bedroom. The child doesn't resent the "intrusion," he welcomes it. The parents do not resent one another when they share the same bed (assuming they have a fulfilling relationship). Having a large family, we have not, until recently, enjoyed the luxury of one child per bedroom. Now, with the exodus of our older children, it is possible. In conversations with our children over the years, however, we have learned that the circumstances necessitating doubling up and, in some cases, tripling up, have been seen by them to represent an advantage as much as a disadvantage. They were able to grow up with one or more roommates (sometimes shifting from one room to another and/or exchanging roommates). Although it is difficult to evaluate the relative contributions all the various interactions within the family have upon bonding, we have reason to believe this necessary sharing of living space has added a lot. We feel it has contributed greatly to the close friendships within the family. At most, we can say this: in our clinical practice, we have spoken with some who have recalled childhood memories of sleeping four or five in a single room, and with others who grew up never having to share a bedroom. When we have questioned each of them on the presence of sibling rivalry in their childhoods, we have not been able to find any correlation that might indicate sharing—whether of things or space—produces rivalries and jealousies. And on the other side of the coin, we have been unable to find stronger bonding, cooperation, or lack of rivalry which could clearly be attributed to any supposed "benefit" of membership in a large family. We have seen intense bitterness in large as well as small families, just as we have observed love and closeness in both. Family size is not the critical factor.

What is important is that each family member be able to recognize what he or she has to gain from a new member. Recognizing the pride that can justifiably be taken in a new member is also important. As parents, we pridefully announce, "This is my son; this is my daughter." Equal pride should be able to be found in saying, "This is my brother; this is my sister, this is a member of my family." The teaching of such pride is a parental responsibility. The older child must be told of and shown the value of the new arrival. "How lucky you are! You have a new baby brother, someone you can help care for, someone you will be able to play with, someone you will be able to teach, someone who will look up to you, someone you will be able to share adventures with, someone you will be able to love." The new baby is introduced into the family as someone who will add to the life of each family member in equal measure, never as someone who will take away anything.

These teachings begin to creep into the conversations months before the baby comes home from the hospital. As soon as the parents know a new one is on the way, the good news should be shared with the children. The baby will be *their* brother or sister. Theirs! The news is cause for celebration, for a party. And with the party, conversation of how they will each welcome the new family member. The new baby will serve as a *rite of passage* for the next eldest who will no longer be the "baby" of the family, and who will now enjoy the status and privileges of older brother or sister, as well as a full member of the family "welcoming committee." In a few weeks the older children will be able to place their hands on mother's body and feel the movements of the baby she carries, and watch as the baby grows within her. The "message" they will want to communicate is that the baby will belong to them just as they will belong to the baby: as members of the same family.

Welcoming the new member to the family, whether it is the first baby or the fifth, should be an occasion for celebration, with the "party" arrangements well completed beforehand. The hours following the baby's arrival home from the hospital should not be spent in frenetic readjustment of schedules, space, and attention. Any shifting around should be accomplished beforehand so that when the new arrival is carried through the door, the house does not at once take on the atmosphere of pandemonium, with parents scurrying from room to room trying to "settle" the infant, heat a bottle, and move furniture. It's a time for introductions, and for getting acquainted. It's a party time. Birthday! Christmas! The Fourth of July! A new member has joined the family! It is an occasion for sharing gifts—gifts the new family member brings to his or her older brothers or sisters, gifts they give in return. We have found a family "tradition" in bringing home from the hospital with the new member small, carefully selected gifts to the older children. These are gifts brought to them by their new brother or sister. They become one more bridge, we feel, toward establishing membership in the family. It isn't perhaps so important how this membership welcoming is communicated as it is that it is experienced. We feel that an atmosphere of celebration best expresses it. In the final analysis, we want all family members to understand that *we are a family*.

Children are insatiably curious, an observation which will come as no surprise to any parent of a child over two years of age. Little by little, as they satisfy their curiosity, they learn. When the tiny brother or sister enters the domain, their curiosity is aroused; they want to investigate. They want to get acquainted, and looking and touching is their way of saying, "Welcome." Most of us parents are too quick to "defend" our newborn from such investigations. We drive the car into the garage, straight home from the hospital. The husband jumps out, runs around the car to open the door for his wife and baby. He takes her arm and leads her to the front door as if fearful that she may drop her precious cargo. Once inside, they may head straight for the waiting crib or bassinet, and breathe a sigh of relief only when the newborn has been safely laid to rest. It may make little difference if they have fed, bathed, and bounced one or more babies before this one. Each one seems amazingly tiny and fragile (do we ever fail to comment on how tiny the little hands and feet are, and how we can't remember how small and apparently helpless is a newborn?). The parents then tiptoe from the nursery making shhhhh sounds. Older children in the family get, at best, only a fleeting glance at their new brother or sister. Naturally they're curious. Mother and father have to examine the baby from head to toe only moments after birth; why shouldn't they also have the opportunity? Just a short period of time sitting on the couch or in a chair with baby on the parent's lap to allow the children to ooh and ahh, to look, and to touch may be the best introduction to the family possible. Newborns are not constructed of venetian glass; they can be touched without risk of breaking. And older children are a little like the family pets: they seldom carry germs which are apt to be caught by the baby. Parents always have the ultimate responsibility and the final say about who does what where the baby is concerned. The point to be stressed is that the baby not be isolated from the other family members, but that he or she be introduced as a full member of the family—a brother or sister—and that the infant be integrated into the family as soon as possible.

As a matter of convenience, the newest member of the family will usually sleep in the parents' bedroom until he or she has given up night feedings. Once that period is over, parental privacy takes precedence, and an elder child (or children) acquires a new roommate. It should be pointed out in passing, however, that there are three disadvantages to such roommate arrangements and that they have nothing to do with sibling rivalry: the baby may occasionally cry during the night; roommates find great enjoyment in entertaining each other; hence, bedtime may not always mean "eyes shut, or right to sleep." And, by ages two and three, the roommates often become conspirators in adventures which can test the patience of the most tranquil parent (early-morning experiments with mother's lipsticks on the bathroom walls, trampoline competitions on crib mattresses). Nevertheless, as veterans of the frustrations accompanying these adventures, we still feel very strongly that the bonding which the roommates develop makes it all worthwhile.

5

No Two Alike

No two children live in the same environment. Nor do their parents. We live in worlds that are, in significant ways, unique. Being male is different from being female. This is not a sexist statement, simply a fact. Whether a baby is dressed in pink or blue, given a doll or a toy truck, or surrounded by "unisex" objects, he or she will inevitably discover a sexual identity. Some of the more vehement feminists seem to suggest that children be protected from making this discrimination. They feel it can only lead to sexist attitudes and feelings of superiority (male) and inferiority (female). But unless gender determines roles, and there is good evidence that it does not, the three-year-old's discovery that she is a girl and her younger sibling is a boy, will not, in itself, determine her interests, attitudes, or self-image. Like brown hair or blue eyes, gender is simply a fact of life. How she may see being a girl, that is, her attitudes toward it, may be another matter, something we will return to in a later chapter. Whatever the psychosocial effects of gender discovery may be, however, one fact will emerge clearly: being (or having) a brother is different from being (or having) a sister. Being the eldest child is different from being the youngest, and both are different from being a middle child. There is lit-

tle evidence that any of these differences are universal,
and, despite endless debates and conjectures, there seems
little reason to believe that birth order per se is a
significant factor in either child development or family
bonding. What seems far more important is role assignment, that is, the roles and expectancies which we, the
parents, assign to the individual family members, and the
roles and attitudes they each assume. We view it as a
major parental responsibility to pay close attention to the
children's role development and relationship to one another and to its effect on their self-esteem. Rights and
privileges follow the child's steps toward maturity. Ordinarily this fact can be understood rather easily by the
child. Therefore, it is seldom that major problems will
arise when the parents explain to their six-year-old why
the sixteen-year-old brother may be given permission to go
places and do things forbidden to him. "Because he is
older," will generally be an acceptable answer. More of a
problem may arise when the children are closely spaced.
What do we do with children ages ten, nine, and eight?
At what age does a "no" change to a "yes"? In the logic
of a child (and it may be a logic which we adults find
difficult to refute), why should one year make a great
difference? Obviously, maturity is never a matter of mere
chronological age, yet no sane parents would set off the
conflicts and bruised ego which would inevitably result if
they were to say, "Jane (age twelve) has permission to attend the junior high dance because we feel she is more
mature than you, Billy (age thirteen)." With children
close in age, the decisions will often seem arbitrary and
perhaps they *are*. Such decisions will fall into that broad
(and often vexing) area of parenting: judgment calls.
These are the decisions which try parents' souls, the ones
which keep returning to consciousness, making us ask
"Did we do the right thing?" There will be no way in

which the disappointments, and what may seem to be unfairness, can be totally avoided. The best parents can often offer is the promise, "Next year you will be able to go too. Jimmy also had to wait until he was thirteen."

It is often much easier to avoid exaggerated age distinctions. An awful lot of pseudopsychological nonsense about developmental "stages" comes about from toys which are designated as appropriate for four- to six-year-olds (but not for three- to seven-year-olds), books and magazine articles informing parents on suitable vacations and outings for the ten-year-old, but not for the sixteen-year-old. If nothing else, these artificial "stage" distinctions can drastically curtail family activities. Our own family has a child age span of eleven years, yet we have as a family attended concerts, explored European cathedrals and museums, visited amusement parks and zoos, volcanoes, and caves. We have dined together on Japanese mizutaki while sitting back on our heels on tatami mats, on pressed duck in Paris, on exotic fish at a Hawaiian hukilau, and countless times on hamburgers at the golden arches. And in all this we have discovered something: that an activity can generally offer something for everyone. A six-year-old may not be turned-on by the same things on that visit to the art museum as a sixteen-year-old. On the other hand, two sixteen-year-olds will rarely share identical interests. People who find life exciting and interesting are seldom bored, they find *something* of interest in virtually everything they do. The goal for the family is to find fun and excitement in being together, sharing experiences in whatever they may be doing.

The sixties and seventies saw a shift away from family activities. Individuality which went beyond mere respect for individual differences was virtually reverenced. Under the banner of "do-your-own-thing," the worst examples of egocentricity were fostered, even glorified. Mothers, fathers, and children each, in their own way, would opt to do their "own thing." This philosophy went beyond self-interest. The message of the gurus of the "me" or "I want it all—now!" generation taught a selfishness which often bordered on viciousness. The adult, as he or she matures, learns that loving—giving—actions through which concern for others are demonstrated, are in our self-interest. Such actions add to our self-esteem and our happiness. The selfishness of a child, even a forty-year-old child, is directed toward only immediate gratification. There is little or no concern for what effect the actions may have on others. Love has been defined as seeking to meet the needs and desires of the loved one. We have observed many parents "patiently" sitting on a bench at the zoo watching their children observe the antics of the monkeys or the lumbering movements of the elephants. Such parents often appear to work hard to maintain their images as "good" parents. They wear expressions of indulgence or long suffering, watching their children having childish "fun." Could it be that consciously or unconsciously they may be seeking to foster in their children feelings of guilt or indebtedness to them for the "sacrifices" they are making as parents? And when older children have been brought along, are the older children resentfully baby-sitting for their younger siblings, or are they ignoring the younger ones while they go off to do their own thing? Often it appears as if the family members are ashamed to be seen together or find the company of the family intolerable. Many so-called modernists have succeeded in persuading an army of children and their hedonistic, resentful parents that responsibilities toward family are hopelessly old-fashioned, stifling to a free spirit, and a stumbling block on the path toward "discovering one's self."

The "do-your-own-thing" advocates have done their job

well. They taught children and their parents that it would be exploitive to ask a child to care for a younger brother or sister, even minimally. A thirteen- or fourteen-year-old might baby-sit for the neighbors for an hourly wage. That would be perfectly acceptable and a fine way to earn spending money. But if the child were asked to look after a younger brother or sister while mother shopped for groceries, that would be an unfair imposition. Child care, so the argument of these advocates of "individuality" goes, is the sole responsibility of the parent (or, in some cases, the society at large), but an older child should not be imposed upon to help a younger one tie a shoelace, go to the bathroom, or learn a spelling lesson. Burdened with such inequitably imposed tasks, the older child might grow up resenting both his parents and his younger siblings. Heaven knows what such unfairness might do to the child's psyche! The resentment and emotional trauma might be avoided, we suppose, if the parents offered sufficient monetary rewards for such "assistance." We spoke with one couple who told us they were having difficulty finding a baby-sitter for their four-year-old for the occasional evening they would like to go out to dinner or a movie. "Don't you have a daughter in high school?" we asked. The wife laughed. "Sure, Allison is sixteen, but she says she won't work for the pay of a baby-sitter. She wants almost twice the going rate, and we don't feel we can afford it." Another mother told us that at those times when she got busy, she would ask her high school son to make a sandwich for himself for lunch—and she would offer to pay him fifty cents if he would also make one for his seven-year-old sister!

On the grounds of the famed Boys Town home for boys in Nebraska, there is a statue which symbolizes this institution founded by Father Flanagan. It is of a young boy carrying a still younger boy piggyback. The statue and its inscription commemorates a time during the earliest days of the home when two boys arrived at the door seeking refuge, the older one carrying the younger on his back. Father Flanagan said something to the older boy about the younger one being heavy. The legendary reply, "He ain't heavy, Father; he's my brother," speaks eloquently of the philosophy upon which this amazing community of homeless boys was built. Is it a philosophy we no longer want our children to hold, a set of attitudes we fear might restrict their freedom? We feel sure all sensible parents would easily reject such a suggestion. Concern for others, a generosity of spirit, and loyalty cannot be obsolete values, despite the strongest effort of any band of self-appointed authorities who, in the name of humanism and liberalism, have attacked everything and anything not directed toward immediate self-centered gratification.

Favoritism is a fear most of us, as parents, have felt at one time or another when we have dealt with two or more children. "Am I favoring this one child over the other?" It is a painful question, one which can rob of us more than one good night's sleep. But perhaps it would be best first to attempt to define what we mean by favoritism, and then to place it in perspective.

Favoritism is an unfair favoring of one person or group over others. Key to the definition is the word *unfair*. We quite naturally favor a courteous salesperson over one who is rude. We favor a community which is friendly over one which is cold to strangers. We favor the child who is obedient over the one who is unruly. These are very understandable, rational, and fair discriminations. They are not exactly, therefore, a favoritism.

We all want to treat our children with fairness. We recognize the importance of justice. We recognize the evils of injustice. We want to treat our children with equality, and we want to spare them the hurt of unfairness. But achieving it is seldom easy. We might all like to find the perfect standard which will tell us when we have achieved that fine balance in which we give to one child the exact equal to that which we give to the other. We're not sure even King Solomon could have ruled with perfect justice each and every time!

Perhaps the first way to escape the dilemma can be found in accepting the fact that *equality* is not the same as *uniformity*. Often, in fact, identical treatment will result in inequality. Suppose one child is addicted to rock music while another strongly dislikes it. We might attempt to treat them identically by taking both to a rock concert. We have treated both identically but not equally. We would not be acting in "fairness" to both if our goal was to reward both equally. Parents will often try to cope with the problem of how to treat children equally at Christmastime. Some will establish a budget and place a price limit "equality" on the gifts. In doing so, they are acting as if the price of a gift determines its intrinsic value to the individual, an assumption we all know to be false. In time, of course, they may shut off any complaints of inequality by the children by pointing out the equal amounts spent, but we would seriously question what such a dollars-and-cents value system teaches children about giving.

Any hard-and-fast rules designed to consistently treat the children "equally" is almost bound to result in unfairness. Duplicate gifts are seldom appropriate. Rarely will the same toy, book, or piece of wearing apparel be desired by two children in the same family. The harsh fact of the matter is that we can never be sure that we are acting fairly. There are simply too many factors involved. We can only try. The major step is taken when we attempt to recognize the unique needs and desires of each child. In doing so we avoid viewing them as children—

plural. They are individuals, therefore we are faced with the monumental task of tuning in to them at that moment in time in order to ascertain their thoughts, feelings, and desires. This extends far beyond gift-giving. Two of our children might be assigned the task of cleaning up the dinner dishes. Would it be fair to relieve one from this duty, leaving the other to finish the job? Offhand, it might not seem so. On the other hand, circumstances can make the question more difficult. We have a daughter who is very interested in gymnastics. Suppose on the evening in question there was a television special on gymnastics, one she had been strongly looking forward to watching. Under the circumstances, we might attempt to work out an agreement whereby her brother or sister cleaned the kitchen on that evening with the understanding that she would tackle the job alone the following evening. We have found that even the time we may expect them to spend on homework cannot be always fairly laid down as a rule to be applied to each child. If one child is having a great struggle with English and mathematics, while another is consistently making straight A's, it would not be fair to impose the additional study needed for the child getting poor grades on the one who is top of the class. We would probably assign additional study time to the one who obviously needs it, while perhaps giving television or pleasure-reading privileges to the other. As much as anything else in the judgments demanded of parents, those in which questions of fairness arise may be most difficult. But then, no parent ever claimed that parenthood demanded only easy choices.

Parenthood includes putting up with accusations of unfairness. Every parent with more than one child has heard it: "But that's not fair!" Children seem to become almost obsessed with what they see as fair and unfair—when it comes to defending what they see as their rights, that is.

Their reasoning may not always be sound, but they will develop almost a knee-jerk reaction, and will make the accusation, "that's not fair," at the drop of a parental demand. Why they do so is rather apparent: they learn it often works to get them what they want. The fear of being unfair is so strong in most parents that children discover the accusation is an effective means to manipulate mother and father. We want our children to treat their parents and siblings with fairness, and we know they look to us for examples so of course we do our best to act with fairness. Since we cannot always be sure we do, we feel vulnerable to the accusations. We get tripped up on our own feelings. It is important, therefore, that we try to sort out what we are reacting to, feelings or actions.

Bending over backward in fairness to children can sometimes be as damaging as being grossly unfair. That cry of "unfair!" from one of our children can stop most of us in our tracks. The accusation may have no foundation at all, but if at the time we hear it we are angry at the child, our emotions can bring on both doubt and guilt. It is the problem of guilt we experience in so many areas of our lives. We experience guilt over feelings rather than actions, and yet it is only on our actions that we should be judged. We all have strong convictions about how we *should* feel toward our children, the first rule of which is: never dislike them. Good, loving, parents always like their children, right? Wrong. No one is passing out halos to children or perpetual patience to parents. But most of us from time to time feel guilty when we discover that at any particular moment we simply may not like one or another of our children—or perhaps all of them. They are not always likable. Oh, sure, we tell ourselves that the five-month-old is not literally trying to drive us to a mental hospital with his crying at three in the morning, but rationality is not necessarily our forte at 3:00 A.M. Frustration does not always lead us to total rationality. But then, we humans are not totally rational animals. More often than not, frustration can set off feelings of *he's-driving-me-crazy-and-I-would-like-to-make-his-life-miserable.* Whatever our feeling at the moment, most of us do succeed in carrying out our parenting in a caring manner. Sure we say no. And we say yes. We give orders. We bestow rewards. And we mete out punishment for misbehavior. It may often seem to the child that we are, indeed, trying to make his life miserable. But are we being unfair? Most of the time, probably not. Nevertheless, it is not an objective analysis of our actions which is so disturbing to us: it is our feelings. Since we cling to the notion that as "good" parents we always feel loving, and never angry or vengeful, we feel guilty when we slip from such an exalted pedestal of virtue.

Is there any way that we can know that we are exercising our parental authority and the power that goes with it in a manner detached from our emotions? In a word, do we have any means of testing whether we are acting justly? First, we hasten to say, parenthood comes with few guarantees. Such certainty, desirable as it is, will seldom be found. There are, however, three possible ways to check on the justice of our actions with the goal of increasing parental justice:

1. *Self-examination.* Stepping outside oneself may never be possible in any total sense. Most of us do succeed over a period of time, however, in learning to view situations (even those in which we are emotionally involved) with increased objectivity. We have found it sometimes helps to sit down with a pencil and pad and write about our feelings, write about the issue involved, write about the decision we will make or have made. On rereading the material, we often arrive at greater objectivity.

2. *Reality-checking through one's spouse.* It is wise to

admit that we are not always best qualified to sit in judgment on our own action. It often helps, therefore, to seek a second opinion. We have found one another's opinions, as co-responsible parents, to be invaluable. We generally are not both equally "emotionally involved" in a confrontation with a child. It stands to reason, then, that the one who is relatively more removed and hence more cool and collected will be in a better position to give an objective opinion in response to the question, "Do you think I was being fair when I told Mary she couldn't go to the party Saturday night?" These reality checks have nothing to do with one parent or the other possessing superior intelligence or judgment. They simply recognize the fallibility and subjectivity to which each of us is vulnerable, especially when we are called upon to play the role of Solomon while the house is coming down around our ears! We grant it takes a good deal of maturity to ask for, and perhaps accept, the opinion of someone else when such an opinion runs smack up against our emotional reaction. But that's the whole reason for asking. If we are certain that we have acted in fairness (and such certainty demands considerable self-honesty), there is no reason to seek another opinion. Nine times out of ten, a second opinion can't hurt.

3. *Reality-checking through another child member of the family.* Other children can frequently provide invaluable reality checks on our fairness to one of their siblings in situations in which they are not involved in the confrontation. Children seem to be endowed with a very simple, yet keen, sense of justice. They tend to see things in black and white. And an alarm bell goes off in their heads when they witness injustice. So, as parents may go to one another, they may go to a brother or a sister to ask, "Do you think I was being fair when I told Mary . . . ?" Some parents have wondered whether to do so might not

undermine their parental authority, or leave the child less secure in the parent's knowledge and judgment. There is little risk of this. Very few parents want their children to see them as infallible. They want to raise them understanding that their parents can make mistakes and are mature enough to apologize when such mistakes or wrongs have hurt the child. We do not want to raise children to believe, "The parent is King, and the King can do no wrong." To seek an opinion from the siblings also conveys an important message: "I value you and your opinions, and I will listen to you."

In the long run, ridding ourselves of tendencies toward favoritism may rest on discovering the origins of such tendencies. When we feel an instant dislike for someone it frequently stems not from any obviously unacceptable behavior on their part (although we may attempt to explain it as such), but from what we are carrying around as "mental baggage" from long before we met them. This mental baggage may be a tendency to *project* our own motives toward others. All of us tend to project on occasion; that is, "If I feel such and such toward that situation, everyone else must feel the same way." We get angry at a child who persists in tapping his fingers on the table. We scream at him, "You're deliberately doing that to bug me!" What we are saying internally is, "If I were to tap my fingers on the table like that it would be with the intent of driving others crazy." But since almost any given action may reflect one or more of a large number of possible motivations, the best we can ever expect to do is to infer motivation from the observed behavior. As it turns out for most of us, we are probably wrong as many times as we are correct.

We also often "tar someone with the same brush with which we have tarred another." If we have a son who has a manner of speaking (laughing, slouching in a chair, scratching his ear) in a way similar to that of the brother we never got along with, we may be lashing out at the hated brother when we are looking at our son. This *transference* shows up in positive reactions as well as negative. A mother may find herself having to guard against the tendency to favor the son who looks very much like the husband whom she dearly loves. Favoritism and the problems of fairness/unfairness take on many colorings and reflect many, nearly hidden, motives.

In the pressure-cooker world in which so many of us live, unfairness may hit a child like a ricocheting bullet. We may *displace* our hostilities. The boss chews his employee out. The employee is understandably reluctant to answer back. But when he walks in the front door of his home that evening, his family would be well advised to tread lightly. At the slightest provocation, he may displace his hostility. It will no longer be bottled up, but will fire off, only to ricochet and hit the nearest person, animal, or chair. The roots of many of our hostile feelings can be found in frustrations we have wisely bottled up in one situation but unwisely let go in another.

Before locking in on a conclusion that our anger toward the child has only one origin, i.e., the frustrating behavior of the child, it would be well to ask ourselves questions based upon some of these other possible sources. And while we feel it is very unwise for spouses to attempt to "psychoanalyze" each other, husband and wife do have a lot to offer and a lot to gain in reality checking when done with love—and when it is requested.

We feel this raises the question and an issue which perhaps might better be placed in a separate chapter. Some would suggest, we are sure, that it should be left out of this book entirely. However, we feel it is so important for any discussion of *bonding* within the family that it cannot be ignored. We alluded to it in the introductory chapter. And we felt at the time we were writing that chapter that it would, perhaps, touch off a storm of protest. We even considered ignoring the issue, but we do not feel it can be ignored. So, to plunge right in, we believe the two-parent family, with both father and mother equally involved in decisions regarding the children, is the best possible environment in which to raise a child. It is the best environment not just because the parental workload is divided. It may not be. It is best because it divides the judgments and decision-making. It is best because it reflects the identities of both sexes, whatever they may be. It is best because it presents to the children comparisons and role models from which they can select the direction they choose for their own lives. Two heads are almost always better than one—and more objective. We bring to our decisions not only our own wisdom, but our own failings. Most often, the wisdom and information of one of us is not superior to the other. One of us is no smarter than the other, and certainly not by reason of gender. We also bring an equal number of weaknesses.

We have listened to those who sing the praises of single parenthood. To them, one is as good as two. We must say that from our experience we have not seen evidence of this. Of course, the occasional exception may be found. They can point out, and we can substantiate, that the conscientious mother supporting her family, teaching them moral values and the work ethic, is probably doing a better job than the mother who keeps the drunken, totally irresponsible father within the household. But to suggest that one conscientious parent can assume the responsibilities of parenting as well as two responsible parents is, to us, absurd. They have presented us with talk-show advocates of lesbian parenthood and a wide variety of "alternatives" to the nuclear family. We feel such arguments may be popular on daytime talk shows, but they ignore some basic psychodynamics of gender. (They usually ignore other rather obvious facts as well. But facts seldom seem to disturb them in presenting a defense for their "lifestyle.") We strongly contend that a mother/son relationship is best balanced by a complementary father/son relationship, and that a father/daughter relationship is best complemented by a mother/daughter relationship. To attempt to ignore this, or even refute it, with suggested alternatives such as, "Well, my son does get a male model from my boyfriend," or "Well, I've told my daughter all about men so she is fully prepared for dating," is deception of the first order.

To go into even a superficial examination of how mother/son, mother/daughter, father/son, father/daughter, and, most crucial, husband/wife, relationships interact within the family and are influenced by gender is beyond the intent and scope of this book. It may also be beyond our current knowledge of the differences between the sexes. Every time a social scientist presents data which might shed light on the question, he arouses the ire of those who are bent on proving their point by creating heat rather than light. Even if we could define and describe whatever differences may exist by reason of gender, we would run smack up against the always observable differences in individuals and their interactions. Generalizations would be totally invalid. Perhaps the best we can do as men and women, fathers and mothers, is attempt to be aware of ourselves, our children, our spouses, and how our views of masculinity and femininity influence all these various interactions. They may well be a major source of favoritism in the family.

Children also frequently play favorites, as we all know from our experiences in childhood. And this favoritism can be expressed in very cruel ways. There is usually little that we as parents can do to protect our children from the

numerous slings and arrows of favoritism they experience
in school and on the playground. Some child psychologists have argued rather effectively that parents should
do nothing, that these experiences are important in preparing the child for the so-called realities of adult life.
Others have counseled parents to contact teachers and
school authorities as soon as they are made aware of such
situations. We have no pat advice to give. We feel that
each incident must be judged on its own. There may be
times in which talking to the principal or teacher may be
effective. At other times, the politics involved may indicate a hands-off policy is best. What we might like to do
to protect our children from injustice meted out by a
teacher or other children will not be always possible.
When to speak up and when to keep quiet is another
question for parents, one which may have no easy answer.
What parents can and should do is to keep a close watch
on favoritism by children within the family.

One-to-one closeness between brothers and sisters may
shift from month to month or week to week, especially
when the siblings are close in age. Loyalties shift swiftly
and dramatically. That should be expected. They result
from shifting interests and activities. They come about
from instant angers and momentary shared pleasures.
They may result from a change in school, a shared or
abandoned hobby, from the development of mutual
friendships, or from sharing the same room. This may be
looked at as simply a process of natural selection. It is neither cruel or exclusionary unless it goes beyond selection
and involves exclusion. If son Jimmy is deeply involved in
model railroads, and daughter Cynthia is equally involved, there would seem to be no obligation on the two
of them to have to include, or even to try to include, their
brother William in their hobby. If William is interested,
and has something to offer (or might with additional

learning, have something to offer) to the model railroad they are building, then it would seem cruel to exclude him. But if the parents were to step in and demand that William be given permission to run the trains and play with the cars when William has shown no responsibility or interest in the model railroad, that would be unfair.

Children do not need to be pushed into including their brothers and sisters in each and every activity. They can be taught kindness and generosity, and they can then be left free to make their decisions on their own. Sometimes, they will reach out to a sibling when it may not be to their advantage. Jimmy and Cynthia may invite William to join them even when they suspect that William will just be in the way. But if William is not included, it may not indicate any unfairness, favoritism, or cruelty. With younger children, a certain amount of clannishness is almost to be expected. Children like to share their secrets. They like to form their clubs. If we take a look at it, we may interpret this as a precursor of what attracts us as adults to join exclusive, and even esoteric, organizations which bestow a mantle of "specialness." Who can say there is anything wrong with wanting to feel special? We all do. Specialness is only cruel when it is built upon arbitrary exclusions which may take on the flavor of prejudice. Children will form in-groups to gain self-esteem. Self-esteem is perhaps the most important thing we want to help our children attain. But when the child's efforts to gain self-esteem result in actions which lessen the self-esteem of the brother or sister, we have to call a halt. With three or more children in a family, if one child is excluded, the consequences work against the goal of self-esteem, and the value of fairness. It is at that point we, as parents, must step in.

This is a continuing problem in many families. Siblings may exclude one child by forming a pact to share "secrets." They join together in an ostentatious manner which says, "We don't want you with us." The harshness and the cruelty of their actions may not be apparent to them, but what they are seeking is not to be cruel but to garner power through what they may see as a minor cruelty. The "secrets" they share may amount to an exchange of trivia, but the outsider involved doesn't know it. All he or she knows is that such exclusion is painful. Some years ago there were sororities, fraternities, and other "blackball" clubs in some high schools. Fortunately, they have been abolished in most high schools as the teachers and administrators have realized how viciously they can be used to exclude the students who fail to meet the criteria of the in-group. While most of us abhor such social discrimination, we can do nothing about it except perhaps protest to the authorities in our school district. In our homes, we have better options. The child does not learn kindness in an environment in which discrimination is exercised in a way which can only be described as abhorrent. This is where the home comes in. If there is no other place in which the child can learn kindness and love, the home must be based upon, and actively live, these values.

Fortunately, such justice and love are virtues which can be easily taught and easily learned. We have said that children have a strong black-and-white sense of justice. They intuitively know what is fair and what is unfair. They are also attracted to kindness, assuming they have experienced the rewards of kindness shown to them by their parents. They find rewards in being kind to others. When we have discussed the hurt that can be brought by exclusion, we have seen the almost immediate understanding that typifies the child's absolute sense of justice. We have found that the short private talk, rather than a scolding, with the offender (the excluder), a talk in which we discuss our feelings, their feelings, and the concept of justice is very effective in avoiding unfairness. In its effectiveness, the talk is certainly preferable in outcome to any demand that, "You must play with your sister." There are times, of course, when some subtle distinctions must be made, and judgments must be set down which say, "Your brother/sister was not being unfair to you." We believe the eight-year-old can understand, once it is explained, why he cannot go on a bike ride with his seventeen-year-old brother and his brother's friends.

Accusations of unfairness can themselves often be unfair. When we appeal to children's sense of fairness and kindness, we most frequently say, "We know you want to be kind and fair, and that you are a very mature, just person." We try to enhance their self-esteem and security by making them understand that we value them and we recognize what they have to offer, in justice and love, to other members of the family.

Scapegoating is a far more serious problem. In scapegoating, one child is chosen to bear the blame for the others, to suffer the punishment for the other members of the family. Scapegoating has three characteristics: First, blame is inevitably aimed at the scapegoat, and it is often unjustified. Second, the blame is almost automatically accepted as valid by the other family members. And third, the family members engaged in the scapegoating derive some benefit from their accusations of blame.

The accusations take on the character of a knee-jerk response—"If the window is broken, it must be Robert's fault." Robert, God bless him, now faces a big problem. He is judged guilty until proven innocent. And proving his innocence is likely to be an overwhelming challenge. It takes on the character of the question "When did you stop beating your wife?" Once children in a family discover that scapegoating is effective, they pounce on it like hungry jackals. They operate as if proof, or even evidence, is no longer necessary. They are ready to believe almost anything, and do accuse on virtually no evidence whatsoever. Their victim will be labeled a "problem child" and they will push their point home at every opportunity. The "innocent" children will quickly see the benefit in having a scapegoat. He or she can carry the burden of the collective failings of the family. In its severest form, the parents join in the scapegoating. The "innocent" children come out of most interactions with the image of "good" children. And since our assessments of behavior are often relative, the "good" child may be seen as a paragon of virtue compared to the "problem" (scapegoated) child. As we might expect, the "good" child then plays on us by acting overly sympathetic to the frustration the parents suffer with the "problem" child, and by being overly compliant and solicitous at those times when the scapegoat is misbehaving.

Whenever there are severe interpersonal conflicts within the family, scapegoating may surface. It is as if the scapegoat is necessary in order to prevent the outbreak of numerous hostilities—on the rationale that "one enemy is better than five enemies." The scapegoat is the target for the displaced hostilities of all family members. The wife, frustrated by what she perceives as the coldness of her husband, may displace her anger toward the scapegoat child. Her husband, frustrated by his wife's sexual rejection, may displace his anger toward the same child. Their children may quickly join in the scapegoating either to displace their angers or to reap the rewards which go with a "good" child image. Scapegoating, thus, can quickly take on the aspects of a collusion in which the family members dump the blame for everything which goes wrong on the shoulders of the scapegoated "problem" child. It is usually only a small, quick step until the scapegoat learns to play the assigned role quite well. The more he is labeled a "problem," the more he becomes a problem. Explained psychiatrically, he "carries the symptoms for the family."

Since scapegoating can rapidly escalate to the ferocity of a pack of sharks attacking a wounded member of their species, immediate and dramatic actions must be taken when it is first suspected. Parental intervention is immediately called for. As usual, the first step should be a serious, and very extended discussion between husband and wife aimed at ferreting out the causes of the scapegoating. This may not come easy if either of them has begun to play a role in the displacement of hostility; parental responsibility, however, demands it. And how do you tell your spouse that he or she may be scapegoating a child? Unfortunately, there may be no diplomatic way. To be accused of scapegoating is to be accused of very unloving behavior, and no parent wants to hear such an accusation; but if the observation is accepted for what it is, a perception of reality by someone every bit as concerned for the welfare of that child as we ourselves claim to be, it can be listened to with an open mind and heart, painful though it may be, and accepted as at least a plausibly valid observation.

If it is only the other children who are engaged in the scapegoating, and the parents are uninvolved, one-on-one discussion with each of the children is probably the best approach. Bringing the scapegoaters together as a group would not only dilute their personal responsibility for what has been going on, it would give them a collective opportunity to justify their behavior. Scapegoating is so serious in consequence that the parental action must be immediate and sufficiently strong to stop it. The message to the guilty parties is, "Or else!" with a promised punishment which is severe enough to deter the behavior at once. If the scapegoating has gone on too long or to too great an extent to stop it immediately, we feel the parents have a responsibility to seek professional help from a psychiatrist, psychologist, or marriage and family counselor.

There are a number of positive steps which can be taken to reduce the chances of painful and destructive sibling rivalry and sibling favoritism. First, parents should accept the fact that rivalry is normal. Achievement throughout life will usually be the result of rivalry. In many respects, life is a game of win or lose. In school, children will be competing for grades. In sports they will be striving to beat their opponents. In almost every area, they will face competition. Rivalry within the family is normal. It is only when the rivalry takes on hostile coloring that parents need to become concerned. There will also inevitably be instances of favoritism. In every family of three or more children, especially when the children are close in age, there will be times when a situation of two against one arises. Often this is understandable and forgivable. When it is grossly unfair and hurtful, it is then time for the parents to step in.

We have found the assignment of mutual tasks to be helpful in handling these antagonisms. Since working together is generally task-bonding, assigning the two children who are at odds to a household task that will call for cooperative effort will have the effect of bringing them back together. Their initial reaction to the assignment may, of course, be negative. People do not like to work together when they are quarreling. But an assignment is an assignment. As parents we have the authority to assign tasks, somewhat arbitrarily perhaps, even if doing so casts us in the role of bad guys. We have employed this technique on more than a few occasions when we have had feuding children. They usually approach the task glowering at each other, but during the hour or two it takes to pull the weeds in our backyard, a transformation usually occurs. They bond, even though the bonding may be based upon a mutual feeling of resentment toward the mean parents who would assign them to such a job. We have also found that it sometimes helps if such jobs are split into separate but equal subjobs. One may pull the weeds, for example, while the other trims the lawn. Such splitting of the job may (and we emphasize *may*) avoid squabbles over who does the most.

We have also, at times, assigned one of the antagonists to assist the other. It is a technique which makes a blatant appeal to ego. "You're so clever with tools, perhaps you can give your brother a hand in fixing his bike," can sometimes work wonders. It gets the two of them working together (task-bonding) while providing the motivation (praise) for the helper. Almost nothing builds friendship more than helping and being helped. We cannot continue to dislike a person to whom we are reaching out and giving.

In any final analysis, destructive rivalry and favoritism can only be dispelled through the building and sustaining of self-esteem by each family member. When we truly like ourselves, we have no need to attempt to put down others. Nor do we feel that we have only enough capacity to love to give our love to one or two. We have more than enough gifts to share with everyone. One of the most important elements of bonding within the family is to be found in this sharing of unique talents. If the newborn infant brings a special contribution to the family— and he or she does—how much more can the five- or ten-year-old bring? If we search to discover the gifts we each contribute, and if we freely give them, we will, in effect, have no competition. Our gifts are unique. We will also be able to recognize the gifts offered by the other members in our family. The children of a family share a

genetic heritage, but they are not cloned. Even in a large
family there are no duplicates. God did not create a boring world. If we wonder at the uniqueness of a snowflake,
how much more must we stand in awe of the infinite variety we find in human beings? Each child is more than an
addition to the family. Through the gifts he or she brings,
all family members are enriched. In a loving family, they
all win. No one loses.

6

Our Daily Bread

Are we *rearing* children, *raising* children, or *bringing up* children? Or are these synonymous? Or are the words we use to describe parenting perhaps not too important? From one time to another, perhaps one description is more apt than another. Overall, we prefer the word *nurture*, defined here according to The Random House Dictionary of the English Language, College Edition:

Nurture (nər-chər, *v.*,-tured,-turing, *n.-vt.* I: to promote the development of by providing nourishment, support, encouragement, etc., during the stages of growth).

It is the "support, encouragement, *etc.*" which challenges parents in their responsibility and opportunity in the formation of the family.

If nurturing children means nothing more than "feed 'em, clothe 'em, and send 'em off to school," the task will not amount to much. Tedious, perhaps, but not too demanding. The rewards, however, will probably be equally scant. When the nurturing is expanded, however, to include education, social development, and emotional needs, and when it is broadened to include the interacting nurturant roles of each family member, the meaning of *nurturance* takes on a challenge which encompasses almost the entire mantle of parenthood.

Our first, and most obvious, attention to nurturance is to the physical needs of our family. Families need feeding, and as parents we are the suppliers to meet these physical needs. Our primary need as we are growing up, and the one we must have met if we are to survive is for food. The moment the umbilical cord is severed, we are dependent on the time and efforts of others to supply nourishment which will enable us to survive. The infant makes these needs known with a cry which is surprisingly loud, considering its small size, but understandable if we consider that it can only survive a very short time unless someone responds.

Most of us grew up taking physical nurturance for granted. Our food was placed before us and we ate it. We didn't have to forage for food. As infants we couldn't have done so. Our parents provided the food and drink which kept us alive. We seldom thanked them. It was their responsibility. And yet somewhere, perhaps, in our unconscious there is a residual of recognition of what they gave to us by physically nurturing us. And perhaps it is from this that we derive our first inklings of love.

Many of our artistic portrayals of the family are related to feeding: the mother nursing the infant at her breast; the holiday dinner; the birthday cake. Mom's apple pie may never have been as good as the soldiers in the field remembered it, but it *was* Mom's. It had the association with nurturance. When we have asked adults to share their memories of childhood with us, we have been struck by the number who have associated eating with their positive memories of childhood—family dinners, picnics, barbecues, popcorn parties, afterschool snacks. Eating occasions have been associated with conversation and laughter, sharing and learning.

When we were children, we didn't give much thought to how the food came to the table. We knew it was cooked in the kitchen, and we knew about trips to the grocery store, but beyond that, the roles our parents played in providing our daily bread, cookies, apples, stew, and milk was a mystery we didn't concern ourselves with. But as we have accepted the roles of parents ourselves, this is no longer a mystery. Food budgeting, shopping, preparing, and serving demands a lot of time and an increasing amount of money. Two or three decades ago, the parental roles involved in providing food for the table were sharply divided. The husband worked to provide the food; the wife worked to prepare it. Today, these roles are less and less distinguishable. Most wives work outside of the home. They provide the money to purchase the food as well as prepare it. And many husbands have developed —and used—cooking skills their mothers would have envied. Joint nurturance in providing food for the family goes beyond rigid roles. It doesn't matter who scrambles the eggs or wheels a cart down the aisles of a supermarket. It is the total nurturing role associated with feeding that is important. And in this there are many ways in which the spouses can share.

In our family, as in most, the kitchen is the social focal point. More conversation goes on in our kitchen than in all the rest of our home combined, and while this is partly explained by the fact that one or more of us seems to always be engaged in meal preparation or cleanup, having a snack or pouring a cup of coffee, the kitchen, with its obvious associations with nurturance, acts psychologically as a magnet to draw us together. (As we write this, we are sitting at the kitchen table—our usual writing area— rather than our office which is decidedly better suited.)

The environment for food nurturance—where and how we feed the baby—is important from the first, every bit as important as what we feed him or her. Parents are not a *part* of this environment. In almost every respect, they *are* the baby's environment. If they are tense, impatient, or irritable while feeding their baby, the baby's feeding environment will be one of tension. An environment is, by definition, the aggregate of surrounding things, conditions, or influences. But not all "things, conditions, and influences" can be given equal weight. We doubt whether the color of the kitchen curtains or the design of the wall paper will noticeably affect the baby's digestion, but the disposition of the parents will quite often have a dramatic effect. How a tiny infant so unerringly perceives the mood of the parents has not yet been fully explained. It may be changes in the muscle tension of the parent's arms. If the mother is breast-feeding, it may be some slight changes in her milk. All we know with certainty is that the baby picks up these changes, and responds. Family doctors, as well as most baby books, routinely advise nursing mothers to stay relaxed and inwardly calm while nursing. Tell this to the mother of a four-year-old attempting to cope with dinner on the stove, the telephone ringing off the hook, and the delivery boy at the door to collect for the newspaper. It reminds one of the saying, "If you can keep your head when all about you are losing theirs, you probably don't understand the problem." There are usually some ways, however, to reduce tension. First, and perhaps most important, *planning*.

Directly and indirectly, food preparation and feeding is the most time-consuming job in most families. Two adults have little trouble adjusting their mealtimes, and neither is dependent upon the other for food. A meal may be delayed fifteen minutes or even an hour without either of them throwing a tantrum or suffering severe hunger pangs. But with very young children, a ten-minute delay in mealtime seems an eternity. The two-year-old cannot prepare his own meal. Thus food preparation and serving, at least for the youngest members of the family, is not at the convenience of the parents. And while children may occasionally be served early, allowing the parents to enjoy a late dinner together (a practice we feel every couple should engage in at least once a week), a meal as a family, with all members present, is too important in its bonding value to be slighted or haphazardly scheduled. It may seem silly to suggest that a seven-month-old infant sitting in a high chair ingesting puréed beets can experience a closeness to his parents and to his brothers and sisters at the family table, but if the bonding experience the baby monkey finds clinging to a cloth mother surrogate is essential to the little animal's well-being (as Dr. Harry Harlow and his associates demonstrated some years ago), can we afford to disregard the possible caring/touching/nurturing benefits a small one may find in the family meal? Bonding, being what it is, is a two-way street, even a three- or four-way street. Bonding at the family meal is not merely between parent and child. It bonds all family members together. And it establishes a pattern for what will become, over the years, the most consistently meaningful environment for family interactions.

We feel it is important to add something to what we previously have said about the father's role in feeding the family. Too often, it is neglected not because men have fled from the kitchen in an assertion of masculinity, but because both sexes have unthinkingly fallen into stereotypic roles: the husband brings home the bread; the wife prepares it; or, in some families, because the wife is the only one who claims to be able to "boil water without burning it." The sexist arguments can be ignored; the absurd never demands an answer. As far as cooking skills are concerned, what can we say? No, most men are not gourmet cooks. Neither are most women. But can most men follow a recipe and turn out a good meal? Of course they can. Probably, we suspect, of quality comparable to the average housewife. Let's face it: how much culinary skill does it take to turn out waffles, fried eggs and bacon, breaded pork chops, spaghetti and meat sauce, fried chicken, or a cake made from a prepared cake mix? What is important is that fathers share in the opportunity to prepare food and serve it to their families. It is indeed sad that so often meal preparation is viewed as drudgery, a mundane task to be avoided whenever possible. In the name of equalitarianism, husbands may be expected to share in the cooking so that the wife doesn't get stuck with it all. The attitude of being "stuck with it" is unfortunate and will inevitably be communicated to children. Dining out has, for many families, become less and less a festive occasion. Many family members eat a third or more of their meals out of the home, even if the "dining out" is only a twenty-minute stop at a fast food restaurant. Does it say something about the quality of family life in the homes of those parents who view feeding their families as an onerous chore from which they seek escape whenever possible? The desire to nurture those for whom we care should seem as natural as the desire to embrace them. And nurturing them through food is a universal gesture of love and communion, whether it be a proffered cup of coffee or the Paschal meal, an opportunity in which both parents have a right to share.

We feel family meals should be more than simply the eating of food. They should be a total sensory experience as well as a bonding experience, and with a little planning and effort they can be. The presentation is important because, nearly as much as the quality of the food prepared, it conveys caring. Perhaps none of us eats that sprig of parsley placed alongside the breakfast omelet, but the garnishing says, "I was thinking about you, and I wanted to make this plate attractive for you." Setting the table attractively with place mats or tablecloths, and perhaps with flowers and candles makes the meal more than just the ingestion of food.

Extra "touches" can usually be added to any meal, and, when added they turn the meal into "dining": cloth napkins instead of paper ones; stem glassware instead of kitchen water glasses; salad plates and forks that have been chilled in the refrigerator; milk served from a pitcher instead of from a carton sitting in the middle of the table. It is sad that so many families fall into the habit of serving meals that are aesthetic as well as tasty only when they are entertaining company. The members of our family are the most valued guests who will ever dine at our table. We want them to recognize this when they see the meal presented to them.

Sitting down to dinner together, all at the same time, is very important. There are, to be sure, times when differing schedules will not permit it, but whenever possible we attempt to have at least one meal each day in which we are all gathered at the table. At that meal, time demands are avoided. We enjoy having a *leisurely* meal together. This has become almost rare in our rush-rush society in which everyone seems always to have someplace to go and little time in which to get there. In Europe and Latin America, families wisely extend their mealtimes. They eat slowly and enjoy their conversation. Who knows, we might discover the joys of both eating well and conversing artfully if we copied their example. There is even something conducive to offering grace when our meals are presented lovingly, and enjoyed as a family celebration.

The quality of food is not something to be ignored if the parents are concerned about the bonding which can take place at the family meals. Parents do not need to qualify as gourmet cooks, nor do they have to buy only the most expensive cuts of meat. They can, however, learn to cook well, and vary the menu so as to introduce their children to a wide variety of tastes. Some of the finest cooking in the world has developed in cultures in which economy dictates less expensive food as an essential part of the diet. Preparing the weekly menu ahead of time, attempting to discover the tastes and preferences of the family members, and developing cooking skills such that the meals are both well prepared and not monotonously repetitive, is one more way of making the family meal an occasion to be anticipated.

We enjoy lingering after dinner. To jump up from the table as soon as the meal is devoured marks an end of conversation. There is seldom a television program so interesting that we would choose to "eat and run." The second cup of coffee isn't needed to justify staying at the table if we are enjoying one another's company. Some of our most stimulating conversations are enjoyed in these postdinner periods.

The kitchen is, of course, a work center as well as a social center (especially in a large family). The children also participate in meal preparation—appropriate to their age and skills. They learn to peel vegetables, to set the table properly, to prepare the salad, and, in time, to prepare more complex dishes. Meal preparation is seldom completely turned over to the children, but year by year they are taught cooking skills. This serves a dual purpose: we want them to each acquire what we have called their "survival kit," the basic skills they will need from the time they are out on their own, and we want to give them the opportunity to participate in nurturing the other members of the family. There are also secondary rewards when we are able to say, "This tossed salad is excellent; Mary made it."

Philosophers and psychoanalysts will probably continue to probe the meanings and symbols of feeding and being fed. But what they will tell us is perhaps no more than we have discovered from earliest childhood: that there is much love and much bonding to be expressed and enjoyed in the family meal.

7

Learning Within the Family

A newborn may cry instinctively when hungry, but learning soon supplants instinct, and the baby learns that its cries, and later its pleas, cause parents to respond with food. The baby suffers the discomfort of a wet diaper. It cries, and it is changed. Learning has occurred. It soon learns to crawl to its parents' feet to be picked up when hungry or when damp. It also learns to identify the voices of those who care for it. Soon, this new member of the human society begins to develop, to learn tastes and preferences. (These tastes will, in the future, be made known in a remarkably assertive and vocal fashion.) A remarkable amount of learning takes place during the first two years, but it is with the beginnings of language that learning surges ahead at an astounding pace.

While some might argue the point, most psychologists contend that we *think* in words, and that our thinking is no more logical and precise than is our use of words. It is for this reason, many claim, that we have little preverbal memory. Most of us have no conscious memory of what went on during our first year or two of life. If the psychologists' interpretation is correct, it is because we could not put these experiences into words. As soon as the child begins to associate *words* with *things*—cookie, mamma, bow-wow, daddy—he/she enters the world of human learning.

Learning occurs almost continuously throughout childhood and early adulthood. We both observe it and experience it. We might assume, therefore, that psychologists and educators have learned quite a bit about the process of learning—how and when it occurs, what will enhance it, and what will inhibit it. The psychology of learning has, as a matter of fact, been systematically studied for many years. Unfortunately, the labors of learning psychologists have produced more heat than light, and the efforts of the educators have produced even less. Sliding through their voluminous research projects, the learning theorists and their harassed graduate students have conditioned the eye-blink reflex in humans and the salivary response in dogs. They have grown bleary-eyed watching rats explore a variety of mazes. They have trained thousands of pigeons to peck at targets. All this has been done in the name of learning: What is it? When does it occur? When is it retained, and when is it lost? The great learning theorists—Hull, Skinner, Spence, Estes, *et al.*—developed complex, vehemently disputed, theories. Their theories were not mere idle guesses but were empirically grounded. They all recognized, perhaps with dismay, that they had a long way to go. Even today, learning (both the phenomena and the process) is less understood than the rhythmic contractions of the heart. In a word, scarcely at all.

Yet despite our ignorance, we as parents face the challenge of nurturing learning in our children. We must accept the benefits of learning (both for ourselves and for our offspring) as well as the responsibilities. And as parents, we must develop the skills which will nurture learning—eagerly and positively.

A lot of learning stems from random behavior—trial and error, reward and punishment. How much is and is not important probably cannot be measured. The infant reaches out, attracted to a bright object on the stove, and is burned. He reaches again, touches a piece of candy, and is gratified. Reward and punishment: punishment or reward. Learning occurs. Soon in his development, often as early as his second year, adults (parents and occasional parental surrogates—older siblings, baby-sitters, grandparents) begin to punish as well as reward. They sternly say, "No!" and they occasionally accompany this with a mild slap on the hand. This sharp "No!" may be repeated a hundred times each day—at least it seems so to weary parents. Two-year-olds may not be insatiably curious and inexhaustible, but it may be difficult to convince parents of a child of that age. In time, however, something is learned.

What is learned and what we hope is learned are, frustratingly, often at odds. Our children learn behavior, pick up mannerisms, and develop habits which annoy, and at times appall us adults. Through positive reinforcement (praise, reward), we hope to teach them to act in ways which we, their parents, find acceptable. We don't always succeed. Years later, we may discover they have "gotten the message," but for many years the learning may seem an utter failure. Other times we employ negative reinforcement (scolding, punishing) in hopes of discouraging what is unacceptable. Often, this also seems less than effective.

In any case, we hope to do more than teach rote behavior. While we want them to learn right from wrong, and behavior which is acceptable and unacceptable, we hope, even more, to enhance their search for truth, and to encourage them to value truth, however tentatively they may grasp it. We want to teach them to cherish beauty and to seek it, to protect all living things, and to care for them, to ponder the mysteries of their world and to live with its ambiguities, to listen to others yet never blindly accept the pronouncements of ideologues. And most important, we want to teach them to love, and in loving, to discover the font of all happiness.

In reality, we don't teach our children. We would be arrogant to believe we do. Gardeners do not *grow* flowers. Farmers do not raise sheep and chickens. They provide environments in which growth is encouraged. We strive to provide an enriched environment in which learning and growth can occur for our children. We may provide some of the stimuli, but we can never force-feed learning. Learning is always a response, either positive or negative. It is the learner who responds, not the teacher. The teacher may even be dismayed upon discovering that what the student has learned is quite different than that which the teacher hoped to teach. The gardener can never be certain of the exact shape the flower will take.

Dr. Lawrence LeShan (*Alternate Realities*, Ballantine Books, 1976) has described what he calls four "modes of being"—what we might call environments of learning. The *sensory mode*, the one with which we are most familiar is "adapted primarily to biological survival. . . . with basic attention to defining differences, boundaries, separations, similarities, and relationships between 'things.' Essentially, they are oriented toward what can be clearly defined as an entity or unitary thing, and are adapted to things perceived as out there rather than in here." This sensory mode has a set of basic laws which emphasizes cause and effect, all information coming from the senses, and concerned with asking and answering questions of "how" and "how to" rather than "why" or to questions of value and moral judgment. The sensory mode can tell us how the atomic bomb works. It cannot tell us why we should build one or why we should drop it. The sensory mode is pure pragmatism. It aims at adaptation. And there is much in the sensory mode we hope our children will learn. But not all. And not to the exclusion of the other modalities.

In the educational nurturance of our children, we usually think first of educating in the sensory mode. It is essential. Children need to learn that fire burns, that mothers provide cookies, and that dogs' tails are not for pulling. We want them to learn to read, write, tie their shoes, and properly employ a fork and spoon. We try to teach them to look both ways before crossing a street, to brush their teeth, and to not accept rides from strangers. Education within the sensory mode is concerned with *facts* (light travels at the speed of 186,000 miles per second, Belgrade is the capital of Yugoslavia, the Gila monster is the only poisonous lizard in North America); *classes* (cows, elephants, and giraffes are herbivores; French, Italian, and Spanish are Romance languages); *generalizations* and *discriminations* (the Thai people are slight, smiling, and delicate-featured; the Catholics and Baptists, while both Christian, differ in their views of scriptural interpretation); and laws (for every action there is an opposite and equal reaction; the freezing point of water is o° Centigrade; students who study the most tend to get the best grades). The *laws* are frequently stated in causal relationships (which may or may not reflect valid observations). Many have become clichés in which familiarity has dulled our critical faculties to challenge them: "Sharks are aggressive and will fearlessly attack anything." "Japanese women are naturally obsequious and follow their husbands unquestioningly." "A rolling stone gathers no moss." "Barking dogs never bite." "Men are rational; women emotional." The pitfalls in such clichéd "laws" are enormous. There is a danger of erroneous "facts," er-

rors in classification, faulty generalizations and discriminations, and ill-founded laws. But more than that, we
may become so enamored of the logic, the order, the pragmatism of the sensory mode that we come to view it as
the only valid source of information, the only way to understand the world in which we live—and the *only* reality
to reveal to our children (or to permit them to explore).

If we make this mistake, we may provide them with
something of value (survival), but it will be to the exclusion of sources of information and truth of equal value—
meaning, creativity, and joy. We doubt many readers
would argue in favor of teaching children solely what
truth can be perceived through the senses, the *what is* and
the *what can be done about it*. Most of us have, at one
time or another, asked the difficult questions: "What is
the meaning of life?" "Why am I here on this earth and
what is expected of me?" "What relationship do I have
with all others, present and past?" "Is there something
that stretches beyond my physical mortality?" "Are my
dreams and fantasies trying to tell me something or
should I try to suppress them, stomping on them for their
'impracticality' and lack of reality?" Yet the moment we
entertain the possibility that there may be something
more than the purely sensory source of information, we
violate one of the limiting principles of the sensory mode:
that it is the only valid way to regard reality, and that all
other ways are illusion. Each modality claims to possess
the sole valid perception of reality. The claim must, however, be rejected if we are to grow fully in knowledge and
truth, and if we are to give life to our children and to the
seemingly transcendental existence of the family unit;
that is, if we are to nurture their understanding and aid
them in becoming educated human beings in the broadest meaning of the words.

Beyond this most familiar, sensory mode, LeShan

discusses a mode which is more puzzling: what he calls the *clairvoyant* mode. Even the word causes many of us discomfort. Clairvoyant! It smacks of crystal balls and tea leaves, psychics and astrologers. But it is not necessarily. Once we leave the sensory mode, however, we leave the anchor post of what we have been taught in a mentality of survival and pragmatism. We leave the security of the purely rational world. We enter the world of scientists and thinkers who live on the outer fringe of an only vaguely perceived universe, one which is seldom, in our present state of technology, empirically verifiable. If the sensory mode tells us *what is* and *what causes what*, the clairvoyant mode attempts to explain what it all *means*.

The clairvoyant mode also has basic limiting principles. The mode is centered upon direct experiencing of the oneness of being and process, "to the essential unity of the cosmos rather than—as in the sensory modes—its separation into parts, into objects and events." In the clairvoyant mode, the entire universe is perceived as a "seamless garment" in which *all* divisions and separations, all boundaries—even that of self from others—are arbitrary and in error. It is a modality that is much less comprehensible than the sensory. In the clairvoyant mode, the most important aspect of any person, object, or event is its participation in the whole—the total oneness of the universe. While the sensory mode views the world in terms of discrete events, persons, and things which interact in cause and effect, the clairvoyant mode denies all boundaries. All things and events *are* each other; they are *essentially* one. The clairvoyant mode has special importance to the formation of the family since it calls for giving up goals and desires for oneself as well as for others (since the separate self and others do not exist). All one is called upon to be is just *to be*. It means, at least momentarily, giving up actions—doing—and accept the state of *being.* This modality, so popular during the sixties and seventies with the followers of the philosophically holistic Eastern theologies, is not adapted to biological survival. It does not help balance a checkbook, plan a vacation, or invent a more efficient mouse trap. The clairvoyant mode is useful to theoretical physicists (Einstein is the paramount example) who wrestle with a view of reality that surpasses the understanding of most of us (who can comprehend only limited *cause-and-effect* physics, i.e., sensory modality), and to parapsychologists, who are attempting to understand the universe in terms of phenomena which are beyond "normal" understanding. Information in the clairvoyant mode would obviously be unattainable in the sensory mode. It would not "make sense." But to the mystic, information gained solely through the sensory mode would be impoverished. It would present only a partial picture of reality, at best. In fact, the mystic might reject the sensory mode altogether.

Through the clairvoyant mode we seek meaning in our existence. We search to discover who we are and the roles we are to play as an integral part of the universe. Through this mode we may be able to glean meaning in the words of John Donne: "No man is an island." The "island" does not, and cannot, exist apart from the surrounding water and from the other land masses. They are all *one.* Through this mode, we may be able to glimpse, however faintly, how we are each inseparable from one another: male/female, adult/child, American/Nepalese. And how what affects one, affects all.

The clairvoyant mode, communicating the idea that we are each and every one of us nothing more than an incomprehensible and indistinguishable component of the whole—the One—is a concept which does not rest easy on our educational foundations of cause and effect, facts, and neat categories. This mode presents disturbing and ever-present questions which are often little understood and are never easy to answer, nor are they easy to dismiss. Reality, viewed within the clairvoyant mode, presents enigmatic propositions: I am you; you are me. Time, space, yesterday, and tomorrow, have no relevance. There is only what *is*. Within the clairvoyant mode, so say the mystics and theoreticians, we may be able to attain feelings of peace, serenity, and security. We may be able to feel a sureness of where we are in the universe. For most of us, however, the truths that may be discovered within the clairvoyant mode will at best be fleeting, and they will always be elusive. The clairvoyant modes, should we be wise enough or insightful enough to admit the possibility of their reality, present us with the maxim that true knowledge may lie in the knowingness of the unknowableness of the known. We will always have far more questions than answers. But then, perhaps therein lie many of our answers.

The third mode of which LeShan writes is the *transpsychic* mode. In this mode, objects, events, and ourselves are *not* perceived as separate from each other (as in the sensory mode), nor as identical with each other (all One) as in the clairvoyant. In the transpsychic mode, all objects, entities, and events are perceived as related to each other and to a larger whole, as the fingers are separate from each other yet related in their "membership" in the hand. We are individuals. We have our individual desires and goals, our unique personalities, our personal responsibilities. We are, however, joined in our common humanity; what affects you will also have an effect upon me. It is within this mode, and with this understanding, that our ethical principles are derived: being interdependent and at all times interacting, we carry a responsibility for each other and an obligation to work for the greater harmony of the whole. Virtuous actions are those which benefit others, and hence the whole. And, of course, each of our actions affects ourselves individually as well. Actions are evil which harm others, create disharmony within the whole, and hurt ourselves. Ethics, morality, and true religious feelings and expressions lie within this modality.

Responsibility, caring, love, and loyalty within the family grow with the development of the transpsychic modes. Other chapters will touch upon values and family interactions which are founded on the development of the transpsychic modality—spirituality, justice, loyalty, etc. Each family member is a separate, unique individual. Together the family members comprise a whole which is greater than the sum of its parts. They are a family. And our individual family, in all its uniqueness, is joined with all other human beings—past, present, and future—to make up a still greater whole. Recognition of this generates many of our feelings of reverence, awe, and humility, and a sense of the majesty of the One responsible for all reality.

Through our sensory-mode learning, we develop the skills necessary to achieve "practical" goals. The *sensory* is the how-to-do-it modality. The sensory mode makes living possible. The clairvoyant mode may provide a reason for living. The transpsychic mode points the way. It gives us direction. Within it, we find purpose and bonding—especially within the family.

There is one further mode through which we discover reality: the *mythic modes of being*. We must admit that the mythic modes are our favorites. They are the ones we employ in play, art, fantasies, dreams, and all creative activities. When Watson and Crick were searching for the secret of genetic transmission, they accepted information from the mythic mode, they followed an "improbable dream," and they discovered the "double helix," the structure of DNA. It is through the development of mythic modes that Beethoven and Stravinski were able to "hear" the music they then gave to the world. The mythic mode enabled Michelangelo to release the magnificent David from his imprisonment within a gigantic block of marble. The world would not have had the gifts of Picasso if the mythic mode had not existed. We would have had no *Hamlet*, no phonograph bursting forth from the otherworld creativity of a Thomas Edison, no men walking on the moon, and no children building sandcastles or sailing off across seas in cardboard box ships with broomstick masts.

In the mythic modes our minds are allowed total freedom. They are not limited by the parameters of the possible and the impossible. Do we yearn to fly to the stars on "gossamer wings"? Can intertwining snakes represent the structure of DNA? Only when dreams are germinated in the mythic modes.

Perhaps we view these mythic modes as so precious because our culture has so often neglected them. Often they have been disparaged. No one values a dreamer, it seems, until his dreams come true. When we were children in school, one of the most severely punishable offenses was daydreaming. Unfortunately, play is frequently tolerated in children for only so long a time as it takes adults to mold them into adults—defined, tragically, as non-artistic, non-creative, non-playing, oh-so-practical-and-serious human beings.

Some parents may say, "Of course we need creative people, and we need dreamers, but I would be disturbed if my children spent their idle hours in a world of make-believe. Dreams seldom have value. It is only *practical plans* which get you anywhere." The concern is understandable, but there is a wealth of evidence that it is only through dreams that mankind, and many of us as individuals, has ever climbed out of the primordial mud to reach for the stars. The dream is parent to the goal. Once conception occurs, the goal takes shape with planning, but it starts with the dream. Dr. Martin Luther King did not stand before the multitudes in our nation's capital to say, "I have a plan for civil rights legislation," or "I have specific goals for the attainment of economic equality among the races." He cried out, "*I have a dream!*"

Dreams are not imprisoned within the rules of logic and causality. They don't have to make sense. The visionary author Jules Verne dreamed of a voyage around the world in eighty days, of rocketing from the earth to the moon, and of exploring the depths of the oceans. During his time, he must have been considered mad, but can there be an astronaut, American or Russian, who has not dreamed dreams inspired by this madman? Picasso broke all the rules. His dreams/fantasies/images led him into worlds of beauty others might have glimpsed, but owing to the inhibitions of a culturally imposed sensory world, dared not explore. He was a rebel, but then rebellion is always an important component of living fully. The rebellion of which we speak is not the mindless rebellion of malcontents. It is the creative rebellion of which the late Robert Lindner spoke. Not so much a rebellion as a reconstruction, a new perception and evaluation. Creative thinking almost always relies heavily on the mythic modes. The greatest thinkers have always gone beyond the accepted thinking of their age. They have rebelled against the *known.* Freud challenged the accepted explanations of what motivated humans and what led to their frustrations. Darwin challenged the accepted explanation of our origin. Einstein challenged the accepted physics of Newton. Whatever the ultimate results of the dreams they dreamed, their rebellious venturing carried us beyond the limits of the world as it was known, and it has changed the world in which we live. The most revolutionary of all, and the most creative, was Christ. He gave us a new way of viewing *ourselves*. He gave us a dream (mythic modality), a challenge (transpsychic modality), and an enigma (clairvoyant modality). He did not teach us techniques; he did not give us specific means to transform our world into one of affluence and disarmament treaties. He told us to "do unto others as you would be done by them." The great rabbi Hillel said all of law was contained in the injunction "What you would not wish done to you, do not do to others." These words of Christ and Hillel contain no how-to-do-it instructions. They challenge us only with a dream, an ideal, and perhaps a direction.

To suggest that play, creativity, and dreams are in some sense one and the same is not particularly original. The contention that they are important sources of knowledge and modes of being does, however, run counter to the educational philosophy popular during the last half century. Much of education has aimed at achieving a sensory, cause-and-effect acquisition of knowledge essential to the achievement of a high material standard of living. By thirteen years of age, children are bombarded with the repeated question, "What do you plan to *do* when you grow up?" Seldom are they asked who and what do you want to *be?* Nor do our systems of education encourage play as an important mode of learning. Most elementary schools provide recess periods (as much to provide a break for the teachers as for the pupils), but this is often directed toward a program of physical fitness, not play. Toys are heavily advertised as "educational." Parents are persuaded to kill two birds with one stone—education and play—with education being given the greater importance in a sensory modality context. Play for the sake of play is, at most, merely tolerated—and then only in moderation. For themselves, adults tolerate it little if any. Recreation and exercise are "acceptable" only when rationalized as an aid to health. Play is viewed as "childish"—a sign of immaturity and a waste of time.

Parents and educators all hope children will learn how to *think*. Why then, we wonder, is the process of thinking not taught? Why have we made our educational system one in which facts and figures are fed into the child's cerebral computer bank to be retrieved at test time? Perhaps it is that thinking, being rare in our society as a whole, has produced few teachers capable of teaching it. Thinking most certainly cannot be taught using the accustomed teaching methods. We cannot say, "Here are ten rules to be followed. They are to be memorized by next Monday," or "Following the method we have learned for thinking, we will not attack the problem of peace in the Middle East." It just doesn't work that way. Thinking is never the application of formulae. Neither is thinking an idle cognitive response or memory trace ("while I was brushing my teeth this morning, I was thinking of taking a fishing trip"). *Thinking* brings together elements, facts, disciplines, etc., which are not ordinarily associated in order to open the doors to new hypotheses, new possibilities. When successful, it results in an exhilaration, a childlike discovery, a reaction of, "Wow! I think I see what might happen if I combine ——— with ———!" These ventures go beyond the usual and expected to uncover what psychologists call the "Aha!" phenomenon—insight!

There are other reasons why thinking is not taught. For one, it's messy! Thinking is, by its very nature, undisciplined. It mixes together in a kind of a mulligan stew all sorts of facts and disciplines that ordinarily don't mix well. It may combine computer technology with jazz. Or biological science with billiards. The combinations are so messy that the professionals in each of the separate disciplines may at once reject the mixture. Even so obvious a relationship as biology with chemistry has frequently resulted in a stormy marriage. Thinking is an exercise in play. We entertain ideas, we play with them, and we may end up thinking. When we plunge into fantasies and savor our dreams, we are taking an initial step toward thinking. It may be fun, but it is always confusing and often messy. Most teachers do not, therefore, encourage it.

Thinking also challenges the status quo. Physicists who were trained in the discoveries of Newton found their world shattered by the theories of Einstein. When William Harvey discovered the circulation of the blood, he threatened the education of doctors who had practiced for years. Thinking often elicits a reaction of, "If your idea is true, why haven't others suggested it?" The answer is: "Thinking is creative. It is original. It is never simply derivative." This is admittedly disruptive. There is a famous research facility in Southern California, a noted "think tank." The facility hires an annual crop of Ph.D.s in a variety of disciplines. In scientific journals, this company advertises for "ambitious, creative" personnel. We were once shown through the institution. The scientist who showed us through brought us to a room in which scores of desks were lined up like tables in a prison mess hall. Each desk was occupied by one of the "ambitious, creative" Ph.D.s. Our guide, noting our dismay, laughed, "If they ever get anyone creative in here, he'll blow the place up."

Despite the fact that thinking is closely akin to play, that it cannot be taught in any traditional manner, that it is messy, and that it tends to challenge the established order, it is essential to making life worthwhile. It is through the mythic mode that we formulate our future, that we shape our fantasies and dreams. The child sits by the ocean, building a castle of sand. Yet to the child it is not a mound of wet sand. It is a castle of walls, turrents, and embattlements. It is encircled by a moat and defended by loyal bowmen. To the child, it does not merely *look* like a castle, it *is* a castle—his castle. It will not fall either to the enemy or to the incoming tide. The material from which is it constructed is impregnable: it is a fantasy. Such dreams will not only sustain him, they will shape his world and make it worthwhile. Perhaps our worlds as well. What better gift can we give our children than encouragement to play and to dream?

Nurturing development of the four modalities—sensory, clairvoyant, transpsychic, and mythic—is a challenge to parents which is not easily met. As in nurturing the growth of a plant, we can provide the proper environment, the soil, moisture, nutrients, and sunlight, and we can protect the plant while we allow it to grow. Perhaps similar nurturance is all we offer our children, but we feel we have an obligation to do so with extreme care. Every child is born into this world eager to grow, explore, experiment, and learn. A friend of ours, a very talented man who would have been described today as "gifted," told us if he were ever to have a child who evidenced high intelligence, he would never enroll the child in school. "I would build a home in the wilderness," he said, "and I would fill it with a library of works of the world's greatest thinkers in science, literature, philosophy, history, and the humanities. Then I would give my child free rein to explore the world about him or her. I would never allow my child to be contaminated by influences which might inhibit questioning. I would never allow my child to be punished for being unconventional in thinking or unacceptable in ideas." Such a radical approach would not be followed by most parents, not because we could not see its logic, but because it would demand a very high price. We are not sure our friend would have taken this course of action had he been faced with the reality of children. He admitted as much. But if we consider his experience, and we soberly attempt to interpret what he was saying, it was this: "We become educated by exposure to the thoughts of others who have preceded us, by personal discovery of the world which surrounds us, and by searching for answers to the questions all such exposures raise." He was suggesting we pursue ambiguity rather than certainty, that we tolerate discomfort and find satisfaction in the search rather than solely in the discovery. He was arguing for the *process* of becoming an educated person, and this is always a process of *becoming*. It is a goal never attained.

As parents, we provide the nurturance toward becoming an educated person by attempting at all times to maintain an environment which is open and encouraging to the exploration of experience and ideas, and by acting as a resource for information both through our own experience in learning and by what contemporary educators call "educational aids": library, video and audio materials, etc. When we can, we like to do it within a context which is fun. We have learned this isn't always possible. The "Aha!" phenomenon is always fun, but acquiring the information, from a diversity of sources, which may trigger the "Aha!" phenomenon may be much less than fun.

Most education within the various modalities is a far cry from what we see in our schools. We may be frustrated by much of what we see in our schools, but we are not fighting them. However, certain evidence must be considered. It disturbs us. By the time the child graduates from high school, only 10 to 13 percent of his or her working hours have been spent in a classroom—considerably less than the time spent in front of a television set, and far less than the hours spent in the home environment. We feel the question of *where* the child learns is less important than *what* the child learns. The child learns everywhere he is present. Every environment is a learning environment. What the child learns often depends on who and what the child is exposed to and how he reacts to the exposure. We have to repeatedly ask the question, "What do we want our children exposed to?" We may be tempted to say, "Everything and anything," but seldom is this true. We don't want our children to learn to lie, cheat, and steal. We don't want them to learn to view the world with cynicism, prejudice, hatred, and self-doubt. We don't want them to learn that they have responsibilities to no one but themselves. We don't want them to learn that being loved is more important than loving. We don't want them to learn that reality is what other people say it is and that they must accept it without question. We do want them to learn that life can be joyful, that it is not a vale of tears in which only the "lucky" can hope for more than survival.

A lot of learning takes place within our family gatherings. It serves as a forum, court, and center for the exploration of ideas. (All too often, it turns into a spontaneous circus.) The ground rules for these brain stormings are well understood. No topics or opinions are "out of bounds." Any family member, regardless of age, can express an opinion—no matter how "far-out." If the opinion expressed is simply an expression of taste (e.g., "I like the songs of John Lennon more than those of Marvin Hamlisch"), the statement cannot be attacked. We want it recognized that different opinions are not challenges and should never be cause for personal attack. We make that a standing rule. On the other hand, if an opinion is presented as a "logical conclusion," based upon factual information, such a "conclusion" may very well be challenged. Any family members stating the conclusion will be called upon to defend it. They will be cross-examined on their sources of information. Their logic may be scrutinized. Debate has long been an avocation of the members of our family. We encourage it. We believe it was Wordsworth who said he planned to send his sons to college for no more than two years. At the completion of two years, he said, if they had learned to use the library, they would have no further need for college exposure, but if they had not, further college would be a waste of their time. Drawing upon documented information—in reading, questioning, and personal experience—we expect our children to develop the ability to present conclusions that can be successfully defended. We encourage them to grow in the skills of critical thought, to learn to assemble information, to draw valid generalizations and discriminations, to accept logical conclusions even when they are uncomfortable, and to be able, in time, to discover exciting "Aha!" associations—insights. If they are able to develop these abilities, then the education, formal and informal, to which they are exposed will make sense. If they are not, their schooling will have been less than worthwhile. In our family discussions, content is less important than process. The topics of discussion we encourage, and their range, are limited only by the interests and information of our family members. One evening we may discuss how nerve impulses are transmitted and how scientific discoveries in this field may affect our lives in decades to come. Another night, we may plunge into a discussion of the amazing scientific discoveries of the ancient Mayans and how these discoveries compared with the speculations of Leonardo da Vinci. In a somewhat lighter vein, we may argue the relative merits of American versus Canadian football. Before a meal is completed, we may have played intellectual handball with such topics as the Komodo dragon of Indonesia and its role in Japanese sci-fi movies, whether God is male, female, or neuter, and a comparison of Humphrey Bogart's roles in *Casablanca* and *The Caine Mutiny*.

When we speak of our "kitchen table" or "dinner table" discussions, we are using something of a metaphor. While many discussions go on during meals, information is exchanged almost continually, and in every physical environment. Parenthetically, the members of our family talk almost without stop. Given the sample topics above, the reader might assume we are talking about discussions held only with older children and adults. This is not in any way true. As with discussions involving sex, almost anything and everything can be talked about at virtually all age levels. With nine children spanning an age range of eleven years, we have been able to make the delightful discovery, that, "They are too young to understand" is more often than not untrue. A six-year-old may not be able to comprehend the politico-economic machinations of the OPEC cartel (who can?), but he can understand a careful explanation of energy needs, supply and demand, finite resources, alternative sources of energy, and conservation. An entire discussion will probably not stay on a six-year-old level of comprehension unless we are talking only to the six-year-old. There will usually be others present ranging in age up to adulthood (assuming we include both parents). The discussion level does not, however, have to be "either-or." In the best of discussions, the ones we enjoy and encourage the most, all family members contribute—and we all learn. Educational and intellectual nurturance is seldom furthered by a "parents teach; children learn" approach. As parents, we have much to learn from our children. Soon after the child utters his or her first word, the word "why?" is discovered. That single

word is asked over, and over, and over again. It is repeated so often that even the most reasonable parent can
be driven to unloving thoughts, but when we think about
it seriously, we can only conclude that it is perhaps the
most important word any of us may ever learn and use. It
is through "why?" that we discover truth and error, acquire knowledge, explore our universe and the galaxies beyond, establish our codes of morality, reject superstitions
and prejudgments, and loose our creative potential. Our
response to the question, "why?" is crucial to our growth,
the growth of our children, and the creation of the world
in which we and they will live.

The question may often seem unreasonable and tedious. We get tired of answering. Often we find we are
stumped, and any attempt to provide an answer will involve us in tiresome research. It will mean work. We may
be called upon to read, study, and evaluate. It may even
lead to questions which challenge our long held, and comfortably cherished, beliefs. And often we will be forced to
admit, "I don't know." Most of us are uncomfortable admitting this to our children, especially when we feel they
have asked a question to which we should have the answer. Faced with the challenge, it is tempting to resort to
the worst of answers: the *non-answer*. The *non-answer* is
an answer which, while not providing any information or
reasoning, tends to inhibit any further questioning.
"What makes water boil?" Answer: "You turn on the
stove." "Why doesn't the sun shine at night?" Answer:
"Because at night we have a moon and the pretty stars."
"Where did I come from?" Answer: "God sent you down
from heaven." "Why can't I color outside the lines?" Answer: "Because that's what the lines are there for." "Why
do we have wars?" Answer: "Because we have always had
wars." In time giving non-answers may lead us to give the

penultimate non-answer of all: *"Just because."* Educationally, a disaster.

When we consistently offer non-answers, we can expect two results: 1) the child will stop asking, and 2) he will acquire a perceived lack of self-worth. The child begins to reason, "What is the use of continuing to ask questions when no informative answers are given?" He lacks information. This is why he asks questions. But he is not lacking in intelligence; he can perceive a lack of information in the answer, "That is the way it has always been." He may not accept it as an answer when he nods slightly and walks away. He may recognize it as worthless. The honest reply, "I don't know" would provide him with much more. The admission of ignorance on the parent's part does not erode respect for parental authority or diminish the parent in the eyes of the child. Children do not need to believe parents are omniscient in order for them to believe that parents are wise, good, and worthy of respect. When our children ask questions to which we have no answer, we should rejoice. Not only does it tell us they are thinking and growing, it provides us an opportunity to search for the answers to questions which otherwise might never have occurred to us. Listening to the questions posed by children, being stumped by them, searching for and finding the answers to their questions, and responding to them, can provide more than a Ph.D. education.

There is no way we can answer questions raised around our kitchen table without resource materials. We will never have that many facts at our fingertips. Fortunately, we have a home library. We consider it absolutely essential to the educational nurturance of us all. It's modest, limited by space and finances, but it is by design and eclectic tastes, diverse. Some works we consider indispensable: an encylopedia, an unabridged dictionary, a world atlas, the World Almanac, and a world globe.

There are also non-fiction works, publications in science, humanities, history, philosophy, and the arts. The fiction ranges from Homer and Shakespeare to Doctor Seuss. We have found that while the average retail bookstore may have a limited selection of resource books (e.g., basic texts in geology, or French/English dictionary), a university or college bookstore is a gold mine, and one doesn't have to be a student to browse and buy.

Almost anything which piques the curiosity of a family member can send us running to the books. Not long ago, for example, there was a television rerun of the movie *Lawrence of Arabia*. It raised a question: "Who was the *real* T. E. Lawrence?" We went to the encyclopedia, read a brief biography of Lawrence, and spent an hour speculating on the personality of this strange, fascinating, tragic man and the times in which he lived. Later, the evening television news carried the story of a young Japanese sailor who crossed the Pacific alone in a small sailboat. This triggered a chain of discussion: "How, when you are in the middle of an ocean, do you know where you are and where you are headed?" We were drawn to celestial navigation, the use of a sextant, and chronographs. We looked to the books. But this raised further questions not so easily answered: "What if the sky is overcast for several days?" "How did people from Polynesia sail to Hawaii when they didn't have chronographs and sextants?" "Yes, and what about the voyage of the *Kon Tiki*; didn't that show that natives of South America could have sailed to the South Pacific islands without any of the instruments we are talking about?" We went back to the books. That evening, we were sitting in the backyard, relaxing after a family barbecue, when one of the younger ones snapped us back to this discussion of an hour or two before—"How can you be sure which star is really the North Star?"

The sensory mode must be given primary attention

since it is our "survival" mode. It does not provide meaning for our lives. It doesn't teach us how to relate to
others. It doesn't teach us how to love and accept being
loved. And it doesn't teach us how to dream and play.
But it does provide us with the cause-and-effect knowledge that will enable us to attain our essential skills.
Within the clairvoyant mode we may toy with extra-
sensory perception, mysticism, or theoretical physics.
Within the transpsychic mode we may ponder the broth-
erhood of man, our obligations to one another as family
members, and the mutual love we can experience as individual parts of a greater whole. In the mythic mode, we
may free the right side of our brains to dream impossible
dreams and indulge in unfettered play. But it is only
within the *sensory* mode that we learn how to balance a
checkbook, change a tire, or iron a shirt. In the world in
which our children will be faced with such mundane but
essential tasks, we have a serious obligation to provide
them with these skills and information.

Many of these skills are better taught in the "labora-
tory" environment of the home rather than in the school.
Showing a son how to toss a salad or to replace a fuse,
showing a daughter what to check for in purchasing a pair
of shoes, or explaining to them the correct way to write a
job résumé, where to find the dip stick in the family car,
and what to look for in a warranty contract, falls quite
properly within the educational setting of the family.
Such information will seldom, if ever, be adequately provided in the schools.

We have personally evolved certain policies, reflective
of our values, in this teaching. First of all, we believe that
both sexes should be taught the same skills. Our daughters have every bit as much reason to learn to change a
tire as do their brothers. Our sons have every bit as much
reason to learn how to cook a full meal "from scratch" as

do their sisters. We recognize that with our limitations we cannot teach them everything they will find helpful in adult life. We can, however, teach them the essentials. And this is our responsibility. Should we teach them to cook a meal from scratch? Yes. Must we teach them the skills of boning a chicken? No. Our upper-middle-class society challenges parents with a frightening number of directives. "You really should give your children music lessons (or riding lessons, or dancing lessons, or tennis lessons, etc., etc., etc.)." A father may not be able to play baseball any better than he can flap his arms and fly to the moon, but he is told, "You really should go out and teach your son how to swing a baseball bat so that he will be able to compete in Little League." Are these self-appointed child "experts" suggesting that parents have an obligation to develop each and every beneficial or enjoyable skill in order that they can pass these skills on to their children? We have spoken with parents who have scrimped to be able to send their children to summer camp, and later on educational tours of Europe. There may be several explanations for what they express as parental obligations to "give their children the advantages." They may want their kids out from underfoot. They may feel they owe such learning experiences to their children. They may want to keep up with their friends in the neighborhood. We don't feel the motives are as important as the question of whether or not the parents share mutually, in accordance with their individual values, in arriving at these decisions. One consideration should be brought into any such decision making, and should be heavily weighed: will this activity add to or detract from the unity and bonding within our family.

In time, our children will develop a number of skills their parents do not possess and have played no part in providing for them. They will acquire interests and skills that will not be shared by the other family members. This is as it should be. Bonding and unity within the family cannot be achieved through any imposed "togetherness" coming from a rule that says, "We will all participate or none of us will." We have found it exciting to watch our children develop their individual interests and share them with us. During the sixties and seventies, many young people were encouraged by self-appointed experts to "do their own thing." What interests they may have developed were not shared, and this left the family members, individually and as a unit, impoverished both socially and intellectually. We have much, however, to learn from one another. From our eldest son, we learned about the ancient sport of falconry, an interest he had developed in his early teens and pursued into adulthood. The rest of us never acquired the knowledge of falconry he possessed, but we did learn much about the sport, and we grew to love his birds. From a daughter, we learned the latest advances in genetics, and the future of gene-splicing. From another daughter, we were able to catch up on our knowledge of French. We bring information to the family discussions which we have gleaned from a variety of sources. Our children bring information from school and their readings. Sometimes it comes from friends and from other outside sources. And once the information is presented, it triggers a multitude of questions. In all of it, there is an interaction which can only be described as *mutual nurturance.*

When the child reaches school age (and this applies to each child individually in turn), parents are presented with a whole new set of problems, challenges, and decisions. Where do we enroll the child in school, when do we enroll him or her, what do we expect of the school, and what role are we to play in relationship to what they may learn in school? Over ten years ago, we published a book, *Power to the Parents!*[1] in which we were openly critical of the quality of education being provided by the public schools. We were not alone. Donald Barr, for example, was but one of the voices raised in criticizing the direction of our educational systems.[2] In the decade since, we have watched the gradual deterioration of test scores for admission to college, reading levels of high school students, and competency levels in basic skills. Teachers have blamed parents and television and the increasing demand that the schools take over providing education in everything from drug abuse to morality. They have complained that they cannot do an adequate job when they are forced to spend the majority of their time maintaining discipline. They have also said, "Give us more money, and we will do the job." For a number of years, the taxpayers were willing to pass one bond issue after another. In affluent suburbs, they provided high schools with equipment and facilities that would have been the envy of many colleges. Educators have also been quick to point out that they are expected, today, to educate children who might in previous years have dropped out of school earlier, and to provide an education to a greater ethnic and cultural mix. Nevertheless, most American parents have begun to question the performance of the public schools. In late April and early May, 1981, *Newsweek* magazine ran a three-part series entitled, "Why Public Schools Are Flunking" (*Newsweek*, April 20, 27, May 4). Nearly half the respondents to a poll they conducted through the Gallup organization thought the schools were doing a poor or only fair job, that too many students did not want to learn, and that too many teachers did not know how to teach. They said, "Too many teachers are

[1] Doubleday & Company, Inc., Garden City, New York, 1972.
[2] *Who Pushed Humpty Dumpty?* New York: Atheneum, 1971.

bad spellers and worse writers, and their own education is a national disgrace." Nearly a third of the students coming out of the public high schools in California entering the University of California are required to take the "dumbbell" English course. They have not learned competency in the use of the English language in our public schools despite the fact that they represent the top 10 percent of high school graduates. We have watched with dismay the deterioration of public education in our own schools over the past ten years. High school teachers who were poorly informed in the subjects they were teaching or unmotivated to do the job for which they were hired, or both, have been the rule rather than the exception. We have read reports of national studies, and we have talked with parents throughout the United States, who have shared our observations and our dismay. If someone were today to ask us what we would do if we were starting all over again, if we had a child ready to enter first grade, we would have to answer, "We don't know." One possibility, and one which an increasing number of parents are choosing, would be to enroll them in private schools. In the *Newsweek* series, the writers state: "Private schools are booming—drawing the brightest pupils from public schools beset with problems." This, however, raises a further question, "How do parents determine that this or that private school can and will provide a better education?" And the further, obvious, question, "Can we afford it?" There are many voices being raised today demanding that the teachers start *teaching*, and that they offer more beefed-up classes in basic academic subjects. We agree that this might help, but we are not convinced that our schools are presently staffed by sufficient teachers who are themselves academically qualified to teach the subjects to which they have been assigned. Their own academic training has all too often been shockingly deficient. As

the *Newsweek* series put it, "Those who can't teach,
teach the teachers." In one California school district, the
teachers were given a test of basic skills. Thirty percent
failed the test at the eighth-grade level! *Newsweek* reported, "The National Education Association opposes
teacher tests, maintaining that they are unfair to students
who might fail after investing heavily in college training.
In 1979, six months after Louisiana began using the National Teacher Examination (NTE) to screen applicants, 33% failed. In 1978, 47% of Louisiana's teaching
applicants failed, even though the cut-off point was
roughly the 25th percentile."

Where does this leave parents who view their children's
education as a serious responsibility? We have been able
to come up with only one universal answer: the parents
must take on the major responsibility. To leave it to the
schools, is to risk a future generation of functional illit-
erates. To demand curricular revisions and to return to
the three R's will help little if the teachers themselves are
barely literate. Parenthetically, we have a friend whose
daughter brought home a note from her teacher. The
note read, "Congradulations! [*sic*] Amy has been promoted to the Forth [*sic*] Grade." We assume Amy was
not promoted on the basis of her spelling competency.
There are many indications that parents are more frustrated with the quality of their public schools than at any
previous period. We feel they have more than sufficient
justification for their frustration. However, all the protests
to the school board, all the demands for increased homework, and all the bills passed in state assemblies requiring
teacher competency tests cannot solve the problem. Parents can no longer delegate the major responsibility for
the education of their children to the schools, content
with their role in "cooperating" with the teachers. They
are going to have to take on the major teaching role

themselves. Furthermore, they are going to have to keep a running check on what their children are being taught in the classroom in order to correct the misinformation. When the child comes home from school with a paper corrected by the teacher, the parents will have to check it for grammar and spelling. The child's arithmetic will have to be supervised by the parent. The parents will have to develop a reading program within the home. The parents will have to repeatedly ask the question, "What did you learn in school today?" and then give the child information which may be necessary in order to correct what the teacher has said. This is, we grant, a time-consuming and frustrating job. Time and time again, parents will find themselves saying, "I'm sure your teacher was mistaken on that; let's look it up in the encyclopedia." The added responsibilities and role demands on parents for the education of their children today makes even more important continual discourse—the dinner-table conversation. It also makes the acquisition of resource material (fiction and non-fiction literature, encyclopedia, etc.) imperative. And, thank God, most of us live within easy access of a public library.

We have listened for years to the arguments of psychologists and concerned parents over the proper role of the school in the education of the child. Should our schools take on the responsibility for the emotional adjustment of our children? Or for their sex education? Or for their ability to drive an automobile? Or for their awareness of dangerous drugs? Or for racial and religious tolerance? These questions are seldom addressed to whether or not we want our children educated in one or another area. We want them to learn everything which will be important in their future life. But who do we want doing the teaching? Take driver education. We want our children trained to drive an automobile with sufficient skill to minimize the danger of injury to themselves or others. Should we, the parents, teach our children to drive? Should we hire private driving instructors? Or should we turn it over to the schools? Even if we are able to answer the question, "Who is most capable of teaching a child to drive an automobile?" we are still left to decide which educational responsibilities we wish to delegate to the schools and which ones we wish to retain. There are, on the one hand, those who believe our schools should be concerned only with teaching the "basics"—reading, writing, mathematics, history, science, etc. Others firmly believe the schools should assume a major responsibility for the socialization, psychological adjustment, and value formation of the student. Actually, there are probably few public schools that could be accurately described in terms of either of these extremes. The teacher in a "basics" school will, from time to time, inject value statements into classroom discussions. And even those schools with the strongest psychosocial orientation show little desire to take over all aspects of the child's emotional development. Nevertheless, who will educate our children, and in what, are questions none of us can ignore. We may delegate the teaching role—in part, but our responsibility for the total educational nurturance of our children cannot be delegated. It rests with us. We may hire a music teacher to give our son saxophone lessons, but the decision to buy him a saxophone and to provide the musical education is ultimately ours. It will reflect our educational values.

We have learned to put our children's formal schooling in a rational perspective, if for no other reason than to reduce our own frustration. First, as we have mentioned previously, we have come to recognize what a relatively small proportion of children's total educational experience comes from the classroom—perhaps no more than 10

percent of their waking hours by the time they complete
high school. Second, even if we conclude that 25 percent
of those classroom hours are devoted to the study of nonsense (or even material we find objectionable) we need
not be driven to an ulcer. If the curriculum is loaded with
one-fourth objectionable material (highly unlikely), we
would probably look for an educational alternative. Let's
suppose that 10 percent (two to three hours per week) is
devoted to objectionable material (and this, too, would
be a very high percentage); this 10 percent figure would
actually amount to only 1 percent of the child's total
educational exposure by age eighteen. Would we be concerned? Of course we would. We do not wish to shrug off
any material to which our children are exposed. But we
compare it with junk food. We hope to provide our children with a balanced, nutritional diet. At the same time,
we know they are going to consume a certain quantity of
junk food. Some of this they will probably eat in their
own home (we are not fanatical when it comes to food
additives and sugar-coated cereals). They will eat some
with their friends, and perhaps some in the school cafete-
ria. We will, of course, keep an eye on their diet. They
will be eating at least two meals a day at home, and we
are quite capable of saying no to requests for a diet of
junk. Over and above that, however, we don't worry
about it. We feel sure that the meals we provide will be
more than sufficient to nourish them. The snacks they eat
occasionally are not going to cause scurvy or rot their
teeth. And so it is with the junk food of the school academic programs. What they lack in intellectual value we
feel we can more than compensate for in our home. We
can correct the errors and counter the faulty reasoning in
much the same way we can if one of our children comes
in from play to tell us his or her friend claims the sun circles the earth, or babies are brought by the stork.

Teachers may have their facts wrong. We can correct it. Teachers may present personal opinions as fact. We can counter them. Teachers can act unjustly. We can explain the lack of justice. Teachers can promote morally doubtful positions, teach nonsense, and confuse students. We, the parents, are the primary educators. At our dinner table, and elsewhere, there is an exchange of information about what is going on in the classroom as well as elsewhere, and this often gives rise to questions. "I think there may have been political reasons also for the United States purchase of Alaska. Why don't we look it up." "But that was Mr. Smith's opinion of our immigration policies; what do you think?" "I think maybe you might have gotten mixed up about what chlorophyll does in plant life; did your teacher explain photosynthesis?" On the more serious matters, the questions of morals and ethics, we accept the fact that the teachers may not always subscribe to the values we hold. If our values are sound, however, and are based upon clear reasoning rather than emotion, these opposing values, whether they come from a teacher, friend, or television program, should present no more than a challenge, never a threat. If we can logically explain how our values are formed and how our moral conclusions are reached, we should be able to aid our children in examining any views they hear expressed outside their home. There have always been parents who fear having their children read or hear views contrary to those held by the parents. In the 1950s there were some who advocated expurgating the works of Marx and Lenin from college libraries, fearing young minds might be persuaded to the Communist ideology. There are some religious leaders who oppose exposure to other religious philosophies. What does this thinking represent? If we are confident that our positions are valid and our reasoning sound, we should have nothing to fear in having our children exposed to other views. We can refute what is invalid. Loving, intelligent parents will always be the primary source of information and direction. We cannot lock our children away from all other influences, nor would we want to. Separating the wheat from the chaff is part of our job as parents. If we take on this job, do it well, and retain their respect, we should have little to fear from what our children pick up outside. If we teach them how to seek truth, how to question demagogues, and how to separate the rational from the emotional, we will have done our job. Children can recognize truth. And truth is all-powerful; it can make us free. This freedom is yet another source of bonding within the family, a bonding which reinforces mutually held values.

8

Self and Family

How do we learn to value ourselves? How do we teach self-value to our children?

To civilized peoples, human life surpasses all other values. We may be willing to sacrifice our lives for a value which we consider of greater value than our individual life, but such greater value is invariably attached to human life now or in the hereafter. The value is seldom attached to a geopolitical or economic abstraction. Sane people do not put their lives on the line for a fatherland or an 8 percent increase in the profit margin. They give their lives in defense of human values. We value each and every individual whether that individual be a derelict in San Francisco's Tenderloin district, a retarded child in a Bronx orphanage, or the President of the United States.

The fully actualized, mature person values not only human life, but all living things. A fireman may risk his life to rescue a dog stranded on a sea cliff. To protect an endangered species, a major building project may be halted. Some years ago in Southern California, a little girl fell down an abandoned well. She was still alive, but trapped many feet beneath the surface. Fire department rescue squads responded. Then, as news of the child's plight spread, people gathered at the site. Many may have been curiosity seekers, the same people who gather to gawk at the scenes of automobile crashes and fires. Others came to offer help. As the news continued to spread through on-the-scene television and radio reports, many rushed to the site who did have something to offer. They were doctors, nurses, construction workers, and well-diggers. The problems they faced were formidable. The well shaft was too narrow for an adult, and the child was wedged far beneath the surface. The dirt walls could collapse at any moment, and time was against the rescuers. With volunteered equipment and skilled personnel, it was decided to sink a parallel shaft to a point below where the child was trapped, and then to dig a cross-shaft. During the hours that followed, Los Angeles and communities within its television range became absorbed in the drama, as scores of experienced men and women worked at a feverish pace. An oxygen hose was lowered into the shaft. A short time later, the little girl's cries stopped, causing all of us to fear for the worst. There was no way of knowing if the child was still alive. The workers went on at a furious pace. Finally, one man, an unemployed construction worker experienced in working in mine shafts, a man who had driven to the site to offer his efforts, was lowered down the rescue shaft. He was to attempt to dig the tunnel from the rescue shaft to the well, entering below the point of entrapment in order to avoid a cave-in from above which would almost certainly smother the girl. The television stations continued to preempt their lucrative regular broadcasting while the efforts went on. The hours dragged. The stations stayed on the air past their usual broadcasting hours. Finally, late into the night, the man who had been lowered long before into that narrow, very dangerous rescue shaft emerged, the little girl in his arms. The prayers of the hundreds who had gathered in the field and the thousands who had sat or knelt by their television sets had been answered. She was alive and well. It was awesome! All that outpouring of concern for the life of one small child! A million or more people were saying to that child and her rescuer, "We value your life; you are important to us; we care about you."

This dramatic rescue occurred over two decades ago. We might ask, "Would people today show equal concern, or have we become so much the 'me generation' that we would turn away from getting involved?" The answer any one of us gives will reflect our own concerns and the extent to which cynicism has infected us. We choose to believe people have not changed, that they are today just as generous and caring, and that they value the life and well-being of others every bit as much. Yet we must admit there is disturbing contradictory evidence that also is presented to us in our daily news reports and interpersonal relationships. How often do we tell others, through our words and actions, even those closest to us, that we value them?

If we agree that self-esteem is important and that a positive self-image is essential to happiness at whatever age, how then do we encourage the growth of self-esteem within members of our family? We can tell our children that they are valued, that they are important and special. Will they, in time, come to believe it? Perhaps. If so, why do we so often neglect this form of nurturing? And we must assume it is seriously neglected if we judge by the number of children and adults who lack self-esteem. It probably is not hostility that impels us to withhold praise and statements of esteem. It may be fear. What if, we ask ourselves, we go overboard in building someone up? Isn't there a danger that the person will become a vain, insufferable egotist? And shouldn't people learn modesty? What about pride? Isn't it one of the deadly sins? What happens to our motivation if we begin to believe we are somebody special—pretty "hot stuff"—won't we quit striving to improve? In a word, isn't there a risk that we may encourage the development of human beings few of us would care to associate with?

There is much misunderstanding when it comes to personality development, how it takes place and how it is enhanced. Most of us have been raised to view humility as synonymous with self-deprecation. Self-put-downs are often not too veiled attempts to curry approval and praise for being "humble." Often, they may be nothing more than individual distortions of reality. Virtue has nothing to do with it. We can each make an honest assessment of our talents and accomplishments without arrogance. We can teach our children to do the same. We can teach them that they are, indeed, very special without risk that they will turn into "stuck-up little brats." The arrogant braggart or the stuck-up brat does not have a positive self-image. Quite the contrary. His abrasive behavior is evidence of a lack of self-esteem, not an excess thereof.

There is ample evidence of what befalls us if we reach adulthood with a poor opinion of ourselves. Psychologist Nathaniel Branden has said:[1] "There is no value-judgment more important to man—no factor more decisive in his psychological development and motivation—than the estimate he passes on himself.

"This estimate is ordinarily experienced by him, not in the form of a conscious, verbalized judgment, but in the form of a feeling, a feeling that can be hard to isolate and identify because he experiences it constantly: it is part of every other feeling, it is involved in his every emotional response.

"The nature of his self-evaluation has profound effects

[1] Nathaniel Branden, *The Psychology of Self-Esteem*, Los Angeles: Nash Publishing Corp., 1969.

on the man's thinking processes, emotions, desires, values, and goals. It is the single most significant key to his behavior. To understand a man psychologically, one must understand the nature and degree of his self-esteem, and the standards by which he judges himself.

"Man experiences his desire for self-esteem as an urgent imperative, a basic need. Whether he identifies the issue explicitly or not, he cannot escape the feeling that his estimate of himself is of life-and-death importance. No one can be indifferent to the question of how he judges himself; his nature does not allow man that option."

The individual, male or female, gives up in the face of what is seen as unsurmountable odds. He settles in his life for what he evaluates as second or third best—in work, marriage, friends, and ultimately in satisfactions found in all pursuits. He feels he can expect no more. He sees himself as a loser, and since his expectations are self-fulfilling, he proves himself to be a loser in his work, his marriage, with his friends, and in virtually everything else. His capacity for becoming an open, responsive, achieving, and loving human being is destroyed.

This isn't the future we want for *our* children, or for *yours*. Far from it. We want, rather, to show them that they are valuable human beings, and that they are valued by us and by the other members of their family. We also want to show them *why*.

The first step toward convincing them of this is a vigorous enforcement of certain "you shall nots." Put-downs are simply not tolerated. They are, within the family, punishable offenses. Someone wisely said, "Treat people as if they have already become what you wish them to be." Only by doing so can you hope to aid them toward becoming the person that others, and the world at large, will view with admiration.

We criticize our children, and they criticize us. Sometimes it is even harsh—both ways. But we feel there is a difference between criticism and put-downs. The put-down is a statement of devaluation. It is a statement which says, "I see you as value*less*." The put-down is an attack on the person. Even said in jest, the put-down is an attack. Sad to say, put-downs are frequently sprinkled throughout the conversations of children. "Hey, big nose!" "What do you want, stupid?" "Where'd you get such a dumb haircut?"

This trading back and forth of put-downs may occupy a long afternoon on the playground while friends shoot baskets. If asked, they would probably deny that they have any intention of hurting one another. As they see it, such remarks are no more than teasing. Any words, however, are like drops of water on a stone. They have a cumulative effect. The physical self-image "big nose" develops will be a reflection of the words which he has ingested and stored in his unconscious. It is possible that nothing is ever totally forgotten, and that our sensory stimuli—negative as well as positive—will be forever stored in our memory banks. If this hypothesis is valid, most of us probably carry around a sizable pile of put-downs stored in our unconscious. For most of us, this pile of put-downs has been growing since early childhood. Some of it came from our parents and some from teachers. And a lot from other children. It is often said that children are cruel. They probably are. Like some politicians who lack the ability to address themselves to the issues, children resort to personal attack; they fall into name-calling. Such name-calling may be passed off as "teasing," but the words of the name-calling are still heard and they are stored in the memory bank of the hearer. It is this memory bank which shapes the self-image.

Put-downs are simply not permitted within our home. The excuse, "I was only kidding," is unacceptable. Put-downs are punishable. Similarly, what we call "negative input" is also unacceptable. It consists of statements and remarks designed to discourage achievement attempts (e.g., "If I were you, I wouldn't even try out for the school play, you'll never make it." "You, play basketball? Are you kidding? You're only five-five!"). Such negative input feeds "you can't" messages into the hearer's unconscious, where they may. become, "I can't" self-sentences.

Self-esteem is built upon a foundation of achievement, and achievement is built upon a foundation of positive self-image. The more we achieve, and can take pride in, the more our self-esteem grows. But in order to achieve, we must believe that we are capable of achieving. We learn our perceptions of reality, including our perceptions of ourselves. These perceptions may not in any way represent a "true" or valid reality, but they are *our* perceptions and we cling to them tenaciously. Whatever we believe we cannot do, we cannot do. We don't even attempt it. As we are growing up, we are taught a number of limitations. These come from friends, teachers, and, all too often, from unthinking parents. As parents, our motives for teaching such "limits" may be loving. We don't want our children to be disappointed and experience the pain of failure. To tell our children, however, that they shouldn't "get their hopes up" if they try for an "impossible dream" or that they should not make the attempt, does not protect them from pain; it only increases the probability that they will make no attempts. "Nothing ventured, nothing gained" is all too true. What we hope to encourage is a venturing which will result—perhaps quite often—in defeat, but more important, will occasionally yield victories.

We feel a great deal of human misery and frustration can be attributed to perceived limitations imposed by self-sentences—the "I can'ts" and the "I have to's." We don't

want our children to believe in limitations. We want
them to have faith in their potential. We want them to
approach challenges with confidence and the belief that
they *can* do anything they set out to do. Of course there
will be times that they will fail. We know that, and so do
they. We also recognize that they will hurt when they
fail. But we know that there will be times, perhaps seldom, when they will experience the exhilaration of reaching beyond their grasp and making it. And those times,
we know with certainty, will make up for the pain.

If we don't encourage them to try, they may not. The
mere suggestion that children be pushed is enough to
drive many educators and some parents into a frenzy.
There have been educators who have argued that *any* failure in *any* pursuit will be somehow traumatic and therefore to be avoided at all cost. These are the psychologically oriented humanists who have promoted "no fail"
schools and non-competitive classes. The results have
been a disaster. Such misplaced compassion has destroyed
the ambition of a generation. Its advocates have failed to
comprehend the fundamental facts of human behavior
and what motivates each of us. Without the possibility of
"losing" there can be no chance of winning, and what we
want for our children is the self-esteem which comes
from winning.

Pushing children to achieve their potential in areas of
endeavor which will be of benefit to them in future years
or will peak their interest is one thing. Pushing them to
achieve what their parents may want for the parents' ego
and/or status is another. We hope to keep our egos out
of it, and think primarily in terms of what will enhance
the self-image of the child. We know what that exhilaration of achievement can do. We have experienced it.
We also know that the achievement must be in an area of
endeavor which has importance to the individual. Doing

one hundred push-ups may not be a world's record. But to the man who has always viewed himself as a below-par athlete, one hundred push-ups may provide a tremendous boost in self-esteem. What we attempt to do with our children is to push them beyond the limits which may be secure—the limits within which they feel certain of achieving. If Jimmy says, "I think I may try out this year for the junior varsity," we answer, "Why don't you show up for try-outs for the varsity?" We know he may not make the varsity team. He also knows it. And we are not saying, "Jimmy, we feel you can make the varsity." Perhaps his odds of making the varsity are no better than one in twenty. We still encourage him. If Jimmy doesn't make the varsity, he will be disappointed. It will hurt. But he will have tried. Even the hurt will not be as bad as he may have expected, and it may make it easier for him to try again next time.

When children do win, there is reason for celebration. There is seldom reason to celebrate when the child or the parent has done no more than what might be expected. This is why since we enjoy celebrating the achievements of one another, we try to avoid discouragement. We want all members of the family to encourage one another to "go for broke." This, of course, extends to the parents. If we forbid our children to engage in discouragements, negative inputs, and put-downs, we must set the example. Husbands and wives frequently make remarks which lessen the self-esteem of their partner. They may do it in the name of teasing, while at the same time they profess love. Yet if love is expressed in desiring only what is best for the loved one, it would seem that any remark which diminishes the loved one's self-evaluation cannot be evidence of loving. Teaching children to enhance the self-esteem of one another must, very obviously, start with the example set by the parents. Do the parents praise one another when they speak to their children? Do they point out the other parent's good qualities? Does the father speak of his wife as the most wonderful woman in the world? Does she portray him as a knight in shining armor? Or do they, in a back-and-forth sniping, make jokes about his bumbling and her poor diction?

Is there such a thing as *overpraising*? Many parents feel that if too much is made of an achievement it can have an undesirable result. They may be right if the praising is done in an unrealistic manner. Performed in a sensible way, it cannot be overdone. We have a basic rule in this: we praise actions and achievements which are "above and beyond" the ordinary, expected level of performance for the child at his or her age—*measured against his or her previous behavior.* To praise any performance which meets only minimal standards (considering the child's age and experience) is a form of put-down. To use an obvious example, let's look at the situation of a husband and wife. Suppose the husband cleans off the ring in the bathtub after he bathes. If his wife heaps him with praise for the consideration and for the superb job he did in wiping away the soap ring, she may be saying, "I didn't really expect you to show such common consideration or to handle such a simple task with any competence." This is a put-down. She is saying, in effect, "I really see you as an incompetent and inconsiderate human being. Therefore, when you cleaned the ring in the tub, I felt you had gone beyond what would normally be expected of you." When a family member goes above and beyond the expected level, praise from the other family members is both appropriate and desirable. If praise is lavished on behavior which is only minimal or average, a put-down may be perceived.

The nurturance of self-esteem extends beyond the mere praising of achievement or even the exhilaration from having achieved. It goes to the roots of valuing oneself. This is perhaps the highest value we can hold as human beings. If we do not value who and what we are, we will never strive to become more than what we presently are. Attempting to instill in our children the value that they can achieve anything they want to achieve and that they are important, valuable, human beings—just for being the persons they are—is not easy in a society which all too often bombards them with the opposite. Self-esteem, for all of us, is bombarded from every side. We are handed guilt trips and messages of our limitations. As adults, we may try to fight this off. Children, however, are vulnerable—very vulnerable. They receive the messages of self-limitation almost continually in their schools. They are put down by their classmates on the playground. Perhaps the only sanctuary they can find in which their self-esteem will be protected is in the home. It is in the home, therefore, that we, as parents, must attempt to counter the negative influences. We're the ones who must attempt to encourage—push—our children to believe in themselves, to let each and every child know that he or she is a very special human being whom we believe capable not only of reaching for the stars but of conquering them.

The genuine achievers will never feel any need to broadcast their achievements. They will not hold a false modesty, but they will feel no need to batter their acquaintances over the head with their winnings. They will accept achievement for what it is—*achievement*. They will have worked for it, and they will be able to enjoy it, with no need to use it to destroy others. It will never be a weapon which they employ against others who have not achieved as much.

Nurturance of self is not limited to encouragement of achievement. It comes about often from a projection of love. If we are loving, we increase our self-love. If we are loving parents, we increase our children's feelings of self-love. Love, being the giving of self, states a value: "I believe I have something of value to give to you."

Praise is not necessarily love, and love is not necessarily praise, but communicating a belief in the loved one's potential may most certainly be an expression of love, a very important one. There are many opportunities to praise our children, and to show them that they do, indeed, have good reason for feeling self-esteem. They each have their own special talents, their own opportunities to "win." They may win in pursuits which surprise us, ones which are not areas of our interest, but it is the winning which is important in the building of self-esteem. It may be in the construction of superior model airplanes, or in playing saxophone well, or in growing plump, rich tomatoes. Achievements are beautiful, special expressions of the fulfillment of the human potential. So long as we tell children, by our praise and acceptance, that we applaud these achievements, they will continue to strive to climb still higher mountains. And as they stack up their winnings, they will stack up self-esteem.

9

This We Believe

We are what we believe in, what convictions we are willing to defend, what loyalties we hold, what beliefs we profess. Ask a man what he is willing to die for, and you will learn what he lives for. You will learn who and what he is.

We speak about *values*, but often the word itself is unclear. It may include preferences, opinions, and tastes. What we mean by values is too often far too broad. Values are more than a preference for strawberry ice cream over vanilla. They are attributes and characteristics which we hold to be of value, those which are good, admirable, and worthy of emulation. They have to do with what is morally and ethically right or wrong, good or bad, virtuous or unprincipled. Within the family, they form our guiding principles, and they direct our teachings and the means by which we nurture our children. Ultimately, the strongest bonding within the family is established by values the parents set forth.

When we were children, we were taught certain values. We were not born with a knowledge of them. Freud may have been cynical when he portrayed the infant as little more than a hedonistic, biting, snarling, little beast. He may have portrayed the dark side of infancy when he held that the one-year-old, given the physical strength, was capable of great viciousness. He was accurate however, when he concluded that moral principles and ideals (what he termed the *superego*) were learned through specific teachings and examples, through limits set by parents. He wisely concluded that these values did not sprout into consciousness as the result of a natural growth process. Parents were, and are, the teachers of what is right and wrong, what principles we should espouse, what beliefs we should hold. Most of us were raised in homes in which we felt respect for our parents and their convictions. As a result, we probably incorporated the values they taught. Through this process of incorporation, a process which includes listening to and accepting the values expressed by our parents and then making these values our own, we became what we are.

We always want for our children something better than what is represented by the world around them. We want our children to incorporate values that will provide them with the best opportunity to find meaning in their lives and to decide upon the goals they wish to pursue. We want them to grow in values which will aid them in viewing others as potential allies, and persons to be loved, rather than foes. And we want them to understand *responsibility* and *identity* where others are concerned. These are our goals, but we recognize they are not easily achieved. As parents, we can do only so much and no more. But we believe we can do a lot, and what we can do, in living and teaching our values, will be the greatest challenge to our parenthood.

The important moral and ethical values have to do with ourselves and what we do in relationship to others. These values can usually be rationally derived. They do not demand faith; they simply make sense in the world as we want it to be.

Even a very young child can be given an understanding of justice as a collection of rights and obligations. They can very quickly grasp the idea that some actions are unfair and therefore wrong, and that some actions are fair and therefore right. The principle of doing unto others as you would have them do unto you is one of simple logic. Even the preschooler can comprehend it and accept it. Parents do not, of course, try to teach a child abstract concepts such as truth, loyalty, honesty, and trust. But the actions which represent these concepts are almost as real in the life of a child as they are in the life of an adult. A child can understand kindness and generosity. When we teach these values, we draw upon the daily experiences of ourselves as well as our children. And we draw upon the experiences and challenges of others.

We want our children to incorporate these values in a way which will have meaning for them. We don't want them to give simply unquestioning obedience to commands of "right" and "wrong." In order to accomplish this, we must present the values through example, and we must support the values by logic. Rules can be presented by simple commands. Values cannot.

For a long time there has been a question as to whether values can be taught as absolutes. Right or wrong moralism has been brought into question. And it should be. We feel, however, that if values are to ever be held with resolve they must be held as absolutes. And they must be taught the same way. Many understandably reject what they see as a rigid morality. They subscribe to an ill-defined "situation" ethic, and they argue that no action is wrong per se, that all actions must be judged within the context of the "situation." If we see a new sports car parked at the curb with the keys in it with no one near, and we get in it and drive it away, is that stealing? "Well," they might answer, "that depends. Perhaps you need a car to get back and forth to work, or maybe the owner has two or three other cars, or maybe it's owned by an oil company that has plenty of money and rips off the public all the time. Perhaps the car is only being borrowed and the police will recover it before it has been gone long." The situation, these individuals argue, determines whether an action is right or wrong. Morality, then, is determined by an ever-changing set of variables. It is a kaleidoscope of grays. As such, it can never be taught. It can never even be understood. The child can understand that stealing is stealing. He can never understand that "situations" determine rightness or wrongness.

Adults have become increasingly confused in trying to make even the simplest moral distinctions. This may be due to the popularization of euphemisms such as, "Rip-off." "Was it a good movie?" "No, it was a rip-off." "The OPEC countries are ripping us off." "Punk rock music is a rip-off." "This wristwatch? Oh, I didn't pay for it; I ripped it off." Are any of these examples of stealing? Do any of them constitute immoral behavior? If adults have difficulty making such distinctions, what can they expect of their children? Even the word *murder*, traditionally defined as "the unlawful killing of a human being" has been, in recent years, applied to legitimate acts of war, abortion, killing of whales, and even the cutting of California redwoods. If murder is defined as ambiguously as this, does it retain any meaning at all? It has been said that we have no *emotional* problems, only *thinking* problems. Further, it has been argued, with great logic, that *thinking* is a function of language. We think in words, and our thinking, therefore, will be only as precise as the words we use. If we "think" in euphemisms, our thought-processes will be as vague as the euphemisms we employ. If we hope to teach moral and ethical values to our children, we *must* do so in absolutes. This means eliminating euphemisms—calling stealing what it is: stealing, and calling murder, murder.

Teaching right-or-wrong values is seldom easy. It is both verbal and experiential. We tell our children what we believe in, and we support what we say with logic. We hope, also, that we reinforce what we say with examples from one day to the next. Our five-year-old brings home a toy picked up at a friend's house. We hope we handle it as simply as possible, in a manner that will not encourage guilt feelings. In most cases it is enough to say, "This doesn't belong to you. It belongs to Jimmy. You must return it to Jimmy." At a later age, perhaps seven or eight, the reasoning behind the value can be explained in terms he can understand: "This belongs to Jimmy. It is his toy. If you take it, it will hurt Jimmy very much. If Jimmy took something which belonged to you, it would hurt you, wouldn't it? Of course it would. And that's what makes hurting others so wrong. We know how much it can hurt and since we don't like to be hurt, we don't want to do things which will hurt others."

We find we draw a lot of teaching examples from the daily newspaper or the news presentation on television. In the first sixteen pages of our daily newspaper for today, we counted twelve stories which raised "ambiguous" moral choices. These were choices which, by the standards of our contemporary society, are not clearly right or wrong. A group of women protesting "sexism and the degrading of women" threw bricks through the windows of stores which were selling (by their viewpoint) pornography. Was their destruction of property moral or immoral? A man known as J. D. Cooper hijacked an airliner. He then parachuted from the plane and he and the money he had extorted have not been seen since. Some people have made him a folk hero; they have even established an annual celebration in honor of his exploit.

But do they admire his achievement and lessen his crime
when they say, "He only ripped off a large company?" Or
what about a group protesting nuclear research in a major
university? The group sabotages laboratories conducting
the research. Are they moral or immoral? A school su-
perintendent directed his teachers to falsify test scores of
minority students because he felt that the tests were dis-
criminatory. Should he be lauded for his high principles
or censored for his lack of ethics? A doctor admitted he
ordered clinical tests which were probably not entirely
called for, but he justified it by saying, "I could get
shafted in a malpractice suit if I didn't cover every base;
it's called "preventative medicine." A patient suffered an
unfortunate but unpredictable side effect from medica-
tion prescribed by her doctor. The patient consulted an
attorney who said, "I think there's a good chance the in-
surance company will settle on this case rather than spend
the money to go to court." The moral questions are
unending.

With a right-or-wrong standard of morality, most of
these judgments might easily be made. But many people
are apparently confused. We asked a group of adults,
"What is stealing?" The answers led to a discussion
which continued for an hour and a half, and there was no
consensus. People were unable to come up with a definition of "stealing." When we called time, one man said,
"We still haven't agreed on what stealing is or is not.
How can we ever figure out what is right or wrong?" A
woman in the group suggested we take a week or two to
think it over.

We do not feel that parents have to raise their children
with such doubts, muddled thinking, and anxiety. We
don't think that they have to trade morality for "situa-
tional ethics." They can present moral issues to their children, discuss the issues, debate the logic involved, and

present conclusions which are supported by reason. They can then openly live the values they possess. When children see Mother undercharged at the store and return the money she did not deserve, a lesson is presented. When Daddy replaces the tool he borrowed from a neighbor and accidentally damaged, another lesson is given. When parents explain that repeating malicious gossip about a neighbor is slander and wrong, and that cheating, whether it be on a test in school or an income tax report is unjust, lessons are taught. Words are never a substitute for example. These examples must be in stark contrast. Only then will both adults and children understand. Some may view such standards as scrupulous, viewing any unwavering principle as morally rigid. But can any of our principles be less than unwavering? If they are flexible, are they principles?

If the opportunity is grabbed, moral and ethical values can frequently be a part of family conversation. Examples are raised from our experiences—those of parents and children alike—throughout the day. The issue of capital punishment may be raised in one of the children's classes. We can explore the topic for an hour or more. A rock star leaves his wife to live with a girlfriend. It raises questions. What commitments do we make when we marry? What are the principles of sexual morality involving others—and why? One of the grammar school children is unpopular, and he is excluded from the team. What obligations do we have to him? A classmate is seen cheating on a test. Is there a duty to report him, say something to him, or simply keep quiet?

In its broadest interpretation, the respect for all living things we have tried to teach our children as an important value encompasses virtually all we hope to have our children in morals and ethics. We want them to understand what they owe to others, both those within their

family, and those who may be separated by many miles
and widely divergent cultures. We do not stress the ideal
of *loving*, although we firmly support it as the ultimate
goal—the only worthwhile goal—to which human beings
can aspire. *Love* is an abstraction, and we are not sure it
can be taught through logic. In any case, it will seldom be
learned before they reach adulthood. And like other ab-
stractions—loyalty, patriotism, faith—it will not be easily
grasped. Ask a child, for example, to define *patriotism*,
and he may say, "Patriotism is when you salute the flag."
What we can teach, however, is kindness. We can demand it, and we can demonstrate it through parental example.

We try to provide "positive reinforcement" for acts of
kindness. When a child acts with kindness toward another member of the family or someone outside the family, we try to remember to praise. It is never done casu-
ally. We define most carefully what we consider to be acts
of kindness. It is from these acts that we draw our examples of more significant acts of charity and love. The opportunities for expressions of kindness are numerous.
They are almost endless. We can offer much to one another in both our words and our actions. We can praise
and compliment one another; we can help one another;
we can support one another. As parents we must lead the
way. We may tell a ten-year-old daughter how pretty she
looks as she leaves for school. We may compliment our
thirteen-year-old son on the neatness of his room or the
excellent job he has done in trimming the lawn. We can
reward acts of respect for living things, and we can punish
unkindness. Always, it is our hope that these values will
be incorporated for their own sake, that they will become
actions which are rewarding in and of themselves. Treat-
ing other members of the family with respect and
kindness is the first rule, but it is much more. This rule,

we recognize, can only evolve into a *value* when it is internally rewarding. We have tried a number of ways in which this might be effective. Many years ago, we began what has evolved into a family tradition. During the weeks before Christmas, we placed a small manger in the center of the kitchen table. It became a centerpiece, a small crib. Beside the manger we placed a bowl filled with short lengths of yellow yarn. The yellow yarn represented straw. For each act of kindness, a "straw" was placed in the crib. This was to provide a bed for the Baby Jesus. The one who performed the act of kindness, usually with no one else present, would place a straw in the crib for himself or herself. The good deed was to be anonymous. Placing the straw would be strictly on an "honor system." The deed could be almost anything. It might be making someone else's bed, slipping a candy bar into a sister's lunch, or doing the chores assigned to a brother. Little by little, the "bed" would fill with straw.

We've used a lot of modifications of this idea. We've always made it an honor system. No one knows who has put in the latest "straw." But given the rationale of kindness, the "straws" accumulate. Christmas morning a small doll representing Baby Jesus is laid on a bed of "straw." At that point, kindness becomes its own reward. All moral and ethical values, kindness, and mutual respect are joined together in the strongest bonding forces within the family. Family members become best friends because they share these values. They remain so because they cling to them and value them. Thus, values are bonding in much the same manner that common interests are. They go beyond the bonding of common interests, however, in that they represent the deepest affirmations of self and the deepest and most meaningful associations with one another. They provide a set of principles within which members of the family can view the world. And in turn, each other.

In the Judeo-Christian tradition, the family is portrayed as the "church in miniature," a microcosm of the larger family of God. The Paschal meal, the observance of the High Holy Days, the home shrines, the ceremonies of christening, confirmation, and bar mitzvah, comprise the religious services of the family/church. In this tradition, the church has relied heavily upon the family as its paradigm. It is impossible to imagine what form religion might take if all family metaphors were removed from the liturgy. We suspect it would be one of utmost tyranny.

Spiritual direction and religious practices within the home, however, raise questions that are not always easy to answer. Even those parents who follow without question a dogmatic and authoritarian religion still must face how they want the beliefs they accept to be introduced to their children. These questions involve more than faith and theology. They touch on issues which are social, psychological, and educational. It is for this reason that we have separated somewhat our discussion of religion and spirituality from our brief introduction to the questions of ethics and morality. Ethics and morals, we believe, can and should be presented to our children with rational arguments. They should be presented in a way which says, "There are sensible reasons for acting with justice and charity, and they are as follows. . . ." These arguments for ethics and morality do not in any way call for a testament of faith. We can explain to our children what stealing is and why it is wrong, without reliance upon religion. We have the arguments of logic to support us. Faith transcends logic, and therefore cannot be derived from logical proofs. Thomas Aquinas, the great thirteenth-century scholastic philosopher, offered a number of proofs of the existence of God. At the same time he argued that faith is both a virtue and a gift. The arguments of logic are one thing; the acceptance upon faith is another. Converts are never won through debating skills.

There is another, perhaps more important, argument for teaching morals and ethics on the basis of logic rather than religious tenets: morality that is dependent upon faith will always be vulnerable to doubts of faith. We have spoken with a large number of adults who have professed belief in a moral code based exclusively upon a religious precept rather than logic. When we have asked them, "How would your life change if you were to find that the Ten Commandments had not been given to Moses by God, that they were nothing but the creative writing of a human being?" The answers we have heard have frequently been, in effect, "I don't know what I would do. I guess my whole life would change." How puzzling! Would he or she no longer find a reason to condemn murder, false witness, or stealing? If our code of morality is based solely on our belief in the God who gives His commandments to His chosen people, what can happen should our faith weaken? Doesn't our moral code also weaken? We feel that morality and ethics should be presented to our children in a rational manner. It should be explained in terms of rights and obligations and the justice we owe to all others. Certainly our belief in God—His relationship to man, His nature, His plan for us, and how we are expected to live in fulfilling it—will be dependent upon the strength of our faith. We may attempt to live our faith, and in living our faith in joy and hope, inspire our children to embrace it, but we cannot argue our children into accepting the moral precepts which flow from it.

Parents may be able to frighten their children into compliance with the dictates of religion if they present them with a fearful God, a bogeyman figure, but what will they reap with such scare tactics? Most probably, they will raise children who will grow up incapable of thinking, afraid of questioning, and clinging to belief systems in which prohibitions—"thou shalt nots"—are the totality of religion. To a child, God is always a parental figure; he is not an abstraction. Children come to view God as they view their parents—loving, giving, understanding, protecting; or cold, punitive, demanding, and cruel. Loving parents do not try to play God, but they are aware of the fact that their children learn to see God through them, and hence to see Him as loving in the way their parents are loving. Such parents do not feel any need to present God as a fearful enforcer of discipline. Frightening children into obedience may be effective in the short run, but in the long run it is as emotionally and intellectually destructive as it is cruel. In previous years, fear tactics were rather common. Santa Claus was presented to children not simply as a jolly old man who brought toys, but as a scorekeeper who rewarded good children and punished bad. Often, God was presented as a slightly more serious version of Santa Claus. He observed our actions; he read our thoughts; recorded our sins; and passed judgment on us. Children were presented with a God who could only be feared. And fear can only encourage rebellion. A theology of fear is not only dreadful psychology, it is abhorrent theology. The Apostle John said, "God is love." And he taught us that love casts out fear. We want our children to live without fear.

The liturgy of the "family in miniature" can only be effective in inspiring faith and love of God if it is focused on joy and love one for another among the members of the family. It can never be enough to say, "Pray together," or, "Read the Bible every evening." Prayer may be nothing more than repetitious words, pious clichés. But it can be an expression of gratitude to a personal

God, an expression of faith and hope, and a means of communication between the individual and his God and between those who share similar convictions.

In prayer, we petition, give praise, and offer thanks. We express our thoughts and our feelings. We feel there can be no more natural setting for such conversations with God than within the home, wherein we feel free to express our personal needs, desires, and reactions. Our family conversations are seldom "formalized." We skip from topic to topic, with many interruptions and digressions. Contributions come from all sides. We often disagree. And vehemently so. Why should our talks with God be any different? Certainly, formal prayers have their place. They strengthen our ties to tradition and to the scriptural foundations of our faith. Talking to our God, however, in our words, does not need to be formal. It is most natural when it is expressed as normal conversation within the home much in the same way that we talk to one another. We see no reason to set limits on what can be said back and forth to one another and what can be expressed as prayer. If God knows what we are thinking, He knows the words we use to express our thoughts. We feel we should be able to talk freely within our home both *about* God and *to* God.

For most of us, religion has formed an important part of our heritage. We have drawn upon it for our identity and our roots. When we visit Israel, the word we most often hear is "tradition." Virtually every square mile is laden with the history and tradition of the three major faiths. "*Tradition* says it was on this spot that Jesus and his disciples . . ." "According to *tradition* it was here that Abraham . . ." "Although not all authorities agree, tradition holds that this is the place at which Pilate . . ." If the Holy Land were to no longer exist, and if every biblical wall, stone, shrine, and grotto were to be obliterated, the theology of the faiths which venerate that small land would be affected not at all. We would, however, lose much of our traditions. And both the theology and tradition are important. The importance of theology speaks for itself; it is knowledge of the God we believe in. Our traditions are psychologically more complex. They are our common heritage, our identity. It is our traditions which contribute so much to our family bonding. Our religious traditions can be drawn from scriptural writings and from ethnic customs. They can also be developed within the circle of our family, even if they are borrowed from other cultures and other times.

Bar mitzvah (and, for girls, bas mitzvah) is a beautiful tradition in which the youth is introduced into the adult community. He is charged with the responsibility of being an adult Jew, of defending his faith and carrying on its traditions. For the Christian, the ceremony of confirmation is similar. The young man or woman is challenged to become a "soldier of Christ." These are ceremonies which are steeped in tradition. Bar mitzvah and confirmation are not ceremonies conducted simply within the walls of a house of worship. They are family celebrations. In times past, families celebrated the anniversary of these spiritual initiations. Each year, the bar mitzvah or confirmation was renewed. These ceremonies or sacraments carried with them meaning. They were more than simply formalities. They were communications of commitment. "You are now an adult," they said, "and you are now pledging yourself to the responsibilities of an adult." At each anniversary celebration, there was a recommitment. Words which were once said, were said again, and the tradition was continued—as well as the commitment. All major religions follow a liturgical year which lends itself easily to family activities and the establishment of family religious traditions. During December, Christian families celebrate Christmas; Jewish families celebrate Hanukkah. Today we hear many complaints of the "commercialization" of these holidays. People say that the spiritual meaning of the Holy Days is ignored. But can we be disturbed by the commercialization if we are not taking part in it? Is there any better place in which to find meaning in these Holy Days than within the family? Certainly giftgiving is part of the tradition, but does gift-giving have to denote "commercialization"? We feel that when our gifts are chosen and given in love, regardless of their price tag, they embody the meaning of the religious significance of these days. Gifts do not commercialize holy days. Hanukkah and Christmas *should* be periods of celebration. They should be days in which family members can share in joy and thanksgiving. The eight days of Hanukkah celebrate the rededication of the temple by the Maccabees following their victory over the Syrians. It is the festival of light, commemorating the miracle by which oil for the lamps, found to be only a single day's supply, burned for eight days. In commemorating Hanukkah within the home, the menorah is lit each night for eight days. It is a beautiful feast, a festival rich in tradition and bonding, and much would be lost if it were reduced to only a single evening of exchanging elaborately wrapped gifts. Similarly, Christmastide begins on the eve of Christmas and extends to the Feast of Epiphany, a festival commemorating the manifestation of Christ to the Gentiles in the persons of the Magi, January 6. But it can extend even further than that. Christmas, like Hanukkah, can be celebrated within the home as a festival extending over many days, and establishing religious traditions within the home which carry the spirited joy of the season. By initiating "traditions" we have been able to extend Christmastide far beyond a one-day celebration, and we have been able to establish religious traditions more meaningful than an ornamented tree and wrapped gifts. Using a little imagination, we feel parents can develop a variety of ways of celebrating their beliefs throughout the liturgical year, ways which will be both joyful and bonding, ways which will at the same time teach the foundations of the faith which the parents profess and the traditions which represent their roots.

The character and the extent of a family's association with the social body of an institutional church raises questions which we feel should be carefully considered by parents, both for themselves and for their children. We do not believe it is enough to follow the advice, "Join a church; become active in your parish." These decisions are too important. Even the decision *what* church is one which challenges us to wrestle with many subquestions. Consider some of the underlying questions:

1. What do *I* believe about God?
2. Do I feel my beliefs are enhanced and my spiritual life enriched through participation in a church community?
3. Does this church community reflect my basic beliefs?
4. Do the practices of this church community (apart from their professed theology) offer something I find of value toward my spiritual (and perhaps social) growth?
5. Do the views which are expressed within this church community—through sermons, study groups, adult and child activities, etc.—support the beliefs I wish to express to my family?
6. Do we, as spouses and parents, agree with the overall church environment that we want for our children?
7. Will this church involvement, with its demands of

time, associations, and activities, draw our family closer together or encourage us to go off in different directions?

Just as war is too important to be left to generals, faith is too important to be left to theologians and ministers. Faith is born out of searching through the dark night of the soul. Nothing is more plagued with doubt, more challenging, more personal. When we speak of a "mixed" marriage, for example we refer to a marriage between persons who profess beliefs in different religious affiliations or labels: Catholic/Protestant, Christian/Jew, Mormon/Unitarian, etc. But these distinctions are seldom enough. If we look beneath the surface, we discover that virtually all marriages are "mixed." Let's say we have two Roman Catholics, Jim and Mary Jane. Jim attends mass when he feels he will enjoy and benefit from the sermon, the community, or the inspirational music. Jim believes that contraceptive birth control should be a matter of individual choice, not dictated by his church. He hasn't said a rosary in years, and he doesn't feel his children should be enrolled in parochial school unless the school is academically superior to the public school. His wife, Mary Jane, on the other hand, believes attendance at mass on Sundays and Holy Days of Obligation is a serious contract with God. She accepts the church's teachings on birth control. She wants the family rosary as a nightly observance. And she is convinced that parochial school is important to the children's religious education. Jim cannot understand how Mary Jane can cling to what he considers "rigid" beliefs. Mary Jane feels that Jim is fastly falling away from Catholicism. Their differences will probably continue to chafe, and stand a good chance of degenerating into a chronic debate, unless they can sit down together and approach their differences with understanding and mutual acceptance. Debates about what are right or wrong, true or untrue, will be senseless. Questions of truth and error in faith are never subject to rational argument. We cannot "prove" the validity of what is always a matter of personal belief.

Jim and Mary Jane can, however, discuss the goals they seek for their family both within the religion of the home and the religion of the church community. While they may hold beliefs which differ as to the nature of God and what He expects of man, their beliefs can be enhanced and their lives enriched if they bury the differences, at least for a trial period, and participate together in the liturgy of their church, and the communion of its members. Unless espousal of very specific, well-defined dogma, is required of the members of the church community, Jim and Mary Jane may find a comfortable home within the church community even if they do not see eye to eye on all beliefs. Both of them may find the social involvement worthwhile; they may find being together with others within the church community helps them to understand those who live in a different world—economically, socially, educationally, and even morally. The church may be a "melting pot." If it isn't, if, in fact, it tends to encourage elitism, they may both wish to sit down together and evaluate what they want for themselves as well as their children.

What role an individual church or parish may play as a community that functions as an extended family is a very important consideration. It is one that husband and wife should consider when they discuss their membership and involvement. The extended family of the church can be divisive or it can be unifying. Organized religion and institutional structures have frequently failed to support family unity. Church membership has encouraged separate, distinct, affiliations in which family members have been called upon to pledge an allegiance which has separated them. Husbands become involved in the Men's Club. Wives are drawn into a women's group. And children spend their time in Sunday school classes and youth groups apart from their family. At its worst, the institutional church has pulled the family apart. This may not have been the intention of the clergy, but it has been the result of those who have seen these splinter organizations as contributing to the growth of religious commitment. We would never suggest that church groups are designed with the intent of dividing the family. We have seen, however, many families pulled apart by church involvements.

We feel bonding within the family is the primary value. Questions and criticisms we raise concerning involvement in church organizations can be directed as well to other involvements. Perhaps no organization deserves a bad mark when it comes to its effect upon the family. And perhaps it cannot be praised. It is simply *there*, and its function cannot be judged on the basis of its effect on the family. Only the parents, husband and wife who are charged with the responsibility of creating bonding, can make the judgment and act accordingly. We contend, however, that for parents who wish to create strong family bonds, and take advantage of the opportunities offered within a society that will strengthen those bonds, any organization, including those within the church, must be evaluated in terms of whether it adds to or detracts from the closeness of the family. The kind and amount of participation which family members may give to their church community should be critically examined. It may very well be a reflection of social needs rather than devotional preferences or theological convictions. One spouse may be a "joiner"; the other spouse less social. One child may enjoy seeing his friends at church each week; another may rebel at being "dragged to that stuffy place."

We once asked a group of adults, "Do you feel your childhood experiences in the church were bonding influences within your family?" Some answered, definitely, "No!" They related dismal stories of weekly tension and conflict between their parents, or between the parents and the children in the family, over what one described as, "the perpetual hassle of getting up, getting dressed, and getting to church on time." The woman who felt such frustration said, "Dad would be hollering at Mom about whether she had ironed his shirt. Mom would be giving Dad a really bad time because the car hadn't been washed and she was going to be embarrassed driving into the church parking lot. They would both be on the backs of us kids. I used to dread Sunday morning more than anything." Her husband, however, expressed positive remembrances toward his childhood churchgoing. "I have very fond memories of going to church with my family," he said. "We would always sit in one of the front pews so we could see what was going on. Sitting in the back is awful for kids—you never get anything more than people's backs to look at. Mom and Dad would sit side by side. I can remember them holding hands, and I can remember us kids sitting on either side. Somehow, it was almost like going to a party every week. One of the things I remember very well was going out to breakfast for pancakes at a restaurant. It kind of continued the feeling of celebration. And at those breakfasts, we could take our time. No one had to rush to get to work or to school. It was at those breakfasts that we would discuss religion and our beliefs. We would usually start out with what went on in our own thinking about the sermon or the gospel readings. Often, Mom and Dad would sort of draw us out about what these teachings might mean in our own lives.

It was a fun experience. Very upbeat. There was a lot of laughter. Church attendance was something we did as a family, and that was great. I feel it drew us together."

Clearly it is the parents who structure the church experience. Through the choices they make and the atmosphere they create, they determine whether church participation will be a positive and bonding experience.

Whatever religion we espouse, we believe its teachings to be true. Implicit, therefore, in religious conviction is the belief that other faiths must be in error. All major faiths hold certain truths believed to be revealed by God. And what has been revealed to the Mormon differs from what has been revealed to the Catholic, Jew, or Muslim. We teach our children truths which we believe, and in turn, we teach them what we hold *not* to be true. In doing so, we tread a fine line. We do not want to teach them attitudes which can lead to prejudice and hatred. History has recorded far too many killings in the name of God. Parochialism can easily lead to social isolation, and we certainly do not want our children to develop a fortress mentality in which they feel they must stay strictly within the company of "true believers" lest they be led astray by "heretics" or brainwashed by proselytizers. If we are living our faith in love and joy, we will have no reason to fear our children being drawn away from it through exposure to those who hold differing beliefs. We can teach our children what we hold to be true, without implying that those who do not accept our beliefs are stupid or evil.

A dear friend of ours once said, "We have only three choices in life: we can develop or accept a sound belief system, one in which gives meaning and purpose to our lives; or we can plunge into such strenuous work and diversions that we have no time to think; or we can end our lives. We will choose one of the three." For many, a personal faith in God and the role He plays in our lives provides such direction and meaning. An understanding of God and His community within the church may also provide insight into the "church in miniature," the family. The love within the family can also serve to reveal the nature of Our Creator and the life He offers us. If God is love, where better to find His presence than within the circle of the family?

10

Our Sexuality

We come into this world as sexual beings. We are born male or female, and we are endowed with a sexual drive. Until this century, little was known of the nature of this drive. Many people felt it was improper to even speculate about the nature of the drive other than to acknowledge the obvious fact that it was tied to reproduction. Hunger and thirst were drives we recognized in infants. They were viewed as both natural and wholesome. But the sex drive was a different matter. Until recently, few "proper" men and women were comfortable discussing what moralists of the past called our "lower nature." While this drive had an obvious importance in the survival of our species, it was not essential to the survival of the individual human being, and hence some wondered if any urge which was so obviously unessential could be satisfied with any moral justification. In the nineteenth century (and for many centuries before) most men and women were not sure. Now, in the last decades of the twentieth century, there are still many who are not.

At the turn of the century, Sigmund Freud was vilified for having suggested that the infant experienced sexual reactions. Living in the puritanical society of upper-middle-class Vienna at the turn of the century, Freud was con-

demned for suggesting that innocent children might be
"guilty" of "lustful" thoughts. If they were innocent—and
who could doubt it?—such thoughts would be impossible.
Yet despite the attitudes and puritanical beliefs of his
peers, Freud persevered in his convictions. He collected
his observations, and he formulated his theory of human
behavior. To be sure, some of his theories have been refuted, even by his closest admirers. No one so prolific
could have escaped error. His observation of sexual response in the infant, however, is today accepted univer-
sally. The sexuality of the newborn is undeniable. The
two-year-old who crawls, walks, explores, explodes, and
charms is a human being who carries all the primary
drives of any other human being, including the sexual
drive.

We earlier touched upon how the child learns to
differentiate between the sexes and to develop a sex role.
Most of us accept the fact that such differences do exist,
that a two-year-old boy and a two-year-old girl differ in
more than merely anatomy. What is not so clear is
whether such differences are due to gonadal hormones or
other physiological factors or whether they result from
socially conditioned sex roles.

The *nature* versus *nurture* argument has vexed psychology for more years than most of us have been alive. The
questions still remain largely unanswered. And this is true
in many more areas than sexuality. If we find, for example, that sixteen-year-old David has a miserable school record, can his poor performance be attributed to low intelligence (inborn) or to an impoverished home environment? If we answer, "environment," how will we explain the honor student who is raised in the same home
and has attended the same schools? Those who argue for
"nature" would say they did not have the same genetic
endowment. Those who argue for "nurture" would try to

point out differences they experienced in the home environment. The problem may never be resolved. What, then, of the differences we observed between the sexes? More men than women have been recipients of Nobel Prizes in all fields. Must we conclude that this is evidence of discrimination against women? Or of the natural superiority of men? Or that women have simply not chosen to enter into and compete in the so-called traditionally male fields? The arguments, pro and con, may go on endlessly, but the only honest present answer is, "We don't know." We do know there are differences between the sexes. And they are real and verifiable. To deny their existence, and some do, is ridiculous. Whatever the basic differences may be, one thing is certain: the home environment is where the child learns what it is to be a man or woman, how they each act out their sexual identities, how they each express their sexual love, and how they each come to know their sexual identities.

These are lessons which are taught, first and foremost, by the parents through the ways in which they act out their own identities and the examples they provide of a man/woman relationship. Children watch their parents very closely (many parents feel too closely). In watching the parents, children learn that Mother is different from Father, not just in anatomy, but in personality, reactions, and roles. Generalizing from this bit of learning, they learn that men differ from women. The ways in which they differ may have nothing to do with gender, but children have no way of knowing this. Daddy is a man. Daddy likes buttered popcorn. Conclusion: *men* like buttered popcorn. The logic may leave something to be desired, but children seldom follow logic. What if Daddy is overly critical or unaffectionate? If the child is a boy, he may grow up in Daddy's image—critical and cold. If the child is a girl, she may grow up expecting nothing more from a man than what she saw her mother receive. Many men and women carry the bitter generalizations they learned in childhood about the other sex. The lessons were first learned at home, then reinforced in the relationships they developed. The girl may, in fact, choose to marry a man very similar to her father, feeling that she can do no better, that all men are critical and unaffectionate. The quality of the man/woman love between the parents is always the cornerstone of the family and the sexual identities the children will develop. If husband and wife fail to develop a continuing love and beauty in their relationship, they will almost inevitably pass on such an ugly legacy to their children.

Teaching a healthy sexual identity and wholesome sexual attitudes is a major responsibility of parenthood. No one else can do the job as well. The schools can't do it. The family doctor can't do it. The churches can't do it, nor can the YMCA or youth groups. No government programs, no books or films, and no well-meaning sex educators can succeed where the parents fail. By the time a child enters kindergarten, he or she will have been taught lessons in sexual identity and sexuality that may last a lifetime. Dr. William Masters said it well: "The best sex education a child can receive comes when he watches Daddy pat Mommy on the fanny and sees that Mommy enjoys it."

A question parents must always face is not *what* do we plan to teach our children about sex, but what *are* we teaching them. Whether they intend to or not, parents will communicate to their children their own sexual attitudes and a picture of the quality of their relationship. The hours husband and wife will spend in discussion of their sexual attitudes, expectations, and even frustrations may prove not only of great importance to their marriage, but of equal importance to the ultimate formation of healthy attitudes in their children. Sexual problems cannot be hidden behind the bedroom door. Children are far too perceptive. They know, even at a very early age, when things are not right between their parents. Every parent has become aware of this. When spouses are currently at odds, the two-year-old may react to the tension with misbehavior or other attempts to steer things away from the conflict and distract his parents from their squabbles. The child picks up signs of the emotional climate even if the differences are not expressed in his presence. Nothing could be more foolish than the parents' attempted justification, "But we never fight in front of the children."

The first overt sexual experience of the child comes when he discovers pleasure in touching his genitals. As parents, we may tell ourselves, quite rationally, that it is in no way a sin or a sexual perversion, but somewhere deep within our own psyches, or guilt feelings, we feel uneasy. Some parents snatch the baby's hand away. Others punish the child's behavior with a slap. Still others merely worry. How strong the negative reaction is probably dependent on the intensity of the parents' sexual fears and the extent to which they may project their negative sexual attitudes. Babies discover sexual pleasure in the same way they discover tastes and sounds, by natural exploration and accidental exposure. The baby does not decide to suck his thumb. Through random movements the thumb is brought to the mouth. Sucking is a normal response, and it is pleasurable. That's that. We don't make moral judgments about thumb-sucking. There is no reason why we should make moral judgments about the infant's exploration of any part of his or her body. If we were asked, we would all say, "Of course we want our children to like themselves, to feel good about who and what they are, and to admire their bodies." We want them to develop a positive-body image and to value the miracle that is the human body, including the reproductive organs of both sexes. There is no way we can convey this, however, unless we free ourselves of negative feelings about what is a normal acceptance and exploration of the body. Whatever the parents' attitudes toward self-stimulation may be, there is no reason for teaching, implicitly or explicitly, that body exploration by the young child is wrong. Parents operate from a rational base when they teach the child that hitting a brother or sister is wrong, but to try to present logical explanations for why genital touching is wrong is an entirely different matter. Will it lead to other undesirable sexual behavior? There is no evidence that it will. All evidence leads to one conclusion, that such genital exploration is a normal component of development. If parents attempt to place heavy sanctions upon it, the results may be other than they might desire. Some of the most severe sexual problems are those which are associated with guilt.

When the second child (or a following one) of the opposite sex comes along, the difference in sexual anatomy can be easily and naturally taught. The elder child may watch as the baby sister or brother is changed, dressed, and bathed. Expectedly, questions will be asked. And it is then the mother and father can explain the marvelous differences between little girls (and mommies) and little boys (and daddies). The older child's observations, and the explanations that are offered, will not, as one mother suggested to us, stimulate any "abnormal curiosity." The questions seek only to satisfy very normal curiosity. Hopefully, children are curious about virtually everything. Curiosity lies at the root of all education. And since education is as important in life as sexuality, we cannot ignore the benefits which may be derived from seeking these answers. Certainly, as parents we have a tendency to project our own anxieties. We may have felt uncomfortable in this or that situation, and hence we expect our children, even when they are infants, to sow the seeds for similar anxieties. But the guilt and anxiety we may have experienced (and may still experience) can only be a product of what has been handed down to us. Whatever we may hope for our children, we hope not to leave them with the same legacy of guilt and anxiety. Sexual curiosity is not the "tiger by the tail" which will be unleashed by the satisfaction of curiosity, and learning, and by which the child will be led into vague but dreadful consequences.

A next common occurrence in sexual development occurs when the child explores his or her differences from another child. Almost every child plays the game of "you show me yours, and I'll show you mine." The game may be played between siblings or with neighbor children. If between siblings, the parents may worry each time the children are in a room alone together. If the "games" are played with neighbor children, they may fear the reaction of the other set of parents or scandal in the neighborhood. It is indeed a strange world we live in that we can so easily be panicked either by our own demons or by the reactions of other, possibly deeply troubled, people. Young children, of course, attach no moral judgments to any part of their bodies. All are parts of the body they were born with. The same God who created eyes, noses, and fingers, created genitals. And children are naturally curious. They are also curious to learn if other children have the same parts, and if so what they have learned to do with them ("How far can you make it squirt?"). And one of the most important questions of all, "How are little boys different from little girls?"

The *differences*, anatomical and psychological, whatever they may be, cannot be ignored. Boys and girls learn very early that they *are* different. The ways in which they differ psychologically is a matter of dispute (nature versus nurture), but every boy is sure he is different from girls, and girls are convinced they are not in any way like boys. In sexual-exploration games, they seek to find out just how they are not alike physically. If boys are kept apart from girls, either by circumstances or design, the curiosity can be expected to increase. In time, they may exaggerate if not distort the differences they imagine to exist. We've talked with many men and women raised in single-sex environments (e.g., boys' school, or girl raised by mother alone) who have grown up with sexual stereotypes that were nearly total distortion. Many found severe problems in their attempt to relate to the other sex because they had learned virtually nothing about the other sex. All they had learned were rumors, and all rumors, as we all know, plant a grain of truth and reap a crop of distortions. These distortions were not always related to ignorance of anatomical differences. Such ignorance is today, among otherwise educated adults, increasingly rare. But if the man has been raised in an all-male environment, he may view females as an alien species.

We are not suggesting that parents encourage "sex games," or that they ignore such activities. It is necessary that children be taught what is acceptable and what unacceptable behavior. We are suggesting only that parents view these activities for what they are: a normal exploration of the child's universe and all its mysteries, both harmless and innocent. Parents can usually discourage such behavior with little more than a patient explanation that there are some things we may do that will upset others. The explanation plus normal supervision should be enough. There should never be a moral position taken that will instill feelings of guilt or negative attitudes toward the body.

Questions about sex often come early, much earlier than most parents anticipate. A three-year-old can ask questions that leave parents open-mouthed: "Why is the lady's tummy so big?" "How did the baby get in her tummy?" The standard advice used to be, "Answer the child's question in a straightforward, honest manner, but only to the limits of his understanding for his age." But the answer raised a more troublesome question: "What are the 'limits' of his understanding for his age?" What will happen, many parents have asked, if we give him too much information for his age? Will it create problems? Will it frighten him? Do children have adverse emotional reactions to "too much" information? We feel the matter of "limits" can be dropped. Children have an intellectual "overload switch." Whether we are explaining the sexual and reproductive facts of life or the workings of an internal-combustion engine, children will accept everything they are capable of accepting within their intellectual limits. If, at some point, the explanation goes beyond these limits they turn off. Their eyes will glaze over in boredom, and we will immediately know we have reached the limit—for that point in their development. Often, children will not only continue asking questions beyond the point which parents expected (and possibly were prepared for), but they will retain a surprising amount of the information. Unless they have been discouraged from asking questions (what a psychology-professor friend of ours calls the "dumbing up" of a child), they will display an incredible capacity for absorbing information. Furthermore, we contend that such information, whether it be about internal-combustion engines or the workings of the reproductive system, can never be harmful if it is given in a healthy way which says, "These are the way these things work." It has struck many observers as very strange that some parents who are strongly opposed to having their children learn about sexual loving seem willing to permit

them to learn through television, how to commit unspeakable crimes.

Will such information "put ideas in their heads"? Our
answers are, "no" and "hopefully, yes." "No," if we mean,
will sexual information motivate children (or adults, for
that matter) to engage in sexual behavior they might otherwise not try. And "hopefully, yes," if we mean will children learn that the physical expressions of love between
their parents are the wellsprings from which the love and
security within the family emerge.

Discussions of sexuality, of physical love, and of males
and females and how they relate to one another should be
as natural to family gatherings as talk of vacation plans or
the best ingredients of a pizza. Such talks should not separate the sexes. The traditional clichéd conversations of
mother to daughter and father to son we feel have no
place in the teaching of healthy attitudes toward human
sexuality. First of all, we find no reason to believe that a
father is better equipped to teach his son the facts of
human sexuality, or that a mother can better instruct her
daughter. We would even argue that a mother may be a
better source of information when it comes to the psychology of women and what her son, as a man, can do to
express his love for his future wife. And it would seem obvious that most fathers would be best able to teach
daughters about the feelings, desires, and apprehensions
of men. We strongly believe however, that there is no
justification for separating the sexes, adults or children, in
discussions of something which is not only natural, but
inherently beautiful. It should be, we feel, something in
which the family can openly express their views as they
openly express their views in so many other areas.

Our sons have learned much about the other sex from
their sisters, and our daughters have learned from their
brothers. We have listened to their conversations, at-

tempted at all times to answer their questions, and offered both our views and our experiences. We set no restrictions on what can be discussed. We not only see no reason to do so, we feel that any such limitations would be counterproductive. Our biological drives and our emotions are as much a part of our humanity as our eyes, ears, and dreams. It is the humanness of our sexuality that we want them to understand, and the human capacity to find meaning in sexual loving that we hope to convey to them. What do you like about being a girl/boy? How do you feel when you are in love? Are there ways in which boys and girls feel differently about sex?

The context within which we hope they will learn of sex and develop attitudes toward themselves and their sexuality should always be one in which self-respect, maturity, responsibility, beauty, and joy are kept paramount. The biological "facts of life"—the anatomy and physiology of sexuality and reproduction—may be the least important information about human sexual response we give our children. The human eye is beautiful, but plucked from the eye socket it is a thing of horror to us. If human sexuality is removed from a setting of love and commitment, and reduced to a mere physiological-drive state and the actions which may be engaged in to periodically satisfy it, it too loses its beauty. This is why our schools can never properly provide "sex education." They can teach anatomy and physiology of reproduction. But that material is science—anatomy and physiology. It is not human sexuality. Schools can teach "sexual" hygiene. That also is not human sexuality. And schools can give instruction in contraception. But they cannot impart moral values or demonstrate the importance of love. If an individual teacher would attempt to do so, it is highly unlikely that the values that he or she might teach would represent the values held by all parents. Even if such a teacher expressed only the finest values, those all parents would subscribe to (if it is possible to even imagine values in any area in which all parents would agree), it is the parents themselves, living their own attitudes and values, who are going to be the *ultimate teachers*. This teaching role parents can never delegate to others.

Discussions of sexual love within the family have to be "ongoing." Children are constantly changing, growing month by month. There can therefore be no single point in time or age at which the child is "ready" for a discussion of sex. Sexuality does not burst forth at the onset of puberty. It has been developing from conception on. The three-year-old has questions about his body, the body of his sister, and the relationship between his parents. So does the twelve-year-old. And so does the seventeen-year-old. The questions differ in some respects, and in other respects they remain the same. The questions will reflect the child's stage of development, what is important to him or her at that point in time. This raises the question, "What if you have a fourteen-year-old and a six-year-old at your dinner table, how do you discuss things in a way which will be appropriate to both?" We have never found this to be a great problem. In a large family, topics are often discussed on more than one level of understanding. The high school student may be talking about the action of enzymes in digestion. A younger brother or sister may be brought into the conversation with some basic facts about how the body converts food into energy. When the youngest in the family asks how the baby gets in the mother's "tummy," the discussion may subsequently be expanded with the older children into discussion of ovulation. As parents in these round-table discussions, we play the roles of moderators and resource persons, but more important, we *listen*. We want to hear what they are saying, what they feel, what they are struggling to understand. We can learn from them, and they can learn from us. In expression of our opinions and feelings, there is complete equality. We may argue for our views, but our right to express them is no greater than that of our children.

These family discussions can result in significant bonding. Sexuality is an area which is treated in our society with great delicacy and often embarrassment. As a result, the trust which is called for in order for friends (or even spouses) to reveal their feelings about sexuality, will draw them closer together (assuming, of course, that such trust is not betrayed). If sexual loving is not discussed openly, there will be a resultant separateness either between siblings or between parents and children. One of the more commonly heard statements is, "I could never talk about sex with my parents." And the child, particularly the adolescent, who feels he or she cannot talk with the parents about sex, in time gives up the attempts to talk with the parent about nearly everything. The same holds true for siblings. Sadly enough, many parents unknowingly encourage the position which says, "Brothers and sisters are never to mention the subject in one another's presence." We reject such a view, and in its stead we argue strongly that anything and everything, any and all opinions, be granted "acceptability" within the family circle. We may argue for an opposing position. We may challenge the reasoning of the position of another family member just as they may challenge ours. But the only limitations which are imposed are those involving courtesy and the respect to be granted to others to enable them to express their views.

Does this include permission to share "off-color" stories and jokes? We feel it should. We also believe that a discussion of the so-called "four letter words" can be an appropriate part of learning. "Dirty" jokes are part of the

206 TO LIVE AS FAMILY

cultural humor. So are the sexual vernacular. To ignore or deny their existence would be tantamount to shutting one's eyes to any other reality on the premise that, "If I don't see it, it won't exist." Sexuality is a part of our existence which unfortunately is fraught with anxiety, an anxiety which is frequently exhibited in sexual jokes. Four-letter words also often reflect our feelings about our own sexuality and our feelings about the other sex. If we, the parents, jump in with an instant admonition, "I don't want to hear those kinds of stories," or "Don't ever let me hear you use a word like that," we may lose an opportunity to explore sexual feelings and attitudes. We are not, needless to say, saying that such jokes and words are "accepted" as a reflection of our own attitudes and the attitudes we hope to convey to our children. We are merely suggesting that they not be instantly stifled without discussion of their meanings, implications, and feelings. Similarly, there is a great deal of sexually explicit material on television and in magazines with which all children are going to come in contact nowadays. Those who are attempting to expurgate all such material through campaigns of various sorts are probably going to meet with far less than success. It would seem to make some sense to bring any problems which may arise through such materials back where it belongs: within the family. Even if we could police all of our children's reading and viewing (a total impracticality), we are not sure it would be the wisest. They live, as we do, in a world of good and evil. We hope to be able to teach them to discriminate between the two and to make choices that are both moral and psychologically healthy. A magazine article, an advertisement, a television program, or a motion picture can form the subject matter for discussion of moral and ethical issues as well as taste, respect for self and others, and the various roles we play in our human relationships. Certainly, as our children have grown, we have monitored their television viewing and we have made choices on the materials they read and the motion pictures they see, but attempting to "sanitize" their world is, in our opinion, neither possible nor wholly desirable.

What children are permitted to express in family discussions and read or view is one thing. What they are permitted to *do* is another. Many social observers have expressed concern at the numbers of parents who permit and even encourage their children to assume sexual roles wholly inappropriate to their age and level of maturity. Some thirteen-year-old girls dress as provocatively as the most sophisticated twenty-five-year-old. Seventh- and eighth-graders attend late-night boy-girl parties that are largely unsupervised. Parents condone children's going steady and spending every available hour together at a time when the children have barely entered adolescence. We have attended junior high school performances in which dance routines differed only in skill from those one might see in Las Vegas. Several years ago in *Power to the Parents!* we wrote: "In the parent's role in the area of the child's sexual development, one side of the coin is *education*, the other side is *supervision*. And here again, our society has given way to a youth culture with responsibility for whatever limits exist being assumed by the children. Children establish the mores of the peer group and the parents fall in line in giving their support. What is popular becomes what is accepted. In less than two decades, the sexual mores of adolescence have moved downward in age almost four to five years. Behavior which was typical of 16- and 17-year-olds has become established for 12-year-olds, and often with at least a passive acceptance by the adult society. This has added a good measure to the already great pressures of early adolescence."

For some reason (perhaps the need for vicarious popu-

larity and sexual conquest) it is mothers who are most responsible for this shift downward in sexual sophistication.
They not only encourage their daughters, they virtually
push them into the dating—and *seduction*—game before
the girls are ready to give up dolls. Of course mother
doesn't admit to such a motive; she says simply, "All the
girls her age are doing it." And for the majority, she may
be correct. If it is the latest "in" thing, mother won't see
her daughter left out. With entry into junior high school,
the ritual of pairing off and going steady begins in ear-
nest, at least for the members of the more hip, "with-it,"
crowd. This raises pressures and real conflict for boys of
junior high school age. As every man can remember, that
period of early adolescence is a time of miserable awk-
wardness for a boy. Often the girls in his class are taller
than he is. The girls are at ease on the dance floor (at
least they seem to be at ease) while he is still trying to
keep from falling on his face. And in the interactions of
boy-girl games, the girls in general are about three to four
years ahead of the boys. The span is further increased if
the dances, mixed parties, and dating are encouraged
and/or permitted by parents. Boys who might still prefer
riding bikes and shooting baskets on the playground now
find themselves in a bind. Although the boy-girl games
may not hold much appeal for them, they may feel com-
pelled to go along with them in order not to risk being
seen as still a "little kid." What we have, in effect, is a
chain reaction of parents prodding daughters to plunge
into the world of adult sexual-social relationships and
drag the boys, however reluctantly, in with them.

"And with what result?" we asked in *Power to the Parents!* "Children who are exposed to experiences and relationships long before they are ready to assume the necessary responsibility for them. And here, incidentally, lies a
further irony: the mothers who often appear the most

eager to push their 12-year-old daughters into the social scene of playing the seductive role, going steady, and the rest, are the very ones who bury their heads in the sand and refuse to consider even the possibility that with the door wide open, their sexy little girl may step all the way through and end up a 13-year-old mother!"

Since we wrote those words, the problems have exploded. Teenage pregnancies have grown yearly, despite readily available contraceptives and massive programs funding "abortion on demand." Sex education in the schools has been an evident failure in stemming the ever-increasing teenage sexual activity. The solution today is the same as it has always been: the assumption of parental responsibility. Parents can draw lines and keep them firm only if they are willing to pay the price of assuming the responsibility and authority of *being parents*. This must mean rejecting the blandishments of other parents and some educators who advocate *conformity-and-popularity-at-any-price*. We grant that in a society which is so heavily other-directed, this may not be easy. But no one ever claimed that parenthood would always be easy. It is at least easier, however, if the parents follow a consistent policy of letting the reins out slowly— very slowly. If adult privileges are granted to the child at thirteen, the parents may face a very difficult task in attempting to rescind those privileges when the child reaches fifteen and they become aware of the consequences of such permissiveness. Buy a sixteen-year-old high school junior his own car only to find that by his senior year his grades have dropped because he spends more time driving around with his friends than he spends studying, and you may face a serious problem. You may trigger World War III when you take away the car keys. The fourteen-year-old who is permitted every afternoon and evening with her boyfriend may quickly get herself in emotional deep water, but the parents will most likely find that they have a rebel on their hands when they try to "cool it."

The responsibility of supervision does not end for the parents until the other responsibilities of parenthood are completed—i.e., until the child is capable of assuming adult, autonomous responsibility for his or her life (or at least has reached the age in which the law entitles them to do so). In previous generations, parents could look to other parents and teachers for cooperation in the supervision of their children and in setting reasonable limits on their activities. Today, this is seldom support we can anticipate. All around us, there are parents who seem to feel that with the start of high school all limits should come off, that ninth or tenth grade is the time for the child to start making his or her own choices with no parental interference. "You can't hold them down forever," is one argument. Another is, "You can't keep an eye on them every minute." We do not advocate holding children *down*. But we argue, and strongly so, that children be given privileges (whether it be to cross the street alone, drive an automobile, or go to the beach with a boyfriend) when the parents, in *their* judgment, decide that the child is sufficiently mature to assume the responsibilities to accompany the privilege. A lot of maturation normally takes place between the ages of fourteen and eighteen, and the fourteen-year-old is rarely, if ever, ready to assume the responsibilities we expect of the normal eighteen-year-old. Yet today, a shocking number of parents are granting eighteen-year-old privileges to fourteen-year-old children. As to keeping an eye on teenage children at all times, of course it is impossible. However, parents can exercise considerable supervision of where the children are permitted to go and what they're permitted to do. To allow a boy or girl of high school to come and go at will is a tragic abdication of parental responsibility. The fourteen- or fifteen-year-old is *not* ready to assume the responsibilities of a close boy-girl relationship. The risks, emotional and otherwise, are too great. We feel, therefore, that as parents we must draw the line on the practice of going steady, which involves always being together day by day. At that age, it is appropriate, we feel for dating, under specified circumstances, to *begin*. But the intensity of the relationship which quickly develops in going steady (as practiced today) is not the beginning, it is almost the culmination. And to the parent who says, "I'm not worried. I've taught my son/daughter the facts of life and how to tell right from wrong so that I know he/she wouldn't do anything out of line," we answer, "Do you believe your child is normal? If so, why would you expect your child to have other than normal responses?" During adolescence, children not only experience the demands of a powerful drive and the upsetting influences of intense emotions but are subject to strong peer-group influence and have unformed values. Often, there is an appalling lack of reality on the part of many parents when this matter is brought up. They might not dream of putting a fifteen-year-old behind the wheel of a powerful sports car, confident that he won't speed "because we have taught him the rules of safety," but they will ignore temptations that may be far stronger and equally dangerous.

Sexual temptations and drive are no stronger today than they were forty years ago. Some things, however, are different. The most obvious is the acceptability of sexual activity for both sexes prior to marriage. Less obvious is what we consider to be one of the more relevant differences: availability of opportunity. Two or three decades ago, teenage sexual activities were most likely to take place in an automobile borrowed from the family. They were fraught with apprehension and had the restraints which would naturally accompany such apprehension. Today, such encounters are more likely to take place in the home of either the boy or the girl. In a high percentage of homes, neither parent is present when the children return from school. Since over 50 percent of families have two incomes, both parents working outside of the home, this has become an overwhelming problem, one for which we have no solution. We do not offer any "pat" answer for how to maintain supervision when neither parent is present. Each set of parents will have to come up with their own answers. But the problem cannot be ignored. If adolescent children are permitted this amount of freedom, problems will arise. The problems will frequently involve their expression of their newfound sexuality.

When limits are set, the sort of limits which say, "No, we will not permit you to go *here* or do *that*," children may rebel, but rebellion can be curtailed if the parents have a favorable alternative to offer. Most favorable, we feel, is the environment of the home. For a son or daughter, a "date" at home is not an undesirable alternative if the home environment is totally positive. Children like to bring their friends home if the reception they receive is warm and welcoming. Again, the question becomes one of what are the attitudes of the parents, how positive is the home environment, and how receptive are the family members (not the least of whom are the parents) toward the guests in their home? How much do the children want to bring a stranger in, how much do they want to show off their parents, how much do they feel confident that their friend will be welcomed by their siblings? If children can take pride in their family, parents and siblings, they will welcome the opportunity to bring friends home of either sex. When we hear parents say, "But my children do not want to bring their friends home," we raise the question, "Have you taken a look at your home and what they might bring their friends into?" If the home is one in which love, mutual concern, and fun is ever-present, the children will be more than receptive to the suggestion that they bring their friends home. Sure, this means effort on the part of the parents. It will often mean additional guests for dinner. It will mean more people in the house. But it will provide an environment in which the parents can observe what is going on in the lives of their children. Where the parents prove themselves to be concerned and loving, the children will seek "feedback" about their relationships. They will want to know how the parents see their friends as well as how they can improve their relationships. Again, communication is of prime importance. If the parents have gained respect from their children, they can expect their children to ask, "What was your impression of ———?" Children want feedback from the parents when they respect the experience and opinions of the parents. The same goes for the other siblings. An older brother may be able to share his opinions of his younger sister's new boyfriend. The brother may not always be right, but his opinions may trigger a self-evaluated reaction on his sister's part. These opinions, of course, are more than expressions of likes and dislikes. Whether or not the parents or siblings find a friend attractive or not is really immaterial. What is important is whether they offer material judgments that can provide food for thought and are offered in good will and with concern. We have consistently found our children to be concerned for one another, and being concerned, they have kept an eye open for what appears to them to be danger signals in one another's relationships. This has been especially true in what our sons have been able to observe about the boyfriends of their sisters and what our daughters have picked up in the rela-

tionships our boys have had with girls. When these observations have been presented with even a modicum
of diplomacy, they have generally been accepted as repre-
sentative of genuine caring. And more often than not,
they have been seriously considered. The same, of course,
holds true of the sharing of parental observations. Where
parents and siblings are seen as loving, caring, and observ-
ant "best friends," children will want to bring their friends
home for an "objective" evaluation.

We hasten to emphasize that bringing friends home is
not primarily for any family evaluation. We want our
children to know—and we feel they do—that it is their
home too, and that we welcome their friends. It is never
easy to say no to places and activities when "everyone's
doing it." We don't want them to feel they are social
misfits, always on the outside looking in. We are convinced they won't, if their home is warm and welcoming,
with more to offer than the local pizza parlor or corner
hangout. It comes down first to the parents, second to the
other members of the family.

Parent-age adults are usually intimidating to adolescents. The young don't know what to talk about with
older people, and "grown-ups" seem to have little interest
in conversing with "kids." When the children's friends
first enter the house, there is often a brief period of uneas-
iness until the ice is broken. The ice-breaking is up to the
parents. They are, quite properly, the hosts—it is their
home. If the parents merely *permit* the children to bring
their friends home rather than welcoming them as friends
of all members of the family, the home is not likely to become a magnet for the children's peer group. Of course,
more than a few parents may respond, "We don't want
kids around the house all the time," but we would ask
them to consider their options: 1) Their children can "do
their own thing" outside of the home—unrestricted (with

all the possible consequences this may entail). 2) Their children can be restricted to the home, cut off from social contacts (with all the resentments and feelings of isolation this may entail). 3) Their children can offer a home environment that will provide a wholesome—and fully active—social life (with all the parental involvement, time, and responsibility this may entail).

We opt for the third. The sandwiches, cookies, popcorn, soft drinks, noise, confusion, and loss of space and privacy are prices we are willing to pay. The ultimate prices of the other options are far too high.

In an era in which the moral and ethical values of parents are often poorly formed or ambiguously expressed, responsible parents have a lot to offer to their children (their firm responsibility) and to the children of others (a responsibility to society, and a gift of love to the individuals).

The beauty of sexual love and the fulfillment of productive work are the two great images and ideals we have to present to our children as they approach adulthood. If we succeed, we will have given them a sense of self-worth and a closeness to others which will affirm our role as parents. The payoff for the parents may come ten or fifteen years later when the children have reached their full adulthood. The payoff makes it all worthwhile.

11

A Special Relationship

For a time we wondered if family loyalty, a value previously accepted by most of our society, would survive the twentieth century. Throughout the sixties and seventies, this value took a terrible beating. All loyalties seemed to be brought into question. Fidelity to country, church, school, and even spouse were denounced and labeled as incompatible with the new consciousness dedicated to the pursuit of individual goals and rejection of all obligation to others.

The so-called "generation gap," as much a creation of the media and pop-psychologists as anything, threatened to become one more self-fulfilling prophecy. High school teachers encouraged students to reject, out of hand, the values held by an older generation. A claque of screaming neo-anarchists denounced those over thirty. They accused the elder generation of having created all the world's ills—war, pollution, corruption in government, and poverty. Parents of an idealistic generation of adolescents were viewed by their children as hawkish, dehumanizing, and obsessed with materialism. Over and over the message was heard: Those who have gone before have destroyed the world; we must now listen to the voices of the young, who will save us.

Teenagers were told they could find counsel and satisfaction only among their own. Parents were told they
must expect to see their children withdraw and reject the
"old-fashioned" values they espoused. Teenagers, said the
spokesmen of the new ethic, would seek the company
only of friends of their own age. They would not enjoy
their parents, admire them, or have fun with them.
Within the family, there would exist only armed camps,
separated across a battlefield determined by age.

The divisions grew even greater within the family.
Women were encouraged to join a misogamic "sister-
hood," and to raise their feminine consciousness of the
oppression they had suffered at the hands of male chau-
vinists. In the name of liberation, the sexes were pitted
against each other. Every group and class seemed at war.
Young fighting old, males fighting females, blacks fighting
whites, rich fighting poor. The wars were no less within
families. The divorce rate began to soar, and it has not
diminished. Children not only disregarded the values of
their parents, they condemned them. The sexual morality
of the over-thirty generation was scorned as "uptight."
The work ethic was disparaged. Patriotism, fidelity, and
responsibility were suspect. Workers burned their facto-
ries; students burned their schools; and feminists burned
their bras.

Aided by sensationalist writers, people became preoccu-
pied with labels, and the labels served to separate us even
further. The "liberal" was the enemy of the "moderate"
who was the enemy of the "conservative" who was the
enemy of the "liberal." We were either militant environ-
mentalists or spoilers of the ecology. We were feminists
or oppressors of women. We were passivists or militarists.
We were swingers or puritans. There were virtually no
differences of opinion which were not dichotomized. It

was almost as if for two decades we sought reasons for civil war.

We can only hope that we have now learned that causes may be espoused, but it is only to persons that our deepest loyalties can be given, and that persons are deserving of greater value than most of our transitory causes. Seldom do other people or values merit greater loyalty than that which we owe to the other members living within our family unit. Blood is not "thicker than water," but the proximity within which we live as a family and the interdependence we experience makes a special loyalty imperative if we are to avoid the pain and insecurity of alienation and betrayal.

First and foremost is the obligation of confidentiality. We feel that what is said within the family circle should be considered "privileged communication." Spouses share many secrets and become aware of many idiosyncrasies in each other that they never reveal to others. The secrecy is one of the unwritten rules of marriage, and we are appalled when we hear of a wife gossiping to her mother or a husband talking to his friend about what goes on behind the closed doors of the home. Such revelations are unforgivable breaches of marital trust. Such obligation of trust should, we feel, be imposed on all family members. To live within a family is to be privy to the weaknesses and foibles of all members. We each make mistakes and suffer embarrassing moments that are known only to the other members of the family. We have each voiced opinions that we would not want revealed outside. The home should provide something of the environment of a confessional, a place where we can each show what may be the worst of us, the most unguarded, and the most vulnerable. And we should be able to trust that our revelations will not go beyond the walls of the home.

This rule is sometimes forgotten by children after they

reach the age at which they develop "best friends." They
are naturally eager to share everything that is going on in
their world, and making the distinction between what is
and what is not confidential, strictly family, information
is sometimes difficult. Parents may have to stress the importance of confidentiality a number of times. Once we
feel sure, however, that our children understand the rule,
any infraction is treated with utmost seriousness. There
are no exceptions, and no excuses. If one of the children
gets a poor grade on a school paper, or breaks a family
rule and is grounded, the others will probably learn of it,
but they know it is not to be talked about outside the
home. These are occurrences that will be discussed between parent and child. We parents will not talk about
embarrassing occurrences with others in the family, but if
the word does get around within the family, it is to go no
further. If a teenage daughter has a crush on a boy, she
should be able to talk about her feelings at home without
fear that what she says will become school gossip. A boy
should be able to rely on his brothers and sisters to keep
secret his fear of snakes or his bed-wetting problem.

We do not feel there are any "outsiders" who can be
made exceptions. Some individuals may enjoy a "special"
relationship with one or another family member or with
the family as a whole, but we do not feel that *anyone*
should be permitted to share in the family confidences
unless "privilege" has been waived. In law, "privilege" is a
right which belongs to the client (patient, penitent client), not to the lawyer, doctor, priest. The client may
waive the privilege, giving his lawyer permission to testify
as to matters the two of them have discussed in their professional relationship. But the lawyer cannot waive such a
right unless permission is given. A similar rule, we feel,
should apply within the home. If the answer to the question, "Do you mind if I tell Aunt Helen about what hap-

pened to you on the way home from school?" is, "No, I
don't mind," the privilege has obviously been waived; permission has been granted by the only one with the right
to waive privilege. "Keeping it within the family," means
keeping it within the *immediate* family. Aunt Helen may
be as close as anyone can be to all members of the family,
but unless she is living within the home, she is not a
member of the *immediate* family. No matter how close
family members may feel to individual friends, neighbors,
or relatives, the rules of confidentiality do not allow them
to share these privileged communications.

Confidentiality is the foundation upon which all family
loyalty is built. When we seek emotional support and understanding, as we all do from time to time, we must be
assured that what we say will be held in confidence. We
must be able to trust the person in whom we confide. It is
sad that so many persons we have counseled have felt
they could not confide in members of their own families.
A wife may confide in her best friend, but not in her husband. He may tell his troubles to a co-worker, but not his
wife. Children often discuss their problems with teachers,
school counselors, adult neighbors, or peers, but they will
not bring them to their parents. All too often, the essential trust in confidentiality is lacking. This trust, along
with the assurances of acceptance and support, may have
been eroded over a period of time. Even a rare betrayal
can destroy the trust. We all need a close confidant from
time to time, not to tell us we are always right, not even
to offer suggestions or criticism, but to reassure us that we
are valued for being who we are regardless of our
weaknesses and mistakes. None of us benefits from being
indulged. If we are wrong, we may need to be told we are
wrong. But we need to know that we can make mistakes,
and expose these mistakes to someone who will neither
betray nor reject us. If family members cannot rely on

such security within the family, they will go elsewhere. This perhaps accounts, more than any other single factor, for the demise of family bonding so noticeable during the sixties and seventies.

Acceptance and emotional-support bonding is, of course, reciprocal: you dried my tears yesterday; I'll dry yours today. You accepted me yesterday when I had not lived up to being the person I should have been; today I accept you. This bonding within the family may be little different from what we expect in all close friendships, but within the family, close friendships take on a special character. They are *unconditional*. Psychologist Carl Rogers, in his theory of non-directive therapy, stressed the importance of the therapist consistently expressing what he called unconditional positive regard. Rogers did not hold that the therapist should condone or encourage immoral or irresponsible actions. Nor did he suggest that the therapist not set limits upon the relationship with the client. He did stress *acceptance* and regard for the client as a person, regardless of his faults and weaknesses. Unconditional positive regard is, we feel, a value to be fostered within the family. It should be an implied contract between all members, benefiting and obligating those living within the home. Family members may debate, argue, and sometimes get into rousing fights, but this contract of mutual support and unconditional positive regard should at all times remain intact and firm. The home should always be a haven of acceptance.

When our embassy personnel were taken hostage in Teheran, the reaction we experienced was one of outrage. We were willing to rush to the rescue, no matter the cost. Only over the months that followed did we learn their names. But the names were unimportant. They were our people. They were members of our family. And they had been attacked and imprisoned; their rights had been violated. In committing these crimes against members of our family, the terrorists had launched an attack against all of us. We set aside our political and social differences to rise in their defense. Our family was under attack, and we joined together. One of the signs which greeted the hostages on their return read, "Thanks! You brought us together!"

A fifteen-year-old expressed this unifying effect within the family when he said, "I guess we have the usual amount of hassles. I fight with my brothers and my sister over the TV and who has to rake the leaves—that sort of stuff. But boy! If any outsider picks on somebody in the family, they'd better look out! We kind of, I guess, draw the wagons into a circle, and those guys find out they're going to have to take on all of us!"

This *all-for-one-and-one-for-all* loyalty in which we come to the defense of any other member of the family is a value that has been seriously weakened by those who have preached an egocentric "personal fulfillment." They have advocated staying within a world of self-centeredness, and they have succeeded, by so doing, in developing a generation of lonely people. Reaching out to others can be best learned within the home environment. If it is not learned within the home, it may never be learned, or it may be learned much later only with the help of professional counseling. The teaching begins with the parents making it very clear that no attacks, verbal or physical, upon another member of the family will be tolerated. Children learn that Mother will not tolerate critical remarks about their father. "Attack your father, and you are attacking me," is the clear message. These messages rapidly generalize beyond the home: "If you make a nasty crack about my brother, you're going to have to deal with me!"

Coming to the defense of one another within the family does not require that we blind ourselves to faults. Jack's sister may have behaved pretty rottenly toward Jack's friend, Ron. Understandably, Jack may have a few well-chosen words to say to her about it. But if Ron verbally attacks her in talking to Jack, Jack should make clear that this is an "off-limits" topic, and that he will not say a word against his sister. In taking this position, he is not denying the wrong she may have done, nor is he condoning it. He is simply refusing to join Ron in the attack. She is his sister, and he will uphold his loyalty to her.

The principle becomes even more important as the family, as both a unique unit and as an institution, comes so often under intense fire. If members of the family make no move to defend one another, whom *can* they call on for defense? And who will come to the defense of family values when they are attacked? Allegiance to the institution of the family rests upon allegiance to one's own family—in a word, to one another.

When we stated this value before a university audience, we were challenged by a woman who identified herself as a high school counselor. "It seems to me," she said, "that the kind of loyalty you argue for can only result in a sort of family parochialism in which the children develop few, if any, friends outside the family. I feel it is far better to encourage children to pick their own friends and decide upon their own values. What you suggest teaches them to place their parents and siblings above their chosen friends. Where does choice come in?"

We disagreed, explaining that strong family loyalty, rather than inhibiting the development of friendships outside the family, aids the emotional development and self-assurance of children, thereby making it easier for them to relate to others. It provides them with the security that they are worthwhile and will be accepted and valued. By being continually accepted and given "unconditional positive regard" within the circle of the family, they will gain confidence to venture into the social world of school and neighborhood. As far as the allegation that it will teach them to place the members of their family above their chosen friends, there is truth in the allegation, but only if it is interpreted as meaning that we teach the priority of family loyalty which takes a place above all other friendships. Unless we place such a priority on family loyalty, bonding within the home becomes meaningless. Where does free choice come in? Membership in the family demands adherence to certain house rules and obligations. In return, all family members benefit. Children are taught these rules and obligations before they are old enough to understand their importance. The rule is taught, and in time the value is incorporated. This applies, of course, to the obligations of family loyalty. When they are young, it would be fruitless to attempt to explain the reasoning involved. By the time they are adolescents, the explanation is not necessary if they have experienced the rewards of such loyalty. Then, of course, they would choose it and champion it. They will have recognized how much having other members of their family standing firmly in their "corner" means to them.

There is another aspect of family loyalty that has taken on importance during the past two decades. It is the duty we each have to avoid doing anything which may cause embarrassment to other family members. Just as we enjoy the status from association with persons or organizations that are given recognition in our society, we may suffer shame when these persons or organizations are disgraced. Many of us have been embarrassed by the behavior of other Americans when we have traveled abroad. We may even have felt a need to apologize and to beg the natives of our host country not to judge all Americans by the one or two ugly ones. It is never fair to judge others on the basis of their associations, but fair or not, we often do judge and are judged by association. And this is especially true of the associations we have with the members of our immediate family. To be the brother or sister of a Charles Manson or a John Dillinger is a terrible cross to bear.

One of the principal reasons given by sociologists to account for the low crime rate in Japan is the high value the Japanese place on the family name. There is a strong duty not to bring dishonor on the family. Many years ago, we held this value in high esteem in the United States, but as families have increased in their mobility, the family name has had a decreasing recognition within the community. Next-door neighbors are often unacquainted. Being recognized as "one of the O'Brien kids" has become less and less common in communities in which the average family of today moves more than once every ten years. To the anonymity which has come from such mobility, has been added an ethic which holds, "Whatever I do is nobody's business but my own."

But no rights can exist without correlative obligations; they go hand in hand. If we invite a guest into our home, we have the right to expect the members of our family to attempt to make our guest feel welcome, to dress appropriately, and to show good manners. They can expect as much from us when they invite their friends over. If their father's name should appear in the paper for drunk driving, the children are going to face what may become cruel taunts from their friends. Right or wrong, the sins of the father are frequently used to punish his offspring. Children will take pride in or suffer embarrassment from the actions of their siblings.

Children can quickly grasp that their actions will reflect on the other members of the family, and that they have no right to "do their own thing" when doing so will cause pain to other family members. We have talked with numerous parents who have been troubled over whether or not they have the right and authority to "impose" standards of dress and behavior on their children. A mother told us she was acutely embarrassed to be seen in public with her fifteen-year-old daughter. "She goes braless," she said, "and she wears tee shirts which leave absolutely nothing to the imagination. Her seventeen-year-old brother says she looks like a hooker. She says all her friends dress that way, so I'm not sure it would be fair of me to tell her that she can't." We asked the woman whether she and her husband attempted to dress appropriately when one of the daughter's boyfriends came to the house. "Of course," she said. "If my husband has his shoes off, he'll slip them on when he hears the doorbell. I may change out of my old wash dress if I know a boyfriend is coming." She understood the point we were trying to make. "You're talking about common courtesy, aren't you? But then why do I feel uncomfortable demanding the same thing of my daughter? I guess I just don't want to seem rigid and old-fashioned." We said we found nothing rigid or old-fashioned in common courtesy and a concern for the feelings of others. As far as *imposing* a dress code on our children, it seems to go to the core of what it means to be a parent. When we counsel parents who seek help with problems of "out of control" children, one of the things we discuss is the dress of the child. In junior and senior high schools, children gravitate to cliques, other children with whom they can identify. Often these cliques are identifiable by their dress. The "goody-goodies" dress one way; the "brains" dress another; and the "hoods" dress still another. If a child has gravitated to the "hood" group, their membership in the group will often come to an end as soon as they change the identifying dress. The group will exclude them. Even the hippies of the Haight-Ashbury during the 1960s, while

espousing individual freedom, were remarkably locked-in
to comformity in dress. No one with a short haircut and a
three-piece suit could have gotten a foot in the door. Certainly we set limits, and we impose rules of behavior,
dress, language, and courtesy on our children. How else
can they learn what is acceptable, responsible, and permissible behavior within our society? As parents, we carry
a responsibility for sharing what we have learned about
acceptable behavior. The fifteen-year-old may not be
aware of the negative reactions others will have to his or
her dress or behavior. Parents have the responsibility to
make such decisions. Parents also have a responsibility to
be aware of how dress, language, and behavior may affect
other children in the family.

Loyalty extends to many areas of family living. It includes reaching out to help one another, whether that be
giving advice on personal matters or assisting a brother or
sister in studying for a test. Loyalty means wanting to do
everything possible to aid other members of the family. It
means recognizing that there is a meaning in the word
"family," and that the meaning transcends any immediate personal interests, and encompasses very special rewards as well as privileges.

The rewards of family loyalty are, in truth, all the rewards to be found in bonding. Loyalty not only contributes to bonding, it *is* bonding. One of the great rewards
of parenthood is the privilege of observing the loyalty that
develops between children. They bond in a way that expresses a deep love. It is an experience which we feel sure
they, and we, will find nowhere else.

There are few rewards for parents which exceed those
they experience when they hear their child say, with pride
and loyalty, "I'd like you to meet my family."

12

Outsiders and Others

The past two decades have seen the emergence of so-called "support groups." These groups have purported to aid in coping with virtually all known problems and challenges. If women face the prospect of reentering the work market after years of housewifery, they are offered the assistance of a "support group." If parents give in to temptations to beat their children, there is a "support group" ready to offer assistance. If a man has recently divorced, there is a divorced men's "support group" to come to his aid. And if teenagers find their parents set uncomfortable restraints on their behavior, they can discover sympathy and understanding within a "support group."

It may take future generations of sociologists to correctly interpret how the support-group phenomena came about and what it had to offer. Do these groups attempt to meet the emotional needs of those who seriously lack self-confidence? Is it perhaps that many feel alienated from others in what some describe as a depersonalized society? Is it nothing more than a cop-out that attracts people to such groups? Self-reliance seems denied by the advocates of many of these groups (although the promoters would deny this). But are such group advocates also denying the importance of self-reliance? Some seem to be.

They state with assurance, "We all need others; none of us can make it on our own." They seem to view the fulfilled individual as one who maintains a complex network of interdependencies. In their ideal world, all of us live in a symbiosis which relieves us of the anxiety that must inevitably accompany personal responsibility.

Support groups of various kinds have made deep inroads into the contemporary family. Parents have increasingly looked to others for both physical help and advice in raising their children. In the not-too-rare extreme, they have virtually turned over all responsibility to others.

The schools are, of course, the most obvious example of what parents have sought as a support group. Many parents have looked to the schools to take over virtually all aspects of child-rearing, ranging from sex education to the teaching of racial and religious tolerance. Parents have asked the schools to give their children a "head start" in reading, writing, socializing, and finding their way to the bathroom. They have demanded that the schools teach the children to respect the property of others rather than to steal, to provide psychotherapy rather than discipline, to teach sex education without teaching moral restraint, and to make the entire educational experience "fun." Going beyond all that, they have expected the school districts and individual school administrators to establish support groups for both the students and the parents. These are expected to be environments in which the students on the one hand, and the parents on the other, can get together with their peers and bemoan their frustrations (receiving in return, of course, the empathetic responses of other group members). If there is one thing which distinguishes the rules of a support group it is that no one is to say, "So why don't you do something about it yourself? Why are you bringing it to us?" Support groups are, by their very nature, anti-self-sufficiency. Implicit in their *raison d'être* is the assumption that the members *cannot/will not* assume responsibility. It is assumed parents cannot decide what is best for their children and set about to take on the effort to achieve such results. It is assumed that only with support can such goals be attained. It is assumed that only with the arguments of others and the help of others can parents hope to persuade their children of what is right and wrong. What happens, then, when the support group is made up of parents who are equally lacking in conviction and any well thought out goals for their children? We feel the present situation in our society answers the question. Countless times we have spoken with parents who were in despair. They felt they totally lacked both authority and influence in the lives of their children. They had attempted to argue on the basis of what they wanted, often without reason. Their arguments have been rebuffed. They had relied upon the arguments of a support group, only to find their children countering with, "You're just saying what Mrs. So-and-so or Dr. So-and-so has told you."

In all honesty, we must say our own profession is not free of blame. During the 1960s, so-called "family" therapy gained a certain popularity. In this technique of therapy, all family members are brought into the therapy session. They are treated as peers. Parents are not viewed as authority figures. The children have as much to "say" as the parents. On the surface, this might seem to be a very democratic approach. What most often happens, however, is that virtually all authority is lost within the family. The family therapy sessions create a *superauthority*, the therapist. The therapist becomes the "parent" who can be cited equally by either parent or child. He or she becomes the arbiter, the final judge in family decisions. Yet the therapist is not living in the home, and the thera-

pist does not have to assume responsibility for the outcome of such arbitration. The end result is that parents
relinquish responsibility that they cannot relinquish. The
children are left floating in a void of non-direction. When
parents telephone us to make an appointment regarding a
parent-child problem, we ask that they come in alone
(i.e., without the child) the first time. We hope to get
from them their perception of the problem as well as a
history of what has gone on with their child. We may
subsequently see the child, and perhaps administer psychological tests, but the focus remains on the parents—
what they are doing, and how they are doing it. We feel
parents need to establish confidence in their roles as parents. They need to feel that they know what they are
doing, have established their goals, and have the ability to
achieve what they believe they should achieve as parents.
It would be destructive both for their children and for
them if we were to step into the role of *superparent*.

Parent-support groups almost inevitably assume a superparent function. They reinforce the self-doubt parents already have. "Should I let my twelve-year-old daughter go
to a beach party with her friends?" When parents take
such a question to the support group, they are confessing
their own impotence. They are saying, "We do not feel
we are capable of answering such a question, or that we
are able to sustain our answer with reason." Their children can be expected to recognize such impotence. And
they do. In adolescent groups, the disdain for parents
most often takes the form, paraphrased in various ways,
"My parents don't know what they believe in, what they
stand for, or where to draw the line."

We cannot say how new a phenomena this is, but one
thing seems certain: parents have increasingly thrown in
the towel. They have sought to find answers in consensual
judgments of other adults—teachers, counselors, and

other parents. In doing so, they have lost the respect upon which their authority rests. They have told their children, "Don't look to me for decisions; wait until I check with my support group."

What can we as parents delegate to others? The answer is dependent upon the question, "What do our children need from us, their parents?" First, of course, they need love. They need to feel that we genuinely value them, and that we see them as special human beings that we are willing to give to and even sacrifice for, simply because they are who they are. The love they are seeking is not a generalized love, the love for all human beings, or a love for children. There are teachers, baby-sitters, and other "warm" human beings who "love" all children. They are giving and even self-sacrificing. But what our own children desire and expect is a gift of love, concern, and self-sacrifice which is "particular"—one which expresses the specialness with which we hold them. There are many people who can love, but how many would we be willing to give our life for? If we are truly committed to an ethic which places others above self, perhaps we can say, "I am willing to give my life for any of my fellow human beings." Most of us, however, fall short of practicing, or even expressing, that virtue. Our love is limited. For our children, limited love is enough. They want no more than the love which we limit to them. And it is this love that we cannot delegate. They have a craving for our love which cannot be met by others. They have a craving for love which is *ultimate* in quality. They not only want it, they need it.

In examining what we can delegate to others and what our children need from us, what can we say of *bonding?* Is there any way in which others can meet the child's needs for *bonding?* To answer, we must ask, "Bonding in what?" No matter how close the relationship may be to a surrogate parent, and no matter how close the bonding to such surrogate parent may be, can family bonding be enhanced by the relationship? Whatever the bonding may be, we fail to see how it can contribute to the bonding of the family as a whole. The child may, quite obviously, establish a very close relationship with a teacher, neighbor, or scoutmaster, but can he find in such associations any means by which he increases bonding with his family?

Within the family, the child finds his security. This security stems from both love expressed by the parents and bonding experiences. All have to do with close association between parents and siblings. No support group can add to the bonding between parent and child or brother and sister. And certainly no support group can enhance the total love within a family.

There is a question of nurturance in all of its aspects— physical, educational, and psychological. To what extent can such needs be met by others? We answer: these needs can never be met by persons who do not have the responsibility and authority of parents fully and on a full-time basis. When we speak of surrogate parents, we are always referring to those who have been given only a limited authority and responsibility. It is delegated for a short time, and generally within designated limits (either stated or implied). If the authority and responsibility is total, both in time and function, then the surrogate parents cease to be surrogate parents—they become the parents. There can be no such thing as "parenthood by committee." The parent holds the final authority and bears the ultimate responsibility. As parents, we may delegate the teaching function to a schoolteacher, a role in religious instruction to a Sunday school instructor, or a role in athletic development to a Little League coach, but these surrogate parents act only within the limits of authority and responsibility we delegate.

These delegated responsibilities raise questions when it comes to decisions regarding the amount of time parents must be physically present in order to fulfill their parental responsibilities.

In recent years, we have been told that mother and father can meet their responsibilities as parents while they both busily pursue careers or avocations which remove them from their children for many hours each day. Proponents of the "new-age" family argue that parenting can be done by baby-sitters, child-care-center attendants, and nursery-school teachers, thus freeing the parents of the mundane, sometimes boring, role of full-time parenthood. Their arguments focus on the needs and desires of the parent, and sometimes on what is said to be good for the child. One familiar argument is as follows: "Staying home with children is a monotonous, nerve-wracking job. I would find myself stagnating and resenting the kids. If I put them in a day-care center, then when I do see them we can enjoy 'quality' time." We feel the argument can be disputed on several counts. The parent who can "tolerate" the child for only a short period each day is probably going to do no more than just that—*tolerate* the child. We have never talked to a parent who argued for such "quality" time who was willing to describe how such time was used or what made it "quality." If spending a very limited amount of time with the child each day increases the "quality" of the time spent, it would follow that the father who is out of the home perhaps ten or twelve hours each day would have high "quality" in the short time he sees his children before bedtime. Judging from what we have observed (and the complaints of more than a few wives), such is often not the case. For many husbands and wives who are employed full time, coming home means relaxing after a strenuous day, withdrawing after a few perfunctory words, and hanging out the "Do Not

Disturb" sign. They have been through the "rat race" of the working world, and they are in no mood to relate to children—at least not with the highest "quality."

Without a parent physically present, the child is asked to function on adult time priorities. He is asked to put his problems, his questions, and his emotional needs on "hold" until the parent arrives home. For an adult, this is often possible and reasonable. But children don't function in the adult temporal world. Five minutes can seem an hour, and an hour can be an eternity. The hurt that brought tears at two o'clock cannot be kissed "all well" at six.

Many parents have also been persuaded that children need the educational and social advantages offered by nursery schools, preschools, kindergartens, and "after schools." In other words, they have accepted the argument that the company of other children (supervised by a "teacher") provides a superior environment. The proponents of these views, generally those involved in maintaining day-care centers and preschools, offer little evidence to support their arguments. Educational research is, on the whole, some of the least empirically sound data published in any serious journal. It is difficult to find evidence that a one-year-old develops social skills in a nursery school superior to those he might develop at home with an attentive parent. We have spoken with many parents who have chosen to place their children in day-care centers or nursery schools, some as early as six months of age. We have listened to them repeat the rationalizations of the preschool educators. But when we have questioned further their motivations, and when we have asked the all-important question, "Would you place your child in a preschool program if there was clear cut evidence that the child could benefit more by remaining in the home?" we have all too often heard parents defend such surrogate parenthood on the basis of parent convenience rather than child benefit. From our experience, we have found no evidence that any such surrogate-parent programs are superior to, or even the equal of, a secure, attentive, loving home environment for the child. We find instead, all too often, that they provide an escape for parents and a convenient dumping ground for children.

We have also listened to the argument that parents who are relieved of the almost full-time responsibility of parenthood, and are therefore able to pursue interests in the "outside world," have more to offer their children. Again, we have seen little evidence that they do, in fact, offer more. The parent who is able to spend an hour or two in the afternoon reading to a child, exploring the mysteries of wild flowers, demonstrating the process of fermentation in bread-making, or talking about how friends are made, is generally offering much more than the parent who has spent eight hours in an office and, by reason thereof, can now share information on closing escrow on a house sale. The "more to offer" argument ignores the question, "What does the child need from me?" We may offer our children the skills we have learned in writing a government grant proposal, but is that what the four-year-old wants and needs from us? The individual who is bored, we find, is generally the individual who is boring. There is no reason why the home environment should be intellectually stagnating. In fact, the demands and time constraints of the home environment generally afford greater opportunity for intellectual growth through reading and other educational pursuits than can be found within the time constraints of a full-time occupation.

Overall, an assumption is made by those who argue for surrogate-parent institutions. They see parenthood as primarily a matter of physical care alone. If you feed a child, wipe his nose, and put a bandage on his skinned knee, you have met the responsibilities of a parent. Some years ago, a well-known feminist said the job of a housewife and mother could be done by an eight-year-old or one mentally defective. Perhaps if she raised children this might have been descriptive of the job she did, but parenthood, as it is assumed by an adult, responsible, loving person is one of the most demanding, highly skilled of all professions. The physical, emotional, and educational aspects cannot be separated. Nor can the responsibilities be adequately met on a part-time basis.

The love and security children need comes first from a reflection of the relationship between the parents. It is from the love of father and mother for one another that the children not only learn the meaning of love, but derive the security that is so essential to their emotional well-being. And since those who are capable of loving generalize their love to others, this love between the parents quite naturally extends to the children. And as they see the love between their parents, they feel the warmth of that love extend to them. If the love between the parents is shattered, the child's perception of being loved is endangered.

Parenthood is by all measures a more extensive commitment than marriage itself, since there is no way in which parents can justifiably turn their backs on it, no way in which they can escape the responsibilities of a commitment which they have made by blaming others—spouse, children, society, or their own hang-ups. Once we bring a child into the world, we are bound, in strictest justice, to fulfill our obligations toward that child. The responsibilities can be awesome. We have no way of knowing ahead of time what they may be. The child may suffer severe impairments. The child may demand countless hours of unanticipated care and attention. But whatever should follow, our commitment is without reservation. We cannot escape it by whining, "But it was an unplanned pregnancy," or "But I didn't realize parenthood was going to be like this." The child is *there*, a living human being, one for whom we are totally responsible. The responsibility rests on both parents. It is what in law is called a "joint and severable" responsibility. One parent cannot be released from the responsibility by reason of the other parent's failure to meet it. It is at all times *total* for each. How many years this responsibility exists may be argued, but only within narrow limits. Some parents feel a responsibility until their children have completed four years of college. Others argue that the responsibility is met once the child completes high school, but that they would be willing to offer support through college (with no feeling of obligation to do so). In any case, the responsibility can be said to extend eighteen or more years. If parents have two or three children spaced, shall we say, over five years, their parental responsibilities will have a duration of at least twenty-three years. A long time, to be sure. Many times it will be frustrating, sometimes boring, often confining, perhaps even heartbreaking. But it is a responsibility that cannot be avoided if parents are to maintain self-esteem and adherence to the dictates of conscience.

We have listened to scores of parents who have expressed frustration at the limits this role imposes. We have spoken to parents who have cried, "It isn't fair! Why should we be tied down by children?" We have sympathized with single parents, widowed or divorced, who have carried an even greater responsibility. And we have recognized the financial pressures of couples who have faced problems trying to survive in an inflationary economy on a single salary and have felt it necessary to have two full-time incomes. What we hope to say is, therefore, not lacking in understanding and compassion. Every husband and wife faces the same set of questions.

Nevertheless, we have not yet seen evidence to persuade us that children do not *need* a parent *physically present* in the home whenever the children are not in school. And this, we strongly contend, extends all the way through completion of high school.

Perhaps the most important minutes in the day-to-day existence of a child are those when the child first arrives home from school. It is at that time the parent has the best opportunity to find out what is going on in his or her life, what problems may have arisen, what questions, and what hurts. Two or three hours' delay is often enough to permit things to "seal over," never to surface for an all-important parent-child discussion. The nurturance provided by a parent waiting when the child returns cannot be put off. It is both physical and emotional. And it is a need which, even if the child cannot express it, is very real. A note taped to the refrigerator saying, "You can have a glass of milk, and there are cookies in the cupboard," will not suffice. Nor is the necessity of a parent present in the home when the child returns from school any less when children reach junior high school and high school age. They need parents to talk to and to share with. They also need parental supervision, as we pointed out in discussing sexual development. Leaving a house key under a doormat or arranging afterschool activities to fill time until parents get home is not enough.

We should probably point out, and strongly emphasize, that we are not arguing a traditional mother's-place-is-in-the-home orthodoxy. We are convinced that neither gender has a monopoly on, or special talent for, parenting. A father can sit down and talk about the day's happenings, pour a glass of milk, and laugh over the latest school joke as capably as a mother. In some cases, parents who are both employed can arrange their work schedules such that one is home one afternoon and the other is home the following afternoon. What is important is that the child be able to rely on having a parent to come home to.

In answer to one argument which is sometimes raised, we see no evidence that children become more dependent or lacking in self-sufficiency when parents are consistently present. On the contrary, children gain self-esteem when they are provided continual support and love by their parents. The more the child experiences love and support, the more he sees himself as lovable and capable, and therefore able to venture forth into the world. The insecure child, on the other hand, is most often the child who has doubted his acceptance and who may have experienced what he perceived as rejection. This child may, in later years, doubt his ability to cope with a world in which doors are closed to him and love is seldom extended.

Does the total commitment of parenthood mean that parents can have no life of their own, no relationship as lovers? By all means, no. The tendency for some couples to virtually give up their love relationship as man and woman, husband and wife, once children enter the home is, to say the least, tragic. Keeping the love, romance, and physical affection not only alive but growing in their marriage is one of the most important gifts parents can give to their children. There is no denying that children bring new demands on time and new constraints on mobility. Most parents find, to no surprise, that spur-of-the-moment evenings out are seldom possible. Baby-sitters must be found, children bathed, fed, and ready for bed. And with the cost of baby-sitters added, new considerations play a part in budgeting a date. Dating once children are added to the family is, however, perhaps more important than before. Parents need time without distractions for just the two of them. The anxiety-ridden parents who feel they can never be away from their children for even an evening are doing their children no favor.

What do you look for in a baby-sitter, and where do you set about to look? Over the years, we have had a lot of experience answering these questions. First and foremost, of course, we look for someone with maturity and good judgment. If you are fortunate enough to live in a neighborhood with a number of high school- and college-age girls (or for that matter, boys), you will probably find you have an excellent opportunity to check out references. Have other parents in the neighborhood, those whose judgment you can rely on, employed this young person as a baby-sitter? What do they have to say? Are you personally acquainted with the baby-sitter's parents? How would you judge them as parents? Does their child-rearing seem to jibe with your own?

In the final analysis, whether the sitter comes recommended or not, parents have to rely on their own observations and instincts when they talk to a prospective sitter. Since there is seldom much time for conversation on the evening you are going out, the first night a new baby-sitter arrives, and since baby-sitters are not generally given extended job interviews, you may want to consider something we tried on several occasions: we conducted a "test run." We hired the baby-sitter for a couple of hours during the afternoon while we were at home (with the explanation, "We need you to look after the children while we finish up some very important work"). This provided us the opportunity to observe firsthand the baby-sitting skills and personality.

Such two- or three-hour sitting engagements served another purpose as well. We often had one or perhaps two favorite baby-sitters we employed regularly, but we considered it wise to maintain a list of backup sitters in case we decided to go out at the last minute and our regular sitters were unavailable. We tried to continually update this list, talking to friends and neighbors, asking for names and references. As a result, we were never stuck for someone to sit.

Beyond maturity, sound judgment, and kindness to our children, we asked little from baby-sitters. They were employed to care for the children, protect their safety, get them to bed at a reasonable hour, and maintain a happy environment. They were not expected to clean the house, wash dishes, prepare meals, or take the dog for a walk. If we found our children safe and sound when we arrived home, and the next morning the children were smiling, we felt the baby-sitter had done a good job. Obviously, there were certain ground rules. The baby-sitter was expected to be attentive to the children, not to sit engrossed in a TV program while the children explored the kitchen cabinets, and not to make our home a social center for friends. Baby-sitters, we feel, should be hired to do little more than look after children. From the experiences of several of our children who have "baby-sat," we have learned that parents who leave housekeeping chores to the baby-sitter often find great difficulty obtaining such "cheap labor." The word gets around. If we suggested to the sitter that the children might enjoy a dish of ice cream before bedtime, that was up to her, and serving it was enough. The dishes could be left in the sink to be taken care of by us in the morning. Good baby-sitters are hard to find. It pays to keep them happy. Bonuses don't hurt either.

We felt it made sense to keep our instructions limited. A sitter who is at all reliable (and who would hire any other?) does not need two pages of instructions and five emergency numbers to take care of children for an evening. Such extensive instruction seldom indicates parental responsibility as much as parental anxiety. We consider it a plus if the baby-sitter lives nearby with parents who would be home in the event of an emergency, especially if the baby-sitter was not yet of driving age or did not have a car. Also, if we knew where we would be for the evening, and if there was an available telephone where we were going, we would try to leave a number, but we did not feel it necessary to always know exactly where we would be and where we could be reached at a moment's notice.

The high school student next door is not the only possible baby-sitter. One alternative which has seen popularity in many communities is a baby-sitting cooperative. In these systems, with minor variations, a group of parents exchange baby-sitting, building up credit hours and paying off credit obligations, always in hours rather than money. Co-ops have the advantage of saving money. They also may have several disadvantages. For one thing, parents might consider before joining a co-op what money value they place on their time. If the going price for a baby-sitter is a dollar or two an hour, is your time worth more than this? There is also less "employer" control with a co-op. The high school student you hire can be given a set of rules having to do with friends, telephone use, and what your children are and are not permitted to do. The situation is stickier when the baby-sitter is the woman who lives three doors down the block. You would seldom feel free to tell her she could not have her friends drop over for coffee while she is baby-sitting your children, or that while she may permit her children to go over to the neighborhood park to play, you do not. Baby-sitting co-ops most often have a social aspect in the relationships between the parents which results in the roles— what can and cannot be expected and demanded—less clear.

There may be other drawbacks. In a co-op, the baby-sitting is generally done in the home of the parent "sitting." This raises several problems. If you and your spouse are going out for the evening, you drop your children off at the neighbors' home, the fellow members of the co-op. Do you feel free to extend your evening out knowing that this will mean keeping them up past their usual bedtime? If it is a hired baby-sitter, you can state what time you expect to be home, and ask if the sitter is willing to work that late. Also, with the baby-sitter in your own home, you are not faced with arousing your child from sleep in a strange bed, wrapping a blanket around it, and driving it home. To the small child (who may even sleep through it), this may be no more than a minor inconvenience. But parents often feel twinges of guilt at waking a child up in the middle of the night.

Two other aspects should be considered in the decision to join a co-op. The sitters will have children of their own. Are their children ones your children can easily relate to and enjoy? How do you handle the situation if it is the turn of Mrs. Smith down the block to baby-sit or your turn to baby-sit and your children and the Smith children are presently feuding? Or if one of the Smith children has a hacking cough, but Mrs. Smith says, "I don't think it's really anything to worry about"? Even more serious, what if Mrs. Jones is the one member of the co-op out of several whom you suspect is an irresponsible parent? Is there any way you can say, "I will let my children stay with any mother except Mrs. Jones"?

Another, even more common, alternative is to use grandparents as baby-sitters. They also may save money, but there may be other, not so obvious, prices to consider. As the old saying goes, "There is no free lunch." If you ask grandparents to baby-sit, and they do so without charge, can you feel comfortable in setting strict rules as to what is and is not to be done with the children?

Grandparents may not know best, but they all too often believe they know best. They know they have had more years of child-rearing experience and despite the fact that your ideas and convictions may express more wisdom, and the fact that these are your children and that you have the ultimate responsibility for what happens to them, grandparents all too often intervene to do what they, in all good conscience, feel is *best*. If parents want their children to have carrot sticks instead of candy as an evening snack, they may be right or wrong in their judgments on nutrition, but it is their decision to make. But what if Grandma comes to baby-sit and brings a box of chocolates? Do the parents feel they can say, "No, we don't give our children chocolates?" Grandmothers, understandably, feel they know best about child-rearing. They believe since they have raised their own children, they are in position to pass judgment on how all children should be raised. They may be right. Often their judgment may be questioned. But right or wrong, the responsibility still rests with the parents. Even the high school baby-sitter may believe that she knows best when it comes to child-rearing. And let's face it, she may. But this does not relieve the responsibility of the parents. The buck still stops with them. They are the ones who are going to have to live with the outcome. And while Grandmother may be convinced that she has all the answers when it comes to raising children, the parents are going to have to live with the responsibilities of parenthood on their shoulders.

Opinions on child-rearing are often in conflict. There are few clear-cut rights and wrongs. When grandparents are brought in to baby-sit, they can be expected to have their opinions. And since they cannot be given a set of rules such as might be given to the usual baby-sitter, the conflicts involved will face both parents. This can exacerbate any existing conflicts with in-laws. If the husband's mother baby-sits the children, and her views on child-rearing are in conflict with the views of her daughter-in-law, and if at the same time, there is any existing conflict between the wife and her mother-in-law, baby-sitting can make matters worse. There is a further potential problem when grandparents are used as baby-sitters. What price will the parents be expected to pay? Grandparents usually do not demand payment when they baby-sit. If they did, the transaction might be cleaner. They take care of their grandchildren because they love them. But for the parents, such services often create a debt. Can the parents decide not to invite the grandparents to a Christmas Eve celebration when they have been using the grandparents as free baby-sitters all year long? Can they discourage the grandparents from dropping over on Sunday afternoon when they have called upon them to baby-sit on Friday evening? "Free" baby-sitting, in whatever form, and under whatever guise, is never *free*. Parents may be willing to pay the price, but they should consider the price before they accept the benefit.

There are other associations which involve surrogate parents. How about the scout troop in which the scoutmaster plays a very heavy, all-inclusive role, as a surrogate parent? Many parents feel that such associations are good for their children because the leaders reinforce the values the parents hold. This goes for extracurricular school groups, church youth groups, summer camps, "educational" group tours, and certain "educationally advantaged" activities—swim clubs, dancing classes, riding classes, etc. In all these activities, leaders often assume the role of "good parents." They often see themselves as providing the understanding, insight, and avenue of communication not available to the child at home. In talking to children, and in talking to leaders of such groups, we

248 TO LIVE AS FAMILY

have seldom found such surrogate parents to be able to offer more than the parents can offer. There are, of course, those rare group leaders and teachers who are able to reach out and offer guidance which is not to be found in the child's home. And many of them can offer love. But in such cases, we find the home environment to be so torn up by divorce, brutality, or simply egocentricity, that almost any concerned and mature adult could offer more. Our conclusion would perhaps be the same if the child were placed in a 1920s orphanage. If the parents assume their responsibilities as *parents*, can they expect a boy scout leader to offer more to their children? It is highly unlikely. Whatever these involvements may seem to offer socially or educationally, parents should ask themselves:

What are the benefits to *my* child?

What effects can I expect on the other children in the family?

Have we (husband and wife) agreed on this involvement, and have we examined our respective roles in it, the cost that may be involved, the demands on our time and that of other family members?

Does the surrogate parent who will be charged with responsibility support our values?

And finally, does this involvement on the part of our child support what we seek to achieve in bonding and love within our family?

Parents do not need to be in competition with their fellow parents and other adults. There is no reason why we should fight for the intellects, philosophical values, and souls of our children. If our values and reasoning are sound, and the example we present is wholesome and productive, we have no reason to fear "losing." There is no reason, however, to subject children to the conflict of having to choose between the sophisticated values of a surrogate parent and the values of the home. Too many other values—popularity, acceptance, etc.—may weigh heavily on the child's decisions.

If we, as a family, have something attractive to offer, we feel sure it will draw others to us. Our family will act as a magnet, drawing others to what is fun, healthy, and life-giving. Our children will not seek surrogate parents. They will live in a home environment in which they can form their own values and goals. Their friends will then be drawn to them and to the environment of our home. We open the door to them.

13

In Sickness
and In Health

Few events can be as disruptive to the family as the illness of one of its members. If the illness is life-threatening or involves prolonged debilitation, the effects can be devastating. All family members are affected, and the resultant stresses can even lead to the disintegration of the family unit. Even less serious illnesses, if frequent, can erode the family. The drain on the family resources in time, money, and additional work can strain relationships to the breaking point.

On the other hand, in coping with the illness of a member, the family may grow in closeness. Adversity itself is seldom threatening to the family. It all depends on the values and maturity of the parents and, through their example and teaching, the children. Regardless of the family's coping ability, however, the stresses associated with illness can never be shrugged away. Everyone is touched. Every family member is forced to change.

The most immediate changes are in activities. Vacations may be canceled, postponed, or cut short. Parties may be called off and invitations to friends withdrawn. Additional chores may be assigned in order to fill in for the sick brother or sister. One of the children may have to

ꜱ

pick up the ill sibling's school assignments. The noise
level has to be reduced. Nursing duties can take parental
time away from other children, and take a toll in loss of
sleep. Meals may be altered. In short, the comfortable
schedule of the family is suddenly scrapped. The illness,
like an uninvited guest who drops in at dinnertime, takes
over.

Following on these changes are emotional reactions.
When a member of our family, someone we care for very
much, is taken ill, we suffer a flood of emotions. They
hurt, and we hurt for them—sympathy and empathy combined. We may feel rage at the injustice of "Why should
it happen to her?" We may be struck with fear of an illness we don't understand, with an outcome we cannot
predict. We may identify with the ill one: if he/she can
get sick, break a leg, or even, God forbid, die, then so
can I.

Some of our feelings may be less acceptable to us. We
don't like them because they make us like ourselves less.
We may resent the ill one who has, through illness,
disrupted our well-ordered existence. We may feel resentment because the illness has made us feel guilty for our
meanness toward him or her in the past, perhaps even the
previous day. There may be resentment generated by fear
of contagion. ("I'm angry at my sister for catching the
flu. She might give me her bug, and I'm supposed to go
on a camp-out next week.") And unconsciously, we may
resent her for reminding us of our own vulnerability to
disease—even to death.

This last, identification with vulnerability to disease,
may, on the other hand, increase feelings of compassion,
especially among family members who have suffered from
the illness. But even if it does, and in most cases we
might view this as very positive, the feelings may have a
fallout effect which is depressing. Will the illness run

through the family? Is illness unavoidable? Is our family fun going to cease?

If the illness lasts more than a few days, a restructuring of the family sociogram is almost inevitable. The sociogram, which may have been relatively secure and stable, is disrupted by any major change affecting one member. The bonding ties to that member with each other member are weakened, strengthened, or in other ways altered. The bond with the ill member and another sibling may suddenly be strengthened which may, in turn, weaken the bond of that healthy sibling with another member. The bond between a "jock" father and his athletic son may weaken when the son suffers a debilitating illness. At the same time, it may increase the bonding with an excessively maternal mother who can now direct even more of her energies toward caring for a sick child.

Reactions to the illness of a family member are almost always ambiguous. Often, they are love/hate reactions, and they are affected by whether or not the illness is acute and short-lived, such as a severe cold, or long-lasting or chronic. The latter may, obviously, produce the more profound effects—whether positive or negative. Whatever the severity or duration of the illness, the reaction of other family members may be as follows:

Compassion: This is a feeling of deep sympathy and sorrow for another's suffering or misfortune, accompanied by a desire to alleviate the pain or remove its cause. It is the reaction we expect from concerned, loving persons. But what if our desire to alleviate their pain or remove its cause is frustrated? What if there is nothing we can do? The compassionate feelings may center solely on sympathy. In fact, sympathy (rather than remedial action) becomes the primary focus. Unfortunately, it often tends to be overdone. Excessive sympathy is never helpful, and it can be harmful. Nevertheless, if we feel we have nothing more to offer, we may layer on sympathy to an inordinate degree.

Compassion is, of course, an emotion we want to encourage. We also want to encourage our children to engage in the actions which are motivated by the emotion. We hope they will learn the meaning of charity. Sympathy, however, especially when it is excessive and borders on pity, is seldom of much help to the patient. The relationships no longer remain the same. Patients are often heard complaining, "Everyone acts so different; why can't they just be natural?" There are some individuals, however, who seemingly soak up all the sympathy they can get. They are the types who seek a lot of attention at all times, and sympathy provides attention. How the compassionate impulses of the family members are expressed must, therefore, like all interactions within the home, be monitored by the parents. It is the parents who must encourage charity while at the same time set the limits on sympathy. People may not be killed with kindness, but if it is expressed in the wrong ways, they can be kept sick.

Withdrawal: Young children are often baffled and frightened by illness in the family, especially illness which strikes down a parent. When mother is confined to bed it is more than an inconvenience to the child, it is a threat to his or her security. To the child, parents simply do not get sick; parents don't die; parents always *are* and always will be. They are the Rock of Gibraltar. To a lesser degree this is true of their siblings. Any serious illness affecting any family member unsettles the child's world. The illness need not be life-threatening to have this effect. When a family member is confined to bed, everyone speaks in whispers. This is unnatural. They don't laugh as much. Equally unnatural. And everyone pays particular attention to the sick one. The well child may respond by withdrawing into himself. He may talk less and spend more time alone. His withdrawal may reflect fear (of the unknown: outcome of the disease, changes in the family), feelings of rejection due to the nursing demands of the ill member, suppressed hostility—often followed by guilt toward the "privileged" sick one, feelings of impotence ("No, there's nothing you can do to help"), and vague anxiety.

Denial: In reacting as if nothing has happened and nothing has changed, the child constructs a shield against the painful reality. Parents may attempt to explain that Jimmy is very ill and may be in the hospital several days or even weeks, but brother Chris may, no more than an hour later, ask if Jimmy can go to the track meet with him the following day. Chris denies Jimmy's illness. The more unacceptable and fearful the reality, the more the defensive denial is apt to be employed.

These reactions, and others as well, may also be expressed by the parents. If the wife and children have seen the husband as the strength of the family, unflappable and stoic, his illness may create severe stress in all family relationships as they struggle to find new sources of strength and self-sufficiency. The mother may have to take over roles with which she is unfamiliar. She may feel overwhelmed, frightened, and resentful. She may in turn make additional, even excessive, demands on her children. Her stoic pillar-of-strength husband may seem to revert to childhood, a frightened, complaining, and demanding little boy in pain. She then finds herself nursing a stranger, reacting to her own fatigue and/or resentment. If she is the one to become ill, her husband may be the one cast in the roles for which he feels totally unprepared. Ironing a little girl's dress or doing the weekly grocery shopping may be baffling. The specific chores and roles are not important. In most young families of today, traditional household chore designations of "men's work" and "women's work" is seldom heard (a very positive move toward egalitarianism and common sense), yet nevertheless, husband and wife will almost invariably have developed proprietary roles. Whether for reasons of convenience, talents, or interests they will have fallen into patterns which result in their performing separate and very distinct functions within the home, roles with which they have become familiar and comfortable. With illness, then, the roles the indisposed spouse has regularly assumed will be thrust upon the other family members. Often these roles will not be assumed with the same expertise, and frustration for everyone will be the result. The newly assumed roles can, of course, be accepted as challenges, but the frustrations will usually lurk there as at least a potential danger. With the illness of any family member, especially a parent, the family members can, with help, pull together. They can assume the new roles and take on additional tasks. They can adjust to their altered life style, whether for a few days or for many months, and they can do so with equanimity and love.

In order to do so, however, they must quickly learn what is happening and what they can expect in the days or weeks ahead. One of the worst aspects of any illness is not knowing what the illness is or whether or not it may turn out to be something serious. With what appears to be serious illness, communication throughout the family is essential. At no time is it more important. All family members need to know, since fear of the unknown breeds anxiety and frustration.

Most illnesses can be diagnosed by a layman. They are minor and do not require medical treatment. There is little, for example, the family doctor can do for a common cold. One home remedy is probably as good as another. There may be times, however, when even a common cold can be puzzling and frightening. Small children have difficulty describing symptoms, and they can appear to be sicker than they are. The infant's fever can have a sudden onset and be alarmingly high with these common upper-respiratory infections, but until the doctor has examined the baby, diagnosed the illness, and communicated his findings, such a "minor" illness will not seem at all "minor" to the parents. "It's nothing to worry about," are the most welcome words the doctor ever speaks. Whatever the diagnosis and prognosis of the illness may be, however, when any family member is ill, medical information should be shared with all family members as immediately and fully as possible. Even a very young child can understand a simple, honest explanation of illness. And he has a right to such an explanation. Many parents feel that discussion of the illness of a sibling or parent will only raise fears in the child. As a consequence, they dismiss the child's questions with, "Mommy isn't feeling very well, but she's going to be all right; the doctor's going to make her well." Such an explanation, however, is a non-answer. Rather than allaying the child's fears, such an answer may serve to increase them. As in all other areas of discussion within the family, openness and honesty are essential.

Unless there is a real danger of contagion, all family members should be given the opportunity to share in nursing care. This may include bringing a glass of fruit juice or a bowl of soup, applying a damp cloth to a fevered forehead, brushing a sister's hair, or simply sitting by the bed, sharing and laughing. Especially laughing. Norman Cousins, in his excellent work *Anatomy of an Illness*, argues most convincingly for the therapy of laughter. Suffering himself from a life-threatening and medically baffling disease, Cousins reasoned that if an individual's depression can both trigger illness and impede recovery, positive emotions—hope, joy, laughter—may be used to fight the onset of illness and speed recovery. With courage, scientific reasoning and methodology, and determination to share with his physicians the responsibility for fighting his disease, Cousins won his battle. Fleming discovered penicillin; Cousins discovered laughter. The latter may be as much a "miracle drug" as the former. While the rationale for the therapy of laughter may seem rather obvious, and it is common to speak of "curing the patient of," in reality the sickroom is often turned into a pretty gloomy place. Friends and family often feel it would be inappropriate, even callous, to bring laughter into the presence of someone who quite obviously feels "rotten." And the sick one may indeed quite understandably find nothing to laugh about. If, however, we view laughter as an important part of the therapy, we healthy ones will do our best to provide it.

It also frequently helps if an effort is made to avoid isolating the ill family member. Being with the rest of the family watching a television sit-com is usually more conducive to recovery than being shut off in a quiet room alone. Silent, darkened rooms don't speed one's recovery from a chest cold or an upset stomach. They just cut one off from others to suffer the misery in solitary confinement. And to the child, such isolation, well-intended though it may be, may seem like banishment.

Health

Some families undergo more than their share of illnesses. Others enjoy robust health, with the members seldom even catching as much as a cold. Doctors as well as laymen used to speak of family differences in "constitution" and susceptibilities which "run in the family." Then, some forty years or more ago, medicine began to look at the emotional, psychological components of physical health and illness. In doing so, the health professionals were rediscovering what the fathers of medicine, all the way back to Galen and Hippocrates had taught: that mind and body cannot be separated, and that what affects one affects the other. Even the new word given to this interaction, *psychosomatic,* implied some sort of dichotomy, but it did, nevertheless, reintroduce an important way of viewing the human being as a total person which had been virtually lost in the mechanistic approaches of previous centuries.

Pendulums swing, and if we are to judge by what has been popularized in the media over the past decade or two, the pendulum toward so-called "holistic" medicine has swung far indeed. The "new" doctor, so it is said, treats the *whole* person, not just his disease. But for the conscientious physician, this has always been so. It is therefore of little wonder that the physician of forty years experience reads such pop articles, and mutters, "What else is new?" And that others, seeing the esoteric cult beliefs which have increasingly sought inclusion under the umbrella of "holistic" medicine (everything from astrology to laetrile) have turned their backs on the new cultism. What is needed, most physicians agree, is a commonsense approach to our understanding of how attitudes and emotional reactions can affect physical well-being, as well as the part relationships within the family play in the mental and physical health of its members. Only in recent years has there been scientific evidence (hormonal, biochemical) indicating how the brain, acting as a control center for the body's immune system, activates mechanisms which ward off disease.

Fundamental questions are still being asked. Is all disease triggered or exacerbated by negative emotional reactions? Do we unconsciously "will" ourselves to be sick? If so, can we change the course of the illness and "will" ourselves to be well again? Is illness, in other words, some-

thing which befalls us, something over which we have
only minimal control, the hostile invader which, at best,
can be only resisted with proper nutrition and availability
of the armamentarium of medical science? Are we all potentially passive victims, wandering through dark passage-
ways of potential pathology wherein lurk dangerous
"bugs" waiting in ambush?

It has been said, "Be careful what you expect in life because you will seldom be surprised." When it comes to illness, this is a dictum that is not easily accepted. Few of
us care to believe that the bout of flu from which we
suffered last winter came about because we anticipated it.

We probably all have evidence to support this hypothesis. Let's take, as examples, two families. Family A—
mother, father, two children—average about nine illnesses
per family member each year. Most are minor (upper res-
piratory, influenza, gastrointestinal, etc.), but some may
be chronic (migraine headaches, colitis, asthma) and in
rare cases one or two might even be life-threatening. (Incidentally, nine illnesses per family member is approxi-
mately what some studies have reported as average.) Thus
for Family A, illness occurs on the average of thirty-six
times per year! Family B, the next-door neighbors, also including father, mother, and two children, average only
four illnesses per year for the entire family. Can we come
up with a plausible explanation for these differences?

The first possibility: Family B may be "just naturally"
healthier than Family A. Perhaps genetics favor them.
Perhaps some people are born of "good stock" while
others are not. This is a difficult hypothesis to test. Less
difficult is a second possibility: that the members of Family A receive a less nutritious diet, engage in less exercise,
have fewer vitamin pills, or less frequent medical
checkups. Perhaps the members of Family A live in a
more germ-ridden environment. This hypothesis is easier

to test. But if we cannot explain the differences by our first two hypotheses, it makes sense to at least entertain the third, that the psychological ambience of the respective homes may differ significantly, and that this variable is more important than the others.

Increasingly, physicians and psychotherapists have found evidence that psychosocial factors in the cause and progress of disease have been given less importance than they merit. Medicine can now cite substantial clinical evidence to support the position that a happy, emotionally sound home environment is also the healthiest physical environment. The family members get sick less, and recover from illnesses more rapidly.

That we feel better when we are in "good spirits" is self-evident. We can all draw upon personal experience to affirm it. The physiological mechanisms through which we ward off disease, and how these mechanisms are effected and/or controlled, by our intellectual/emotional states are still not fully understood. We have learned a great deal in the last thirty years but we still have much to learn.[1]

From our observations and those of others, three things seem pertinent: 1) our emotional environment, 2) our expectancies, 3) our attitudes of self-sufficiency.

In a negative emotional environment (stress, conflict, lack of satisfaction in relationships, frustration in attaining goals), the body's immune system, the biochemical and hormonal defenses which deter ever-present, potentially hostile organisms from successfully attacking, break down. Flu bugs, cold germs, even cancer cells are always with us. Our natural immune system keeps the upper hand, and the diseases don't win a foothold. Something

[1] For further readings, we suggest: Benson, Herbert, *The Mind/Body Effect*, New York: Simon & Schuster, 1979; Lewis, H. R. and M. E., *Psychosomatics*, New York: Pinnacle Books, Inc., 1975.

happens, however, to this natural protection when life turns sour. The man who feels trapped in a dead-end job, the woman who is unhappy with her sex life, the child who feels rejected by the other kids at school, become suddenly very vulnerable. While the emotional environment of the home and family is not the total world in which any of us live, it may very well be the most influential when it comes to our physical and emotional health. It is therefore understandable that each member of the family may play an important role in the health of all family members through his or her contributions toward maintaining the home as a happy, loving, tranquil environment. Positive attitudes of the family members serve as an antidote to what might otherwise be a stormy and unhealthy world. Expectancies, including those which involve health, tend to be self-fulfilling. This has been well documented. When we were children, we were told exposure to damp, chilly weather would make us "come down with" a cold. Researchers refuted this notion, of course, but a lot of us got our feet wet as children and, sure enough, came down with colds. This serves as a simple example of the self-fulfilling prophecy in illness. The extent to which people predict their illnesses is often amazing. "I just know I'm going to get a headache." "We're going to Mexico next week and I'll probably come down with you-know-what." "My job is sure to give me an ulcer." "At my age, I expect to have high blood pressure and prostate trouble." These kinds of predictions prove to be depressingly accurate. If parents, then, *tell* their children they are going to be ill, more often than not they will be, given the child's usual inclination to believe the parents. Not that parents set out to make their children sick, but the expectancies of the parents become the expectancies of the child—and the results are self-fulfilling. Teaching expectancies of health and refuting expectancies of illness thus becomes an important part of any family's health program. In our experience, and those of many, many parents with whom we have talked, playing down illness (or the potential of illness) is a very important factor in maintaining family health. This does not mean that we deny the existence of illness or the suffering of the child. It simply means that we do not feel it is wise to dramatize aches and pains, especially to the child. We feel that it is wiser to say, "I'm sure your sore throat will be all well tomorrow and you will be able to go out and play," than to say, "That could mean a strep infection, and you may have to go to the doctor." It goes without saying that we will take the child to the doctor if he or she is not better the following day or the day after. We are aware, however, of the capacity of the mind to exacerbate illnesses and increase the probability of their occurrence. We feel it is unwise to give sickness a head start. The power of suggestion is too powerful to take such risks. And recognizing this fact, we prefer to convey positive suggestions.

In every area of life, a belief in self-determination is important. It is especially important in physical health. We want to instill in our children the belief that they are responsible for their own destiny, that they are the captains of their fate. We recently spoke with a man who had undergone cancer surgery. Approaching what for most of us would be a terrifying and unknown ordeal, he called the operating staff together around the table before they administered the anesthetic. He thanked them for "assisting me in my battle against this invader." He accepted the disease and what could be done to fight it as his responsibility and his battle, not the doctors'. He chose to view the medical staff as his "seconds." He saw himself, however, as the guy in the ring. (He won the battle.)

Research in behavioral medicine has consistently

pointed to the importance of such a view—individual responsibility—in both the maintenance of health and the
treatment of disease. It may be too sweeping to say that
we always make ourselves sick and we can always make
ourselves well, yet there is impressive evidence of the importance of holding just such a view. We might look at it
this way: if we stay confident of our ability to influence, if
not control, our physical health, do we lose anything if,
per chance, some illnesses are actually beyond our control? Given the research findings of the past two decades,
it would be foolish to disregard personal responsibility for
health. This is an attitude we very much want to teach
our children both by example and instruction. Specifically,
we want to teach them that they are not physically passive, potential victims of invading germs. Just as learning
is as much or more a measure of the student as the
teacher, recovery from illness is as much a product of their
determination to fight the disease as it is the medications
that their doctors may prescribe. We very much want to
teach them to minimize their minor aches, pains, and discomforts. Almost all physicians agree that the majority of
the patients sitting in their waiting rooms suffer from ail-
ments which will be healed as quickly by nature as by
medical intervention. It makes sense, therefore, to be medically conservative, to not turn every pimple into a boil,
every cold into pneumonia.

"I'm so tired in the morning I can hardly drag myself
out of bed," is an all too common complaint. But suppose
we ask the complainer, "Do you think you would feel
that way if you were scheduled on an early flight to Tahiti
for a vacation in the sun?" What answer would we get?
Our physical reactions are very frequently influenced by
our hopes for the immediate and distant future. We have
all heard stories of the scientist who having completed his
research, died, the author who finished her novel and took

to her sickbed, the pioneer who saw his family safely across the plains, then succumbed to a terminal illness. When we feel we have reached all our goals, we have little or nothing to look forward to. Having something positive to anticipate is perhaps the best preventive of illness and the best cure of disease. Why not, therefore, create as many things as possible that we, as a family, can look forward to? Not a single thing, perhaps, but a number of small and large anticipations. Perhaps a TV movie with popcorn, or a weekend tournament of miniature golf, or a picnic, or an upcoming vacation. The anticipations might include little more than a fun-filled family dinner or a good session of sharing jokes. If we can help provide a *reason* for staying healthy—in anticipation of what tomorrow will bring—we will have given our family something approaching an immunization against both mental and physical illness.

Nothing we have written in the preceding pages should be interpreted as expressing any opposition to professional medical care or established preventive medicine. We firmly believe medical science has more to offer today than could have been conceived of even a half century ago. Childhood diseases which took the lives and health of children and gave parents countless sleepless nights even three decades ago are now a thing of the past. The family doctor is, and will remain, an important ally in the maintenance of the health of the family. Dr. Spock's famous works saw us through several children and their minor symptoms. We do find overwhelming evidence, however, that family health is most often obtainable and sustainable through a working partnership with a family physician who is concerned with the total emotional and physical environment within which his patients are living, and who recognizes them as co-equals in the maintenance of health, and with parents who are motivated to establish rational, healthy (and happy) attitudes within the home. An obligation is pledged in the words of the wedding ceremony, "in sickness and in health," which pledges us to a heavy responsibility—to care, to empathize, and to heal. They are the responsibilities which we can all recognize as perhaps challenging us to the highest demands of loving. "I will love you" may very well be synonymous with "I will do my best to make you healthy."

14

The Working Family

If you had been a fifteen-year-old living on a Kansas farm during the 1930s, you would have learned very well the meaning of family work. Everyone on the farm had jobs to do. Each contributed to the family income. Children as well as adults knew what was expected of them; each carried a share of the load. As they were growing up, the children were economic assets. They worked in both the fields and the house.

The mom-and-pop grocery or the family restaurant offered similar opportunities to children. Children could work in the family business at tasks which were not just "make work." For some children, these jobs served as their appenticeship for their future occupations. For others, the jobs provided responsibilities to assure them that when the day came that they would be on their own, they could make it in an adult world. Working side by side with their parents in adult jobs was an additional rite of passage.

With the end of World War II (a historical benchmark from which we measure so much change in our society), the 160-acre family farm underwent dramatic change. The gigantic mechanical combine eliminated the need for threshing crews and large numbers of farm laborers. Farmers added hundreds of acres to their farms or they sold out and moved to the cities. Farming became agribusiness, and highly specialized. There were very few farm chores left for the children of the family. In the cities, the supermarkets drove the family grocery stores out of business. The twelve-year-old who used to stock shelves and help carry out grocery bags could find no work in the supermarket. He or she was underage for these union jobs.

Child labor laws were increasingly tightened, and even where they did not prohibit children from working in a family business, the social climate had changed. Parents began to feel they might be *exploiting* their children if they put them to work preparing vegetables in the kitchen of the family restaurant.

Some child psychologists and educators climbed on the stump to argue that children who were "forced" to work in family businesses would miss out on important opportunities and joys of childhood—hobbies, play, afterschool group activities, etc. "Children should be allowed to be children," they said. They would have a lifetime in which to work and keep their noses to grindstones. The later years of childhood, rather than serving as an apprenticeship for the assumption of adult responsibility, became an extended period of play. The sixteen-year-old cruised the streets in a sports car and watched endless hours of television reruns. Work came to be viewed as an onerous demand to be postponed as long as possible.

Parents were often easily persuaded to go along with this view. Many took pride in being able to say, "Our kids don't have to work as we did."

Even those who believed that work experience, especially within a family business, might be good for their children, had no business in which the children could participate. Dad was putting in forty hours a week programming computers. Mom was selling real estate. The most children were asked to do was a few household chores, and, with smaller houses and more appliances, the chores demanded little in time or effort. The parents worked; the children played, and the divisions widened.

We previously spoke of task bonding, and emphasized its importance in the total bonding within the family. No task bonding can be more substantial than that which results from all family members working together toward a single overall goal. The benefits to be derived make it worth the effort to create a "working family."

The effort will frequently be substantial. It will demand time on the part of parents as well as children. It will mean that parents not simply assign chores to children, then leave them on their own to perform them, but that the parents be actively and equally involved in the projects. The essential of task bonding is *mutual* effort; members working side by side. Within a family, this means all members—both parents and all children capable of making a contribution, however minimal.

Before returning to consideration of task bonding, however, we might examine other advantages in family work projects:

There are a number of skills in what we have chosen to call the "survival kit." We want our children to develop all these skills, at least to a level of proficiency which will serve them well when they have homes of their own. Painting a room without leaving streaks on the trim is one of them. Replacing the caulking in a shower stall may be another. And preparing a sauce for spare ribs, shampooing a carpet, sharpening kitchen knives, balancing a checkbook, ironing a pleated skirt, shortening a cuff, replacing shingles, repotting a plant, and typing a business letter may be included. They are all components of the "survival kit."

Two or three generations ago, sixteen- and seventeen-year-olds struck out on their own. They married and started families. They had to have the necessary skills for survival. Today, however, we see young men and women in their mid-twenties who lack even the fundamentals. Twenty-six-year-old college graduates often cannot cook a pot roast, change a washer on a kitchen faucet, or manage a household budget.

Children want, and need, to feel they are *contributing* family members, not free-loaders. They enjoy the self-esteem they derive from being able to look at a job in which they have shared, in a job well done. To enjoy these rewards, they must be able to recognize independent responsibility, a task they can see as fully their job. If the family as a group sets about to paint the living room, the child likes to be able to point to the north wall and say, "I did that." Children want very much to see themselves as growing into adulthood, to see themselves as attaining self-sufficiency. They may still be living at home and dependent upon their parents for support, but they want to be able to say, "I don't need help; I can do it myself!" It is the opportunity for such feelings that we want to provide.

Most of us don't own a family business in which we can all work together, but there are still many projects available in the maintenance of the home. Saturdays can be designated as house-cleaning days, with the various jobs divided among the family members. Cleaning the garage can be an all-day project for the entire family. So can the spring yard work. All the members can collect their discards while cleaning their rooms and the garage, and can spend a profit-making day selling them at the flea market.

And there still are opportunities for family businesses, even if on a part-time basis. We have close friends who began to sell Halloween pumpkins several years ago. They enlisted the aid of their children. As the business prospered, they expanded it into another part-time business of selling Christmas trees, and as this, in turn, grew, they added additional tree lots. A couple of years ago, at the close of the Christmas tree selling season, the family rewarded themselves with a vacation in Hawaii. They had all earned it, and the *task* bonding they experienced on the job added to the *experience*-bonding rewards of the vacation. The children gained in maturity and responsibility as they worked at an adult job. The parents, along with the children, were rewarded in the bonding that occurred. And the entire family benefited from the income.

We liked the reward they gave themselves. We believe work deserves to be rewarded. There are, of course, rewards in living together, enjoying one another, and enjoying the basic support which comes from our work. But we also enjoy the special rewards we give ourselves from family work projects well done, just as our friends did with their Hawaii trip. When we have all pulled together in efforts beyond the usual, we feel we deserve additional rewards. When we have given a seminar, the children have often pitched in to help in the housework and meal preparation, and they have aided in making name tags, distributing materials, and even participating in panel discussions. Once the job is over, it is time for a party to toast all members of the family. Often it has been a special dinner out or a movie, sometimes a day at the beach, and a few times, a weekend or even a week away on vacation.

Work and play form an almost inseparable combination in their bonding effects upon the family. Bonding effects are the same, regardless of the psychodynamics by which the bonding occurs. When all of us as a family pitch in to wash and polish the car or decorate the Christmas tree or help the youngest ones dress in costumes for a party, bonding occurs. It is senseless to question whether the bonding is derived from mutual "work" or mutual "pleasure." What *is* important is that bonding does result. And with the bonding, comes pride in what we, as a family, have accomplished. When we gaze with pride on our achievement, we do so as a family.

15

Taking Flight

A very few years after parenting begins, it comes to a close. The front door, banged open and shut so many times in response to scraped knees, squeals of elation, cries of anguish, and endless goings and comings, closes for the final time on the child, now an adult.

The world out there is waiting for them, and they feel they are ready for that world. They have their survival kit in hand, assuming we have done our job in providing it. They have an earning potential, one which will assure them self-sufficiency and hopes for the future. They do not leave in defiance. Nor are they tempted to stay at home because they fear the challenges out there in the "cold world."

Leaving the "nest" should be a day of rejoicing for all concerned. It should be a *commencement* of the autonomy of adulthood. While there may be a few tears, they should be tears of joy, very much like the ones we shed at graduation ceremonies and weddings. If our children have matured as we have hoped for and worked for, and if they have acquired the education and the skills which they will need in order to earn a living, they will be ready to leave home. Furthermore, they will have reached the point at which they *should* leave home for their own

274 TO LIVE AS FAMILY

benefit. If they continue to live at home after they reach this level of development and maturity, they will do no good to themselves. Everything concerned parents attempt to do during the years children are growing up is aimed at preparing them to assume all the responsibilities of adulthood. Along the way children take a number of steps, large and small, toward achieving independence: there is the time they cross the street alone for the first time, the day the training wheels come off the bike, the first day they go off to high school, the day they get a driver's license, and the day of the first paycheck. Step by step, children collect skills and develop the self-confidence to employ them.

At each step, the question for the parents is the same: is he/she ready? And each time, the answer is the same: "We think so; we hope so; we pray so." We parents do all we can to prepare them for these steps. We do everything we can to reduce the risk. We cannot, however, reduce the risk to zero. If we wait until such time as we feel comfortable and totally free of anxiety, we will probably have protected them far too long—to their detriment. The overprotection will not mark us as conscientious parents, only as parents more concerned with our own anxiety than with the development of our children.

When children reach the "age of emancipation," they may not be, and probably will not be, totally *ready* to meet the challenges of adulthood. They are close to the eighteen-year-old who signs a major-league contract to play baseball. He seems to have the talent, but he needs three or four years seasoning in the minor leagues before he is ready to take on all that will be demanded of him in the big leagues. We can only hope that we have prepared our children well enough that we can have confidence in their survival. If they can survive, they can probably eventually "make it." We expect them to experience rough bumps along the way. We hate seeing them suffer the bruises, rejections, and financial tight scrapes, but we recognize that learning seldom occurs when teaching comes wrapped in cotton batting. They will undergo experiences which will be painful. We don't have to make them painful. We don't even want them to be painful. If they could sail through this transitional period with no bumps and bruises, we would rejoice. But life seldom works that way.

The decision to leave the nest is usually made by the child. It may be made by the parents. Under the best of circumstances, it is a mutual decision, based upon all available evidence which says, "The time has come."

Before embarking on any discussion of how these decisions are made, and by whom, it might help if we defined our terms.

"Leaving the nest" means just that—*permanently leaving* the parental home for life of independence as an adult. The eighteen-year-old who goes off to college with tuition, board, and room paid for by the parents, has not left the nest. He is no more independent than his fourteen-year-old brother. This is not said in criticism; it is merely an observation, a statement of reality. The twenty-three-year-old living with her parents, paying only a token amount for board and room, is not really on her own. If she then marries and moves in with the parents, sharing the spare bedroom with her husband, she has not attained the status of an adult, and neither has her husband. Marriage alone is not sufficient to confer autonomy. We have spoken with a number of young people who have told us they were out on their own, but when questioned further, proved to be still very dependent on their parents. Parents themselves have told us of how their children were "out on their own," without the parents' recognizing the extent to which they were still providing for them. Parents very frequently have a difficult time saying, "This is where we draw the line; from now on it's up to you."

We have invested two decades of time and effort to provide our children with the skills necessary in order for them to function independently. Yet when the time comes to say, "Sink or swim," we find ourselves backing away. We hedge. We stall for time, and we delay closing the door for the last time.

If our twenty-year-old decides to get a place of his own, overextends his limited credit, and can't make his car payments, do we step in to bail him out? If we do, how will he see himself? And how will we, his parents, see ourselves? If a twenty-five-year-old daughter loses her job and decides she wants to move back home, do we say, "We will always be here when you need us"? If we do, can we say that we have contributed toward helping her reach adulthood?

These questions reflect broader and far more vexing questions: What do we owe to our children? What do they owe to us? During the growing years, the answers to these questions are easy. As parents, we owe our children nurturance and protection in all the ways of which we have spoken in these pages (and probably in ways we have overlooked). Our children owe us compliance. They have to abide by the rules of the family. They do not owe us love or respect. If we conscientiously fulfill our roles as parents and give love to them, we will earn their love and respect. But we can't demand it of them. They are obligated to abide by the rules, and to submit to the authority of their parents, for one reason, and one reason only: authority flows from responsibility. Parents are charged with a great responsibility. In shouldering this responsibility they must make countless decisions. They will bear the burden of the outcome of the decisions they make. In carrying out their responsibilities, they take on the mantle of authority: the children have a responsibility to follow their direction. When we decide our children can go to the beach with their friends, we take on the burden of the possible consequences. Whatever may happen will rest on our shoulders and our consciences as their parents. Rationally, we may be able to say, "There was no way we could have anticipated these consequences," but we will hold ourselves responsible for any outcome. And since the responsibility begins and ends with the parents, the children have an obligation to adhere to the reasonable dictates of the parents.

The question which then arises is: when do these reciprocal obligations end? The answer, we feel, must rest on a number of considerations. The twelve-year-old cannot strike out on his own even if he wants to. He is dependent upon his parents, and is incapable of functioning independently. At the same time, his parents cannot cast him out. They have an obligation to care for him. That much is clear. But what obligations continue after the child has completed high school and is, at age eighteen, legally an adult? If he is physically and mentally competent, he will be capable of getting a job and holding it down. It probably will not be a high-paying job, but it will be a job. Out on his own, he won't starve to death. As an eighteen-year-old, he can choose to leave home. He can decide to travel around the world, join the Army, enter a monastery, become a rock musician, or set about to discover a cure for cancer. He may decide to go to college. On the other hand, he may decide that college is not his "thing." To the eighteen-year-old, the choices seem endless. The whole world seems to be his oyster. And that is as it should be. For the first time, after almost two decades of submission to authority, the high school graduate has the right to make his or her own decisions.

Parents, on the other hand, may feel they know what is best for their children. Why shouldn't they? They have, on their side, the weight of experience, education, and cautious judgment. But the one thing they lack at that point in the child's development is authority. Almost overnight there comes a dramatic change in the respective rights and obligations of parents and child. It is safe to say that no one involved is prepared for these changes. They are suddenly *there*, and they must be coped with.

Changes in the relationships are seldom recognized. They are even less often verbalized. Both parents and children know that *something* is different, but they are not sure just what. What has happened has been a "contractual" shift. The old "contract" is no longer in force, but the parties to the contract have avoided coming to the "bargaining table" to negotiate the terms of a new "contract." Since so much is still the same, the changes seldom seem to demand immediate action. Things tend to drift along as usual, as if nothing at all has changed. In time, however, changes that have taken place without notice bring to the surface new relationships which give rise to conflict.

We believe that many misunderstandings might be avoided at these periods if the parents called a meeting with the child to iron things out. This might be called during the child's final year in high school. The purpose would be to discuss both the child's plans for the future and the terms of a new "contract."

Such a discussion will inevitably cast all participants in strange new roles. They will be called upon to interact as equals, and at first this will create discomfort.

To ask our child what, if any, plans he has once he graduates from high school, and to *resist telling him what we think he should do*, is not the easiest thing in the world, considering the fact that we have spent eighteen years handing down parental edicts and giving parental responses to what he has had to say. Post-high school education and career choices, however, belong to our children. They will undoubtedly need a lot of good advice, but needing it and accepting it are very different things. Whether our children ask us for advice is up for grabs. If we enjoy a good rapport, they probably will, but we must recognize the fact that they have other sources of information available, and other influences operating. From their school counselors, readings, and conversations with their friends, they may make preliminary decisions for themselves before we have any opportunity to talk with them. The important thing is that we, as their parents, stand ready to offer what information we have and to give advice—but only if we are asked to do so. In some cases, our information may be very limited. We may also have limited advice. But whether our information and advice is limited or extensive, we feel it is important that we offer only what has been asked for—nothing more.

This is a self-imposed limitation, one which most of us find difficult. Parenting is a long-standing habit. Year after year we have said, "Let me tell you what I think you ought to do. . . ." We now decide this is inappropriate, and that since we do not give officious advice to other adult friends, we should not push such unsolicited advice on adult friends who also happen to be our children. By refraining from volunteering our opinions, we take a major step toward recognizing them as adults. It can mark the start of a new relationship and a new "contract." We want to let them talk, to tell us of their plans and their dreams, and to let them know that we are receptive and supportive. That is enough.

Whether we call it "cutting the cord" or "leaving the nest," the step into adulthood and emancipation can be traumatic. We want to listen to them, but beyond that we want to say, "You are nearing the big day, your graduation from high school. We know you will have impor-

tant choices to make, and if you feel that we have information and advice that may help, you know you can call
on us. Perhaps we will have something to offer you; that's
up to you to decide. One thing we want you to understand, however, is that whatever choices you may make,
they are *your* choices. They may not be the choices that
we would make, but that isn't important. You have your
own life to live, just as we have had our own lives to live.
We will not in any way try to tell you what your choices
should be. We also want to tell you something more: we
feel you are capable of making it on your own, regardless
of where you decide to go from here. We are proud of
your capability, and we feel confident you will achieve in
whatever you decide is right for you. Up until this point
we have pretty much told you what to do and how to do
it. Often, we have told you when to do it. From now on,
what direction you will take will be up to you. Anything
we may have done for you and anything we may have
given you has been of our choosing. We have very much
enjoyed all the years we have lived with you, and anything during those years which we have done, and which
you may have enjoyed, have carried no attached strings.
We have been more than repaid by everything which you
have given us. You owe us absolutely nothing in return.
We have already been paid—more than enough. Now,
the slate is wiped clean. You owe us nothing, and, in
turn, we owe you nothing. We do not want you to feel
obligated to spend Thanksgiving or Christmas with us
when you might rather be off on a trip with your friends.
We don't want you to feel that you owe it to us to go to
college, or to become a doctor, lawyer, accountant, or en-
gineer because you think it might please your parents. If
you want to become a rock musician, go after it. If you're
drawn to become a plumber, anthropologist, cabinet-
maker, or chiropodist, we will be on the sidelines cheer-

ing. We want very much to see you attain your goals, whatever they may be, and we are willing to help you. You must understand, however, that we reserve the right to determine what we feel we can offer you from this point forward."

What we are, in fact, willing to offer is based upon our judgment of what will be in the best interests of each one of our children as well as ourselves.

The offer may include financial and other aid while attending college or trade school. Too often, however, higher education is merely taken for granted by both the parents and the children. The parents may believe that a college education is essential. The child may enter college with little or no thought as to why—simply because all of his or her friends are doing the same. Many parents feel they have an obligation to send their children to the college the children select. The parents may go deeply in debt in doing so only to find that their child has little motivation for college. With the cost of private colleges and universities reaching unbelievable heights, parents may sacrifice their own financial future for what could prove to be a dubious investment. Not all children are interested in academic pursuits. Others have vocational interests which do not call for a college education. And there is more than enough evidence that a college degree is not the sole key to success. We want to see our children pursue the vocational interests they choose. If they do, and they work diligently to achieve their potential, they will most probably achieve success as well as happiness.

For some, this will mean some amount of college. We have been fortunate to live within a short drive of a state university, several community colleges, and three or four private colleges and universities. There are no tuition costs at the community colleges, and only a nominal cost at the state university. When each of our children approached completion of high school, we offered the following contract:

"If you choose to go on to college, we will be happy to help you. You can continue to live at home. We will offer board and room. It will cost you nothing while you're in school. You can pay for your tuition, books, and other expenses. If you do decide to live at home, we will expect you to continue to do your share and to function in all ways as a member of the family. A part-time job should easily take care of your expenses."

We spent many hours discussing our values, what would be in their best interests, what we felt were our parental obligations, and what we genuinely *wanted* to offer to our adult children. From these discussions, we arrived at the terms of the contract we offered. We do not feel there is any one "right" contract. We do feel the parents are the ones to determine what is "right" for their family. Whatever the terms of the contract, it should serve to clarify the change in relationships which is occurring, and to clearly mark the conclusion of the child's dependency.

If children know they are now recognized as adults and expected to assume the responsibilities of an adult, they may avoid seeing the parental home as having a revolving door from which they can move out to be on their own only to move back in once the bills pile up, a job is lost, or a romance turns sour. In some homes, this turns into an almost endless cycle. Three months and a couple of hundred good meals later, the child moves out again. Indulgent parents may watch this repeated year after year. The parents' insecurities and confusion over obligations may prevent them from ever bringing parenthood to a close.

Leaving the nest may not constitute as clean a break as it perhaps should. Parents may understandably have an urge to "give the kids help in getting started" through financial assistance in various ways (e.g., purchasing furniture, contributing the down payment for a house, buying a car). This can continue over a matter of years such that the child, now an adult, remains at least partially dependent. Often, we have seen more harm than help as a result. The sooner the young man or woman can feel completely capable of "making it" without assistance, the sooner he or she will gain the self-esteem which comes from maturity. For most it will not be easy at first. It probably wasn't for the parents. But the eventual rewards make the struggle worthwhile.

When the adult child marries, there is yet another change in the relationship of parent and child. Married sons or daughters are no longer members of the parental family. Once married, they have families of their own. They will have one family, and one family only—the one they establish with their spouse.

Marriage changes the relationship with the parents and siblings alike. The emotional adjustments demanded are often not easily made. The bonding which has been built over many years is suddenly drastically altered. You are still close, but the child's primary loyalty is no longer to parents and siblings. Accepting the fact that this child is no longer a family member owing allegiance to the parental family is often quite painful for all concerned. The parents can usually help the transition by discouraging too frequent contact. The new husband and wife need time to begin building the foundations for their marriage and autonomy. We have seldom seen a marriage which was in any way helped by continuing close contact with the parents of either husband or wife. We feel the most loving thing parents can do is to convey, quite clearly, "You now have each other; you have your own family to establish, and your own traditions to build together. Look to one another for your answers; not to us."

We have spoken with countless couples who have spent every major holiday, year after year, with the parents of one or the other. It has never occurred to some that any other option was open, that they might spend Christmas in their own home holding hands before their own Christmas tree. They have either sought to maintain the dependency role of the child or they have been made to feel obligated by their parents. The result has been that they have built no memories and traditions which are theirs alone.

The first time we received a photograph of a Christmas tree in the home of one of our daughters and her husband, it was a very warm, sentimental experience for us. It brought back wonderful memories of our first Christmas tree and all those which have followed. Did we wish they had spent Christmas with us? No, not really. Christmas together in their own home, by the tree they have decorated together, opening the very special, private gifts they have wrapped for one another, sharing that first Christmas morning cup of coffee together, and later working side by side on their first Christmas dinner is a far more important memory—one we want them to cherish for many, many years. It's one more important step in the bonding we hope they will experience.

When the last child leaves home, it will mark the close of one chapter in our lives. It will mark the beginning of another, a new one we anticipate with the same joy we have experienced during these years as a family. If you are around at the time, you may see a little car heading off toward a sun-drenched beach. The noise you hear will be tin cans and old shoes tied to a rear bumper.